I0099685

THE FOUNDATION YEARS OF
ELIJAH MUHAMMAD
(1959 - 1962)
VOLUMES 1 & 2

Unpublished & Rare Writings
of
ELIJAH MUHAMMAD
Messenger of Allah
(1958 - 1962)

Nasir Hakim, Editor

By
Elijah Muhammad
(Messenger of Allah)

Published by
Secretarius MEMPS Publications
111 E Dunlap Ave, Ste 1-217 - Phoenix, Arizona 85020-7802
Phone & Fax 602 466-7347
Email: secmemps@memps.com
Web: www.memps.com

THE FOUNDATION YEARS OF ELIJAH MUHAMMAD VOLS. 1 & 2

Copyright © 2003
Secretarius Publications

ISBN10# 1-884855-43-1

Printed in the United States of America

DEDICATION

TO ALL THE BELIEVERS AND FOLLOWERS
OF
ELIJAH MUHAMMAD,
MESSENGER OF ALLAH,
WITHOUT WHOM, WE AS FRACTIONS
WOULD HAVE NO EXPECTATION
OF EVER
BECOMING WHOLE.

~ ~ ~ ~ ~

THE
MESSENGER
IS A SWORD
IN A MAN'S HAND

~ Sayings of Elijah Muhammad, Vol. 3

PREFACE

It has been approximately 40 years since these articles have been written. Many of the truths in them are not being taught today. You will find some of them in certain books compiled by Elijah Muhammad and then others may surface every now and then in photocopy or a citing here and there.

In any case, these articles represent those submitted to various new organs of the early 50's and 60's. Some of these newspapers are no longer in business and others have simply gone through economic and social change prompting them to change their name and management.

In the early days, when there was no Muhammad Speaks newspaper, which had become the official newspaper of the Nation of Islam, Elijah Muhammad submitted articles to various local papers for publication. Some of these newspapers were the Herald Dispatch, Amsterdam News, The Crusader and the Pittsburgh Courier.

In various instances, after submitting articles, the Brotherhood of the Fruit of Islam (FOI) would begin distributing the papers in an effort to get the articles in Black people's hand. The sharp increase in distribution produced leverage with the paper that gave an "insurance" that the Messenger would be published. It was due to the Nation of Islam's distribution of many of these papers that pushed it into the status of mainstream in the black community. Previously, these tabloids were no more than nickel and dime shopper guides.

Some of these articles are included in parts of Elijah Muhammad's books, as pointed out in their respective acknowledgements, making it clear that all of his books are actual compilations of previous speeches, articles and lectures. Considering the Messenger is one of the most prolific writers of our time, many of his articles were not included in his standard books. This work fell to those of us who understand that the guidance we need in his absence is in his literature. This is nothing new to those who mind.

Our motivation for publishing these articles is simple. There are many truths that Messenger Elijah Muhammad taught that are not available today. We, therefore, are rising to the occasion to satisfy this vacuum. *"In the absence of the Trainer, the training will rise up and meet the occasion."*

We trust that if the reader reads something he or she has read before, it will only enhance their knowledge base. There, however, are many items that will be fairly new to you. We hope that whatever experience one has, it will be one that benefits our nation and in this way, regardless of when or if you have read it, you will act upon the principle contained herein. For as Elijah Muhammad, Messenger of Allah, said, "Mere belief counts for nothing, unless carried into practice."

~ Nasir Makr Hakim
Minister of Elijah Muhammad,
Messenger of Allah

INTRODUCTION

"We believe that the offer of integration is hypocritical and is made by those who are trying to deceive the black people into believing that their 400-year-old open enemies of freedom, justice and equality are all of a sudden their friends. Furthermore, we believe that such deception is intended to prevent black people from realizing that the time in History has arrived for the separation from the whites of this nation.

If the white people are truthful about their professed friendship towards the so-called Negro, they can prove it by dividing up America with their slaves. We do not believe that America will ever be able to furnish enough jobs for her own millions of unemployed in addition to jobs for the 20,000,000 (now approximately 40-50 million) black people as well." (The Muslim Program, Belief 9)

This is one of the Muslim Beliefs established by Elijah Muhammad, Messenger of Allah. We, His followers, believe as he believes. Within the past 40 years or so, America has stepped up its campaign of trying to convince blacks in America that they want to live side by side, ride the bus side by side, go to school side by side, work side by side, eat, drink and intermarry. Yet, one must still ask if after all this and introduction, tolerance and now dissipation of Affirmative Action, have blacks to date got anything of significance?

For many of the well-to-do blacks in America, it seems that the greatest aspiration they have is to do exactly as their former slave-master's do, even to intermarrying with them. Accompanying these steps is the acquired mind-set and "new politically correct loaded language" that all people have red blood and that we therefore are all part of one human family. Nothing could be further from the truth. Have we forgotten (for those who have known at any point) that the United States of America is an experiment in democracy? Who said the experiment was over?

If one looks closely at the meager tokenism offered to symbolize freedom, justice and equality for the once slaves here in America, it will insult anyone's intelligence. White America had never been serious at offering anything to blacks that would in essence represent, nor lead to, self-independence. Their offers have been and still are nothing more than pacification. There has never been, and still isn't any substance to what they've offered their once slaves to compensate them for the losses incurred as a result of not only forced chattel slavery, but the systematic robbery of their God-given identity and human rights. When looking at what's being offered by this country in comparison to what has been taken, one can start seeing the hypocrisy. I say start here, because it is only the tip of the iceberg.

Elijah Muhammad, Messenger of Allah, had pointed out for over 40 years the true interpretations of biblical as well as qur'anic scripture; wherein, both books speaks of a time when God Himself would come and raise up, or resurrect a dead people. What we didn't understand is that it would

vii

not be a physically dead people, but a people who had been mentally dead. This mental death would be a direct result of slavery in America, and as before mentioned, the blacks having been systematically robbed of their self-knowledge: original names, language, culture, religion, and God, consequently rendered them categorically "dead" when it came to knowing, functioning or acting like civilized humans. In fact, the mental robbery coupled with a government system, which made it law to treat them as live stock and chattel, this effectively rendered them on the level of beast; thus property.

The scriptures further prophesied that one day God would come to this people and raise them up from this mental death. Due to the fact that the slave-master didn't want any foreigners near his "property," this wise God came "like a thief in the night without observation, while men slept." Having come among the people, He didn't attempt to raise them all Himself, but to search for one to teach and that one was missioned to teach the rest. The God Who was to come and did come is Allah (God), Master Fard Muhammad, and the one He raise up first, otherwise, known as the First Begotten of the Dead, is none other than Elijah Muhammad, Messenger of Allah (God).

God's coming, finding and raising up a people, whom the Bible refers to as "Lost Sheep," is prophesied to take place approximately 400 years after them being in slavery; whereas, after that time He would come. His intent was to raise a Messenger, and mission that Messenger to restore us to what we once were before being made slaves, re-educated us back into the knowledge of ourselves, civilize us, dignify us, and qualify us to be fit once again to interact with other civilized nations as an independent nation, which means a total and complete separation from the slave-master and the slave-master's children.

Our own personal experiences with white America has proven beyond a shadow of a doubt that they are disagreeable to live with in peace; however, what Elijah Muhammad, Messenger of Allah has pointed out, is that the whites know scripture too and know that this is the time for separation of blacks and whites, and they want to keep us among them as a prey; consequently, they are pushing the offer of integration, not for the purpose of reconciliation or atonement, but to cause as many of his once slaves and their children to go down with him and his country. Integration is a bait for those who have wanted to be accepted by America all their lives and now feel their time to take part in America has now arrived. To sum this relationship up is like being a slave at the bottom of a large luxurious boat for all of your life and now you and the slave-master now see another boat sail towards you with black people in control, and instead of your slave master either allowing you to own a place on his boat (which you and your parents built with free labor) or helping you to relocate on the boat coming for you with your people, he opens up his boat to you and allows you to come up to the boat, puts you third in charge of driving (something mentally unchallenging) and lets you wear one of his old captains hats, then tells you that the boat now belongs to you too. Your mind is already set for that and it would be natural to understand if you would accept that, but the deception comes in when the Whiteman knows that he brought you up top because he didn't want you to see the large hole at the bottom, and if he allows you to believe that the boat is as much yours as his then you'll fight harder for it than he would. This in essence causes the once slave to turn enemy against his own salvation and people, when in fact this is the time of his own independence and freedom. The slave-master knows that the slave is completely ignorant as to what true freedom is and therefore keeps him blind, deaf and dumb to that knowledge and truth that would enable the slave to make an intelligent decision.

So today whites are permitting blacks to participate in a vast number of posts, even to government. They have become so confident in their deception, they will even allow once-slaves to run for the highest office in the land. Reverend Jesse Jackson ran twice and now they're working on the experiment of Collin Powell. The past few elections would make one believe that of all the highly qualified potential nation builders our race has to offer, we can find none to send to represent us but a couple of homeless Baptist preachers, who have no more to their credit than sleeping in the Lincoln suite at the house at the invitation of the president, who as well, was accompanied by someone other than his wife or twisting the arms of corporations to extort money from them in the name of justice for their brethren. This shouldn't come as a surprise, because their predecessors trained them this way.

Historically their greatest project is the civil rights movement. It is "programmed" common knowledge that the Reverend Doctor Martin Luther King, Jr. spearheaded this movement and eventually staged the March on

Washington; however, the common man's knowledge is in need of correction.

It was the government of America who made it possible for Negro once-slaves, ignorant lower class whites and poor immigrants to march and make up what is known as the civil rights movement. Martin Luther King didn't have that kind of money, nor did he have that type of logistical background and independent thinking necessary to pull that off. In fact, in the 60's, if the government wasn't with it, it didn't happen, at least not more than once. To this day, if it wasn't for government and government money, none of these civil right organization would be standing. These organization are tolerated, mainly because it diverts attention from the real program of independence for so-called Negroes that is only taught by Elijah Muhammad and the Nation of Islam.

It is human rights, of which we are being deprived. The right of self-determination. The rights of freedom, justice and equality and independence. We are not seeking to stay with white people, because God has said that He intended to destroy this country. God's coming and raising one to teach the rest, is for the purpose of separating us and putting us with our own kind. The white-man's ploy of integration is for the purpose of deceiving as many of us as he can to stay with him so he can effectively take a final swipe at killing as many of us as he can. This too is substantiated by the long track record of the white man's history.

White scientists are constantly trying to prove that blacks are genetically inferior than whites. There are many studies underway trying to prove that blacks have a genetic inclination for crime and violence. In other words, they are trying to prove that blacks are naturally criminal. This attempt is not surprising, for white America has been putting lies into law for years, which they say is based on some "study." What you can expect is that regardless of what finding they "develop," they would have still cultivated the thought amongst their people. By highlighting every negative thing they can about blacks in their media, they will be manufacturing a "self-fulfilling prophesy" themselves. You had heard that the O.J. verdict "had" to be along racial lines, because since the jury was predominantly black, they didn't want to convict "their brother." Their emotions kept them from rendering a "just" verdict.

There is no people on the planet who are more racist than white people. Regardless where you find them or what time, their own history bears out over and over again that not only have they killed millions of darker peoples of the earth, but they have done so for the purpose of colonization, exploitation and eventually domination as world rulers. If there is anyone who knows racism, natural criminal inclination, and ethnocentricity (belief that one's ethnicity is superior to others), whites collectively have written the book.

To get the black people of America to see that whites world-wide are their natural enemy is very difficult. One of the best characterizations to illustrate the seriousness of this issue can be depicted in a relationship between a large bird of prey and a lamb. The German philosopher, Friedrich Nietzsche, 1844-1900, wrote,

"There is nothing very odd about lambs disliking birds of prey, but this is no reason for holding it against large birds of prey that they carry off lambs. And when the lambs whisper among themselves, 'These birds of prey are evil, and does this not give us a right to say that whatever is the opposite of a bird of prey must be good?' there is nothing intrinsically wrong with such an argument - though the birds of prey will look somewhat quizzically and say, 'We have nothing against these good lambs; in fact, we love them; nothing tastes better then a tender lamb.'"

The moral of this observation is that whites understand their relationship to us and we have been intentionally blinded of the "right kind" of education which would make us mindful of them. Consequently, it puts us in the position of taking our open enemies for friends and instead of securing an existence that would sustain our way of life, we have a history of being eaten on a daily basis and being satisfied with just begging for the right to choose when we will be eaten. Why continue marching to Washington asking the birds of prey to stop eating lambs and try grass for a change. To do so is not natural.

The offer of integration is a ploy or trick to divert from your ship that has come for you in exchange for theirs, which no longer has a bottom. They know this, which is why they finally offer it you as a last swipe of vindictiveness and enmity for you.

This book points out the brutal and realistic interchange between them and us and how they think. The basis of their treatment of us is the natural course of their nature, which is why it is perpetuated regardless of geography or time. Yet, the time would bring about a change and instead of fighting our way into begging for a place near them, we are faced with the choice of fighting for a place of our own - with God's help.

TABLE OF CONTENTS

ALLAH COMES FROM HEAVEN INTO HELL

Since the coming of our Saviour, the Mahdi, the One Spoken of in the religious scriptures of the past as the Son of Man and the Messiah, Who came in the Person of Master Fard Muhammad, many great and wonderful events have taken place among our people (so- called Negroes of America). The majority of my people have not realized the blessings we are receiving or the great love that Almighty Allah has for us. There is none who loves us to the equal of our Savior, Master Fard Muhammad (God in Person). He, Alone, came into this part of the earth filled with all manner of evil and corruption to reach us the ways of righteousness. For this is the land (America) that is like unto ancient Babylon which was destroyed because of her sins and corruption.

Allah Comes From Heaven Into Hell

He (Allah) came out of Heaven into Hell (North America) to save us from destruction that is hovering above this nation. America's inescapable and timely end is set as in the rising and setting of the sun. As I have made clear in my last two articles, we of all people and of all nations did not know who we were before the Coming of Allah, therefore, we have been open prey to our enemies (White Race). In fact, all nations of the earth have taken advantage of the poor Black man and woman in the mud in the part of the earth.

Though our first parents brought to this country were not ignorant to the knowledge of themselves, they were soon either killed by the white slave masters or died from grief.

1

The slave masters then subjected our fore-parents children to their filthy lust and wicked deceiving teachings. Thus, we have been reared today from the soil of corruption and from the seed of their hate, murder, violence and blood. It is not easy to separate you from their evil influence and practices when you believe all the lies the slave masters taught us ABOUT OURSELVES during these past 400 years.

Lost And Found Nation of Islam

We (so called Negroes) have been named the Lost and Found Nation of Islam, a name or title given to us by the religious scientist of the East to describe so-called Negroes of America who would be lost for over 400 years, and who in the last days of this present world would be found wandering blindly in a strange land like helpless lambs in the midst of ravaging wolves. If you are yet in doubt as to the truth of this history, I ask you to name another people who have been lost from their native land and are presently living in a foreign land with no desire to return home because the enemy, who captured them has killed within them to reclaim their own. Name another people, who do not know their native tongue and speak only the master's language. What other people besides so-called Negroes have the religion and history of that people been so concealed and hidden, leaving no possible chance for this knowledge to escape except by the Will and Power of God, Himself? There are no other people who fit this description but the so-called American Negroes.

ALLAH SAYS: ACCEPT YOUR OWN

The acceptance of one's own is justified by the law of justice as an act of self-pride and intelligence. If we object to the acceptance of our own whose own can we accept without bring classified as fools without self-pride? Self, comes first by all civilized people. What is our own? Spiritually, Allah answers that: we are the righteous and were made other than righteous by the devils who enslaved us and robbed us of the knowledge of self and our own. If Allah (God) has numbered us as being members of the righteous nation, the original the first people in the Sun, then our OWN includes everything in the Sun.

Lost and Found People

The whole of the universe, we are recognized throughout Asia and Africa today, as being their lost and found people. Mr. Lomax learned this on his recent visit to Africa seeking the inside story of his people for his slave masters. Most so-called Negro journalists are only the devil's informers of the secrets of the black man!

The Asiatic and the African are now closing their doors against all so-called American Negroes, except those who confess Islam -, the Muslims.

The Negro leadership, both religious and political, because of their love for the white race, white Christianity and their hatred of the black nation and their religion Islam (the true religion of God), are rejected by the Islamic world which includes Asia and Africa.

3

Made To Serve Enemy

We must agree on common sense, that we were brought here by our enemies (the white race) and made to serve them. We are the product of our enemies own makings. Whatever we are today, it is the work of our enemies (the white race).

Today, they despise and hate us, the product of their own making! They scorn, make mock of our laziness, ignorance, filthiness, drunkenness and our hatred of each other!

Since the black man of Africa and Asia are not such people as we are, then who is to blame? They (white race) spent 400 years in making the so-called Negroes what they are today.

Allah (God) desires to make us a people for Himself and if we submit to Him, he will give us back our OWN, (the mastery of the Universe). We cannot exist further under other than our OWN, for there will not exist other than our own, after this great, final war between Allah and the devils.

Height of Ignorance

The desire and want of the black man and woman of America to mix blood with the devils is the height of ignorance! nearly 90% of the so-called Negroes would forgive the devils for the evils done to their parents and selves today, if the devils only accept them as his own, Even the preachers, who should know that there is no such thing as a forgiving of the devils by Allah (God), preach that their people should love the devils and forget the past!

Allah cannot forgive the devils and keep his promise to the prophets, that He would destroy Satan, the devil, who had deceived the nations of the earth.

Why not accept your OWN? You are the best, the most beautiful, the most powerful, the FIRST and the LAST! Love your OWN, and keep your OWN!

AMERICA WILL DESTROY HERSELF

"For thou hast said in thine heart, I will ascend into Heaven, I will exalt my throne above the Stars of God (this throne represents a false religion, opposing the true religion): I sit also upon the mount of the congregation in the sides of the north." Verse. 13.

Interpretation

Here Satan, the devil makes an attempt to equal himself with Allah (Jehovah) who created the heavens and the earth; Satan had no part in the creation of the heavens and earth, therefore, cannot ever be the equal of Allah, in power. But in his heart, he secretly believes that he can with his newly acquired knowledge of gravitation and the power of the atoms.

Satan believes that he has conquered water, land, air. Now, he seeks to conquer the space to get out of the confines of the gravitation of earth and he thinks he will be independent to the power of Allah to destroy him and to be Allah's equal in power over life on the earth.

Satan Exalts Himself

He makes or exalts himself above the very chief scientists (the Stars of God) of Allah's in wisdom; he seeks to establish and mount his religion and followers above the true religion and follower of Allah (God).

He will sit upon the mount of the congregation (make himself like God over the people; the vice-region of God) in the sides of the North. Not in the East (The Holy City of Mecca) where the congregation of Allah assembles-the Muslims.

It is the religion of Christianity with its head in Rome called the Pope or Father of the Christian Church, who has tried to set organized Christianity above the true religion of Allah (Islam) and to turn the people from the spiritual center of Allah's Mecca, Arabia.

Had Army of Elephants

The Pope tried to do this even by war in the year 570 A.D. with Abraha, the Emperor of Ethiopia, with an army mounted on elephants. As history shows, this was a miserable failure. They may, according to the Bible (Rev. 20:9) attempt to attack the Holy City Mecca again by air at their final end, but that too will be a failure.

The religious history of Rome shows many false Gods at its head. She is backed by the wealth and might of the white race. (See Rev. 17:1-7.) Mecca is backed also by wealth and power, but of Allah and the Nation of Islam for which every Muslim on the Planet Earth would die before they would allow any nation or nations to attack and destroy the city.

The devils have always desired to be the rulers of the people of God. This is the nature in which they were created (grafted). The devils were given the power to rule the righteous people of the earth for six thousand years. Now, that time is up! But they desire to remain the rulers of the people. This desire cannot be removed from them by just telling them their time is up! "I will ascend above the heights of the clouds; I will be like the Most High." (They dress like the righteous and claim to be worshippers of God and one of His prophets - Jesus) Verse 14.

It is the Most High Allah (God) in Person Who is High above the clouds on a man-made planet from the earth. Its machination cannot be equaled by the devil scientists.

Took 20 Years

It took the original machinists twenty years to build the "Mother Plane" that you see today flying through space and stars at night at a speed and height that the devils cannot ever be able to attain. Isaiah, Chapter 14:13,14 is the root of the prophecy.

In Thessalonians, Chapter 2:4-12, the description fits the white race well in their works of trying to ascend to outer-space planets, and their religion, Christianity, and their calling the heads of the church, "Father."

So, my people, I warn you: do not be deceived by the devils and their great showing of tricks of which you may think them to be the equal of Allah (God) and the angels of Allah (God).
NOTE: The 2nd Chapter of Thessalonians says: that the coming of god is after the workings of Satan (the devils) "and with all their deceivableness of unrighteousness in them that perish; because they received not the love of the truth, that they might be saved." (Verse 10).

It is the so-called Negroes who are referred to in the words: "they received not the love of the truth." (Whom the white race has deceived). The truth that the so-called Negroes are afraid to believe is the Truth of the white race being the real devils, the ever enemies of Allah, the Prophets and the original nation of the earth. (The Black, Brown, Yellow and Red races).

AN EVIL AND INDECENT RACE (WHITES)

The people of `paradise' who followed Yakub 6,000 years ago had no idea that he intended to disgrace and destroy them. He was cast out and doomed to total destruction. He carried with him 59,999 original black people. this is the devil's same intentions today, to deceive and tempt the original black people here in America to go with them to THEIR CERTAIN DOOM. This is in the minds of white Americans' religion - tempting and deceiving the so-called Negroes to make them deserving of hell fire with them. My People, I am warning you!

The Devils are now using one of their greatest weapons (temptation) to destroy the black people or cause them to take part in their doom which was prepared for them the very day they were created. They are aware of you, they see you, but you do not see them.

THOUGH ALLAH in these last few years has manifested them to you and me, your love for our enemies, the devils, is so great that you are blinded and cannot see them as devils. They are the enemies of God and the entire Black Nation.

Real Devils Are Enemies

YOU DISPUTE the truth of them being the real devils - the enemies. You are even fools enough to teach the love and worship of them to your own children. It is a shame and a disgrace! You become so displeased with god and His servant for teaching you the truth of them that you call

11

the truth "hate" or rather charge the Messenger of God with teaching you to hate white people! (the devils)

Your hopes in making such charge against the Messenger is that maybe the devils will put a stop to such true teachings -even by imprisoning or killing him and his followers as the enemies of God's Messengers did in the past.

I AM AFRAID you are going to be disappointed in your ignorant and wicked wish for your flesh and blood. Today, the bearer of truth is protected by his Sender, Allah, To Whom be praised forever. I only desire to see you saved from that which you have no part; only that which you take of yourself. I warn you against letting this evil tempter tempt you into their world of evil and indecency that you may share their doom.

Filthy, Wicked Show

The so-called Christian race (the devils) are putting on one of their most filthy, most wicked shows that have ever been produced by a human being. They sing filthy love songs, filthy kissing and dancing, showing off their nude bodies on the television to your families to incite the evil, filthy, immoral practices into your children and yourself. The Bible and Holy Quran both warns us against accepting these devil's filthy temptations. Read Bible, Luke 8:13: James 1:12, Matt. 26.41; Deut. 4:30; Rev.3:10.

There is much more you may study that you might know the devils whom you in the past have not known; but now, the truth has come to us from the Lord of the Worlds! Why should they now tempt us after seeing and having knowledge of the evil, filthy doings? The Christians or devils display NO shame.

THEY ARE bold and shyless, they are pig eaters, alcohol drinkers which help make them shameless, they go indecently dressed, according to the Holy Quran (7:17,20,21,26.) And it (Quran) warns us of the shame devils deceived our fathers in "Paradise" 6,000 years ago. They (devils) led them out on an island into the Aegean Sea, stripped them of both the clothing that covered their shame and the wisdom and knowledge of themselves and God. And today they (the devils) are playing the same trick on you and me and the whole of the Black Nations. READ THE FOLLOWING verses of the Holy Qur'an:

> *"O children of Adam, we have indeed sent down to you clothing to cover your shame, and clothing for beauty, and clothing that guards against evil - that is the beast." This is of the Messages of Allah that they may be mindful, not the devils (the white race) seduce you, as he expelled your parents from the Garden, pulling off from them their clothing that he might show them their shame. He sees you, he as well as his host from whence you see them not, (electronic devices make this possible) surely we have made the devils to be the friends of the disbelievers - (7:26,27)."*

BATTLE IN THE SKY

The battle in the sky is near. The vision of Ezekiel's wheel in a wheel is true if carefully understood. There is a similar wheel in the sky today which very well answers the description of Ezekiel's vision. This wheel corresponds in a way with the spheres of spheres called the universe. The Maker of the universe is Allah (God), the Father of the Black Nation which includes the Brown, yellow, and Red people. The Great Wheel, which many of us see in the sky today, is not so much a wheel as one may think in such terms, but rather a plane made like a wheel.

This wheel-like plane, it's like was never before seen. You cannot build one like it and get the same result. Your brains are limited. If you would make one to look like it, you could not get it up off the earth into outer space. The similar Ezekiel's wheel is a masterpiece of mechanics. Maybe I should not say the wheel is similar to Ezekiel's vision of a wheel, but that Ezekiel's vision has become a reality. His vision of the wheel included hints on the Great Wisdom of almighty God, Allah; that really He is the Maker of the universe, and reveals just where and how the decisive battle would take place (in the sky).

When guns and shells took the place of the sword, man's best defense against such weapons was a trench (ditch). Folsom gas and liquid fire brought him out. Today, he has left the surface for the sky to destroy his enemy by dropping and exploding bombs on each other. All this was known in the days of Ezekiel, and God revealed it to

15

him, that through Ezekiel, we might know what to expect at the end of this world.

The Originator and His people, the Original Black people, are supremely wise. Today we see the white race preparing for the sky battle to determine who shall remain and rule this earth, Black or white. In the battle between God and the disbelievers in the days of Noah, the victor's weapon was water. He used fire in the case of Sodom and Gomorrah; in the battle against Pharaoh, He used ten different weapons that included fire, water, hail storms and great armies of the insect world and droughts, and finally plagued them with death.

The Holy Qur'an says that: "the chastisement of Pharaoh was like that which God would use against His enemies in the last days."

Throughout the Bible and Holy Qur'an teachings on the Judgment and destruction of the enemies, fire will be used as the last weapon. The earth's greatest arms are fire and water. The whole of its atmosphere is made up of fire and water and gases. It serves as a protected coat for arms against any falling fragments from her neighbors. Ezekiel saw wheels in the middle of a wheel. This is true; (the universe in the universe. It is made up of revolving sphere). There are wheels in the wheel. The present wheel-shaped plane known as the Mother of Planes, is one half mile by a half mile and is the largest mechanical man-made object in the sky. It is a small human planet made for the purpose to destroy the present world of the enemies of Allah. The cost to build such a plane is staggering! The finest brains were used to build it. She is capable of staying in outer space six to twelve months at a time without coming into the earth's gravity. It carries fifteen hundred bombing planes with the most deadliest explosives; the type used in bringing up mountains on the earth. The very same method is to be used in the destruction of this world.

The bombs are equipped with motors and the toughest of steel was used in making them. This steel drills and takes the bombs into the earth at a depth of one mile and is timed not to explode until it reaches one mile into the earth. This explosion produces a mountain one mile high; not one bomb will fall into water. They will all fall on cities. As Ezekiel saw and heard in his vision of it (Chapter 10:2) the plane is terrible. It is seen but do not think of trying to attack it. That would be suicide!

The small circular made planes called flying saucers, which are so much talked of being seen, could be from this Mother Plane, of which Mr. Keyhoe claims in his book that he saw. This is only some of things in store for the white man's evil world. Watch and read this article for it is the truth. Believe it or believe it not! This is to warn you and me to fly to our Own God and people.

BLACK MUSLIM LEADER ADDRESSES 5,000

Muhammad Predicts Complete Separation of U.S. Negroes, Whites by End of Decade

Elijah Muhammad told 5,000 local members of his Black Muslim sect Sunday that Negroes in the United States will separate themselves completely from the whites, their "enemies," by the end of this decade.

It was the black supremacy leaders first appearance in Los Angeles in four years. He makes his headquarters in Chicago.

"There will be a resurrection of the dead of our people by 1970," Muhammad said from an Olympic Auditorium speaks' platform he shared with heavy-weight boxing champion Cassius Clay and other sect leaders.

Clay Tells Conversion

Muhammad surrounded by a guard of 50 men that was changed three times during his talk, reiterated his position that the white race is evil and that there can be no justice for Negroes in the United States.

Muhammad said that time is running out for the American Negro to make his decision to turn his back on the white.

"You must quickly make a choice between God and Satan," he said.

Clay a sect member who calls himself Muhammad Ali, said it was Elijah Muhammad who made him boxing champion.

"He taught me how to talk," Clay said, "and it was my talking that won the championship for me."

The boxer said that in 1960 he smoked, drank and had " a hundred girl friends."

Newsmen Searched

"I said then," Clay continued," if I get to be champion, I'm going to get me one of those white ladies."

The fighter said that after listening to the voice of Elijah Muhammad though, he realized the white race was inferior to the Negro and grave up vices taught by the whites.

Newsmen were the only whites allowed into the auditorium. They were thoroughly searched for weapons, and were not allowed to enter unless they turned in matches and pen-knives. Non-Muslim Negroes also were searched before they were admitted.

Although Mexican-Americans were given a special invitation to attend the meeting, none could be seen in the audience.

THE BLINDNESS OF THE NEGRO PREACHERS

Allah (God) has brought to us the light of Truth. This light, the devils (white race) hope to put out with the help of the mentally blind, deaf and dumb Negro Preachers. Just as Pharaoh thought he would be able to put out the light of Allah (Jehovah), that he kindled in Israel through His servant Moses, with the help of his spiritually blind magicians (preachers). But they met with Musa, (Moses), Allah's servant, there, the false light of the magicians was put out by the true light of Allah (Jehovah).

This king had no love for Israel, just as the President of America and the American citizens have no love for their so- called Negroes. Pharaoh was afraid of the light that was kindled in Israel by Allah (Jehovah), though His servant Musa (Moses) so that he became angry. He began to plan the death of Musa and the future of Israel by killing off the male babies of Israel. He was afraid, says the Holy Qur'an, that the light of truth preached by Musa (Moses) would change Israel's beliefs in Pharaoh's false religion, which he had made Israel to believe. So it is with this modern Egypt (America) and its rulers and people. They know they have blinded the poor so-called Negroes to the knowledge of truth. They pose as Divine representatives to the black man; while at the same time, being the real devils, leading the Negroes away from the true God and true religion into a false religion. They mislead them under the name of a true prophet of Allah, named Jesus. These devil-made and hand-picked leaders and preachers of our poor people, the devils have made to help crush and put out the real light of truth revealed to

21

me from Allah, in the Person of Master Fard Muhammad. He (Allah) is the Negroes' long-awaited Jesus Christ, our Saviour and Deliverer, and the Crusher of our enemies (the devils). It was made manifest how rotten blind and fearful the devil-made preachers are, on September 10, 1961, at Griffith Stadium, in Washington D.C., on the subject: "Christianity vs. Islam." There, Elder Lightfoot Solomon Michaux made no attempts to challenge the truth that I used in condemning Christianity as a Divinely revealed religion. and no attempts to challenge me that Jesus was not the founder of the religion of Christianity; that he (Jesus) was only a prophet, as Moses and the Prophets that followed in history after Moses, and Jesus was not the Christ. He wasn't the Son of God any more than any other righteous original man. It is false and wrong to accuse God of getting a son out of wedlock, and it is false to believe that God is a spirit, while all of God's people are made of flesh and blood.

In secret, this Elder Michaux had agreed at my home that Thursday before the 10th of September, that he believed in what I was teaching and that he believed the white man to be the devil. But when he spoke behind me that Sunday, there were devils sitting in the meeting and he, Michaux, wanted their friendship so he turned to them and shouted, "I love white people." Such double-crossing, hypocrite preachers cannot be trusted with good leadership for their already blind, deaf and dumb people.

According to some newspapers and magazines, Reverend Martin Luther King say that he doesn't like the Black Muslim's basic beliefs, - Black Supremacy. Because, he says, Black Supremacy is as bad as White Supremacy.

Reverend King, in such words, makes himself either neutral or a hypocrite on both sides - the black and white nation; due to his fear of the devils. The Negro preachers never speak, actually, the truth of what is in them. He speak the way he thinks will please the white devils. He cares not for the friendship of God and his people, (the so-called Negroes). He is after the friendship of the enemies of God and his people, (The American Whites). Reverend Martin King is very lucky to have one Negro following him, who openly tells the poor, down-trodden black people in words, that he never wants to see or live under the supreme ruler-ship of the Black Nation - for they would be just as bad as white Supremacy! He has never lived under his own people's rule. He never has seen the black man lynching and burning the black man. He never had the experience of having to go on freedom rides, sit-in strikes under black rule, to force them to serve him. Mr. King and his followers are showing the world that they love white supremacy, and hope it will rule them forever.

Reverend Martin Luther King is not trying to teach and make the lazy, white lovers, who are followers of his to unite and do something for self. But rather, he is aiding them to never have a desire to do for self. But to live by begging the white man to share his wealth with the Negroes and force the white people to share in everything that the white man has and not worry about doing for self.

This is the worse teaching I have ever heard of in this modern day, of the rise of the Black Nation. The Reverend King would not be able to live where the black man is going after something for self. The scared, rotten, white-poisoned preachers should be driven to the rear of the people until they learn that we, the Black Nation, the first and the Last, under the Guidance of Allah, will rule successfully ourselves, without the help of these devils. STOP depending on OTHERS and help SELF; unite and seek a place on this earth that you can call your own as other Nations. Stop seeking the love and recognition of the devils.

THE COMING OF THE SON OF MAN

"And then shall appear the sign of the Son of man in heaven; and then shall all the tribes of the earth mourn, and they shall see the Son of man coming in the clouds of heaven with power and great glory."
Matt. 24:30.

Here in the plainest words is the Son of Man in the Judgment Day. We are not told by either Moses or Jesus to look for God on the Judgment Day to be anything other than man. Spirits and spooks cannot be the judge of man's affairs. Man is material of the earth. How long will you be ignorant of the reality of God? You are poisoned by the devil's touch. Why are you looking for a God that is not in flesh and blood as you are? Spirits can only be found in another being like yourself. What pleasure would you have in an invisible world? And on the other hand, what pleasure would spirits have in this material universe of ours? Your very nature is against your being anything other than a human being.

These are the days of the resurrection of the mentally dead so- called Negroes. The Son of man is here. His coming has been fulfilled. He seeks that which was lost (the so-called Negroes). Many are now receiving His name, and that name alone will save you. The wicked nations of the earth are sorry and angry to see the Son of man set up a government of justice and peace over this, their wicked and unjust world. They see His signs of great power to execute Judgment on the world of the wicked, in the heavens (sky), and they mourn.

We must have a new ruler, and a new government, where the people can enjoy freedom, justice, and equality. Let the so-called Negroes rejoice for Allah has prepared for them, what the eye has not seen, the ear has not heard and that which the heart has not been able to conceive. The enemy knows this to be true and is now doing everything to prevent the so-called Negroes from seeing the Hereafter.

CORRUPTION

"Corruption has appeared in the land and sea on account of that which men's hands have wrought, that Allah may make them taste a part of that which they have done, so that they may return." (Holy Qur'an 30:41)

THE WORLD approaches one of its most darkest periods since the creation of the Caucasian race; the intensity of it is increasing hourly. A high temperature of madness is troubling the heads of the nations, regardless to the great advancement of science in every field of wisdom. The great progress that they have made should bring joy and happiness, but instead of joy and happiness, trouble, sorrow, fear and trembling - and the worse is yet to come!

There is a great financial waste on a mad-war race - arms that are made today, become obsolete tomorrow. Every nation is trying for the best and for the most destructive weapons of war. Billions of dollars are being spent on useless experiments; the currency is all but worthless. The great army of informers - nearly everyone will deceive the other. The above verse says that is, "On the account of that which men's hands have wrought." Man makes his own happiness or trouble. With his brain, he is able to think the thought or idea; he forms an image of it and the ears, eyes and mouth bear witness; then the hands fashion it into shape, the image of the mind.

SO THE WHITE RACE has prepared their own DOOM with their own hands - the great fortification at sea and land, the prevailing corruption on the islands of the seals. The great mistake made by the white man was in bringing the so-called Negroes from their native land and people,

27

putting them in chains to rob them of the knowledge of self and labor; and administering merciless beatings and killings for four hundred years. Now, the God of Justice says; as Thou has done, so shall it be done unto you.

ALLAH (GOD) has chosen the so-called Negroes to be His people and offers them heaven at once on their submission to His Will. He invites them into the true religion of God;

> *"Then set thyself, being upright, to the right religion before there comes from Allah, the day which cannot be averted; on that day, they will be separated." (Holy Qur'an 30:43).*

The Day mentioned that cannot be averted is the day of DOOM for the enemies of Allah. There is no future for the so-called Negroes in the white man's world. For four hundred years, the slave-masters and their children have not offered them anything but a job to work and serve them. Twenty million people cannot depend on a job in the factories and on the farms of white people, which benefits the owners, not the so-called Negroes. We must have some of this Earth that we can call our OWN. There we can create our own jobs, and the labor will benefit the Negroes. The slave-masters and their children have never given the slaves (the so-called Negroes) a fair chance to go for self. They have not had an equal opportunity, and probably will never get one as long as the white man is in power. The white man is against equal justice and equal opportunity for the black man.

LAST WEEK, a Mr. George E. Stokowski, news- writer, seemed to be angry and upset over the progress that the Truth, (Islam) is making among the so-called Negroes.

Mr. W.D. Fard, Whose proper name is Allah, has brought this truth to awaken the so-called Negroes into the knowledge of self, God and the devil, and Mr. Stokowski charges the progress of this truth to be from a violator of the narcotics law, who served three years in San Quentin Penitentiary.

NOTHING COULD BE WORST THAN THESE CHARGES! We will make Mr. George E. Stokowski prove this lie, regardless to the cost! Allah (God) has brought the knowledge of the truth to us, and this truth is preventing our people from practicing their evil habits. The devil wants to stop the so-called Negroes from believing the truth.

DECEIVED

We now are seeking the respect of the Nations of the earth. To get this respect or recognition, we must lay aside many old ignorant habits practiced from birth. Being loud to self or in the public is not good manners. Too much joking, yelling at one another in public, using ugly indecent language, swearing at each other calling each other names, singing foolish and filthy songs, dancing and shaking, twisting the body in public, lusting and looking with wanting eyes at each other, smoking drinking the fire spirits, is no good. Chewing or using tobacco in any form, form fitting clothes, the wearing of shorts by women or men in public is indecent. Going barelegged in the public, gambling games of chance and whistling is forbidden.

Keep the body and mind clean. Take frequent baths. A total bath should be taken daily. Stop eating swine flesh. It is a Divine prohibition flesh. Two-thirds of our ailments can be traced to the eating of this poisonous animal called the swine (Hog). Go cleanly dressed. If you have only one suit, keep it clean. Keep your house clean. The woman should never invite or allow strange men to come into her home in the absence of her father, brother (the son of her father) or husband.

Show respect to self and others. Respect and honor men in authority whether they respect you or not. Provoke no one. Do not steal nor take advantage of one another because of the freedom to do so. Do not quarrel and fight each other, for we are brothers - same flesh and blood.

Would you like to continue destroying your own flesh and blood? Protect your daughters and women from doing evil and filth. Protect them from the love of strange men. Rid yourself of laziness - be smart and industrious. Do good and righteousness regardless to whom or where. Be not wasteful, help to build a better future for self and kind.

Patronize your own people's business. Spend your dollars among your own kind. Serve One god, Allah, One religion - Islam. Be not divided, have love and unity of brotherhood first among yourselves. Help to secure a home on this earth that we can call our own. Do something for self and kind in the way of building a better future where we can enjoy peace and security, free from the shadow of death of our enemies.

I am so sorry that illness last Sunday, the 25th of June, 1961 prevented me from keeping my appointment with you in the Nation's Capitol. Allah is the Best Knower.

I have made visits and have mixed with our people (most all of them) and the above habits are the things being practiced by us that they (Nations) do not like, along with the love of our enemies and the hatred of self and kind.

AMERICA'S DOOM

They say that they (white race) love the scriptures of the prophets of God and are followers of Jesus; then let that which they claim to believe be their judge. If they claim to be believers (of which they are not) in, the scriptures of Allah's God's Prophets, (surely they brought the truth and that which they predicted would come to the wicked and the righteous in the last days), the truth of them is made manifest in our time.

America's price that she must pay for her evils done to her slaves (the Lost-found members of the original nation of Islam from the Tribe of Shabazz) who are nick-named, "Negroes" by the slave-master, is the same as that price paid by Pharaoh and his people.

Must Reap What Is Sown

The only difference is that Egypt still exists, while America will not. She must reap what she has sown. She hates her black slaves. She takes pleasure, daily in robbing, beating and killing them as though her black slaves once robbed and killed them. Her hatred for her slaves can easily be seen and heard in the evil, filthy, name calling of the slaves.

She has never attempted to mistreat her aggressive nations, and those who war against her in such evil manners as she does her helpless slaves (so-called Negroes), who know nothing; only what their slave masters have taught them.

They are trying their best to imitate their teachers, the slave master. This is due to the born fear and ignorance of self and their masters.

They will fight to death for the independence of the slave-master, but are too afraid to accept independence for self, or even to leave their slave master for a home among their own kind.

33

Not Learned Love of Self

They have not learned love of self and kind as other nations, they love their open enemy, the slave master, (the real devil). I still say that the history of Pharaoh could not have been made a better picture and warning to America and her slaves. The very plagues, almost 100 per cent, are mentioned and prophesied in the Revelations of John, the last book of the Bible, which brought an end to the symbolic "beast," except the fire does not run side by side with the water and hail, as in the case of Egypt under Pharaoh, According to both books, (Bible and Holy Qur'an).

Allah (God) used Pharaoh as a sign of the chief enemy's (devil's) destruction in the last Judgment of the opponents of God and the righteous. Read (Bible-Exodus 9:16-17) what Jehovah said to Pharaoh,

> *"and in very deed for this cause have I raised thee up, for to shew in thee my power; and that Name may be declared throughout all the earth."*

Jehovah's Wonderful Story

No reader of the Torah and Qur'an can say they over-looked this wonderful story of Jehovah's power, which crushed the power of Pharaoh in such manner as could be called a mockery of the proud king and his boast of power over Egypt and Israel, his slaves. It is the power of the white world that the world boasts they have, that is powerful enough to destroy whoever tries to attack and destroy them.

America, since she hypocritically professes to be a believer in God and the Prophets will not say as Pharaoh said to Moses, for fear of losing the so-called Negroes, who believes in the spooky slavery teachings of Christianity.

Today, America has the help of the Father (Pope) of the church, through the present administration in Washington, as we have never seen before. The Catholics are going all out, in America to convert the so-called Negroes and the black people in Africa.

Mocked the Idea

As Moses stood before Pharaoh representing Allah as the Lord of the Worlds, the proud wicked Pharaoh mocked the idea by suggesting that he would build a tower to attack Moses' God and Pharaoh said,

> *"O Haman, build for me a tower that I may attain the means of access to the heavens that I may reach the God of Moses, for I surely think him to be a liar."* (Holy Qur'an 40:36,37).

This "Haman" must have been Pharaoh's chief construction engineer of the war department. Note, that Moses made no mention that Jehovah never told Moses where He came from.

Sign of the Judgment

We must remember, that the judgment of this Pharaoh's rule and his people is a sign of the Judgment of the powerful rulers of today by the unequalled weapons that Allah has prepared to use in destroying them.

These terrible and dreadful weapons, are both, on the earth and in the heavens above the earth. But yet, these rulers mock the idea of Allah being able to destroy them and their advanced wicked science without hurting one Muslim (the righteous).

The present wicked rulers have learned and now see, through their powerful telescopes, the power of Allah hanging and moving in the sky as well as you and I, who are able to see some of it with the naked eye.

Allah has made the retired ex-general, Keyhole, take pictures of this power of Allah over our heads, which is almost identical to what Allah showed me in the sky in 1932.

Jesus prophesied of it coming in the clouds of heaven and Ezekiel gives us a faint picture of it in his vision of "a wheel in a wheel," high above the earth.

The foolish disbeliever of today say and do the same as the disbelievers before them. Remember, Jehovah killed the mocking, proud Pharaoh and his people for the evil they had done to Israel.

The symbolic prophetic beast of the Revelation was destroyed for his persecution of the symbolic "woman" and seeking to destroy her child at birth, Pharaoh and his people sought to destroy Israel by killing off all the boy babies; Herod sought to destroy Jesus by the same Method.

What means and methods are now in the working to destroy the so- called Negroes from becoming a ruling power? Wait for the answer! Remember, Israel was persecuted severely by Pharaoh and his people.

Rome and the Jews persecuted Jesus and his disciples. The Revelation's symbolic "beast" persecuted the symbolic, "woman" and her child. The "Beast" and those with him were destroyed in a lake of fire. Pharaoh and his people were destroyed by drowning in the Red Sea. The Jews and Romans lost their independence and the power to rule the world.

What and how will America lose her power and independence to rule the world? Watch for the answer.

THE DOOM

It is forbidden for the righteous to have friendly relations with the wicked, who are the enemies of God, His prophets, His scriptures, and His religion of peace, ISLAM.

> *"O you who believe, take not my enemy and your enemy for friends. Would you offer them love, while they deny the TRUTH that has come to you? Driving out the Messenger and yourselves because you believe in Allah, your Lord! If you have come forth to strive in My Way and to seek My Pleasure, would you love them in secret? And I know what you conceal and What you manifest. And who ever of that does this, he indeed strays from the straight path. If they overcome you, they will be your enemies, and will stretch forth their hand and their tongues towards you with evil; and they desire that you may disbelieve. (Holy Qur'an 60:1,2)*

My people the TRUTH (Islam) has come to you, why not believe? Is it because you are guilty of loving your enemies, and the enemies of Allah (God), His Prophets, and His True religion of peace, Islam? Is it for the love of your enemies that you seek to give the lie to Allah, (God), His Messengers, Prophets and His religion? Allah has made manifest to you, His enemies, (the white race). They are His enemies, your enemies, the enemies of our fathers, and our nation, the black, brown, yellow and red man.

The poor NAACP black leaders, who are yet blind, deaf and dumb, are in love with these open enemies of Allah (God) and their own people, the so-called Negroes. The so-called black leaders are against separation from these universally known enemies of the black nation due to their open and secret love of membership in the white race and a position as a permanent servant in their house and country. These are the same enemies who forced our fore-fathers into servitude slavery for 300 years and still own them as their property under free slavery. The (NAACP leaders) boast that they have equal rights with the master in the U.S.A. Whatever is the master's, it is also the slave's. They believe the master should beat and kill his brothers to enforce equal rights between the slave and the master - what a foolish people! They think that they, not the white race can live without each other and therefore should not be separated. It is an open and universal fool who loves his enemies and the enemies of his God and people.

Ask these dumb leaders, who is it that deprives them of freedom, justice and equality? They will say, the white man. Ask them who was it that enslaved you, lynched, burned, beat and killed you out of the law of justice all over America? They will say the white man. Ask them who killed God's Prophets and crucified Jesus? They will say, the white man. Ask them who was it that started the war in Europe and in the 30's, and on Ethiopia? Was it the black nation (Islam) or the white race (Christianity)? They will say the white man. Then ask them, does not your Bible teach "who-so-ever therefore will be a friend of the world (the white race is the ruler of the world) is the enemy of God? (James 4:4)

They will say yes. Then ask them, have you not heard that Allah has revealed to His Servant (Elijah Muhammad) that this is a race of devils and that by nature they cannot love justice and righteousness? They will say yes then say, O foolish of all the people, why not believe and seek your God and people like yourselves? Did not they (the white race) stretch forth their hands and tongue against Martin Luther King and his followers in the South, when he tried to force the white brothers against each other to enforce the law of integration - a law which would mongrelize the white and black people? Yes but you yet love the enemies of Allah (God) and yourselves; so wait and see who will be happy and who will be unhappy.

THE DOOM DRAWS NEAR

"And affliction is combined with affliction. To thy Lord on that day is the driving" (Holy Quran 75:29, 30).

A rich and powerful people living in luxury, having everything that their souls desire. Feeling secure from harm coming to them because of their strong and powerful fortifications, and well-trained, well-fed armies. Having armed planes and ships carrying death to one another; stock piles of bombs of death waiting for the hour to be released on the nations. No peace, no safety in such a world that you and I are now living in. The people of Allah (the so- called Negroes), are mentally dead to this time, as the people were in the days when Moses was sent to Pharaoh to bring Israel out of the bondage of the Egyptians, into a land where they could enjoy self independence.

Instead of them (Israelites) being happy to hear that God was ready to deliver them from Pharaoh and to give them a goodly land, they set to contend with Moses and to help Pharaoh oppose Moses and Jehovah. They knew not that they were fighting a losing battle, until Jehovah began plaguing Egypt. With armies that the Egyptian armies were helpless to fight, Jehovah brought both Israel and Pharaoh to their knees, in submission. As the Bible's second book (Exodus), opens with war over a chosen people, it closes also with war for another people. Pharaoh was drowned in the Red Sea and the Beast destroyed in a lake of fire.

43

American is more guilty of mistreating the people of God (the so- called Negroes), than Pharaoh or any slave masters that recorded history makes mention of. The doom of America is at her door.

This is the Great Judgment of the most powerful nation on earth of the white race, but she is the most wicked of all. America will not do justice by her slaves (the so-called Negroes). She claims they are free, but is aware of the fact that they are mentally enslaved and by no means know how to go for self. America has always mistreated the so-called Negroes by beating and killing them to put fear in the others; shooting them down in the streets and highways for little or nothing. She (America) takes her slaves to be her worst enemies. She has never treated any enemy that she has warred with, as she has and still treats, her harmless slaves. They have made the Negro to even love them and have them killing their brother-slave to satisfy the blood- thirsty, merciless masters.

Allah has now chosen the poor Negroes to be His people, and will slay you as He did Pharaoh and many Kings and empires who were even stronger than you, according to the Holy Qur'an and the remains of their civilizations are found under the sand in Egypt and Arabia. Affliction upon affliction shall come upon you. Dust storms, hail storms and other destructive storms have served as a reminder for America, that Allah (God) is after her. Now if droughts and earthquakes follow, you should not be surprised. You must give up the so-called Negroes to meet their God and live on some of this earth that they can call their own.

THE END

We are fulfilling that which is written of us in the scriptures, (Which we must read: Matt. 5:11, 10:23, 23:84, Rev.12:13.

My followers and I do not belong to the slave masters anymore. We belong to Allah (God) in whose name we are called; this is universally known. But as it is written: "You will be persecuted until the help of Allah comes (Holy Quran). That help is very near

America 's jails, I was told, are filled. Some of them are so overcrowded, that many of the prisoners have to sleep in the hallways. But yet, she (America) rejoices in persecuting the Muslims under false charges, just to discourage our poor, blind, deaf and dumb people from accepting the truth (Islam) and returning to their true God, Allah, and His true religion, Islam.

Prey to Government

We, the original people, are a prey to the government of America. Who must now be freed and separated from our enemies, the slave masters and their children if we are to ever enjoy peace, freedom, justice and equality.
Twenty million of our people cannot depend on another nation for existence. We must look to God and self as other nations had to do, or continue to beg our enemies (white slave masters) for jobs to exist among them, instead of asking and demanding a chance to go for self, to create our own jobs.

This is a disgrace to the leadership of 20 million people who do not want the responsibility of caring for self. Well, the time is very near when you'll have to go for self.

Something of Past

America's and the entire white race's ruling power over the brown, red, yellow and black nations of Africa and Asia will soon be something of the past. No longer will those nations bow to the Western powers. America's DOOM is sealed, and is inevitable, according to the word of Allah (God) to me.

Allah desires to make Himself known to the world, that He alone is God and has appeared among us in the Person of Master W. Fard Muhammad.

Both Bible and Qur'an teach of the presence of God in Person at the end of the world of Satan, the devil's rule. We would be foolish to disbelieve that such character is not present and is not directing the course of the nations today.

Allah Against Whites

The American white race is the number one people whom Allah's anger is directed against as Jehovah's anger was against Egypt in the time of Moses. Jehovah's weapons of war used against Pharaoh and His people were the forces of nature: flies, frogs, lice, diseases, rains, hailstorms, fire, water and finally the drowning of Pharaoh and his armies in the Red Sea.

The same forces of nature are prepared to be used against America with the following additions: terrifying storms (which now harass America); the loss of friendship of the nations; a specially prepared enemy people under the name "Gog" and Magog" whose skill and power will cover the earth for a while; there will be no friends for America; snow, ice and earthquakes, even droughts and dust storms, the natural powers of water, wind, terrific cold out of the north, fire from the sun, agitation of the high seas by the magnetism of the moon and sun (which will aid in the destruction of America's sea power).

Sins Are Greatest

This is referred to in the prophecy of Jesus; Read: Luke 21:25. also Isaiah 27:1, Rev. 8:7, 8, 9. America's sins are the greatest! her sins are even worse than all the nations of the earth combined. She sees and knows her doom is near. So she seeks to trick her slaves (so-called Negroes) to share this doom with her. But she knows that her once slaves have a chance of escaping so she hypocritically offers them social equality under the name "integration" which she knows the blind, deaf and dumb will fall for, while it is an open trap of death for both sides.

My people do not realize this, nor will they believe this until they are hurt or it is too late, or that this is the end of Satan's world, (power over the Black Nation of Islam) and must be told in the plainest language.

This is the work of Allah, not you and I. Read your Bible and Holy Quran. America has always hated and mistreated her slaves (so-called Negroes). Today, she backs up the police departments throughout the country to beat and kill poor black men and women.

47

We have always been submissive to these cruel, merciless enemies - like lambs are to a pack of hungry wolves. Stop tricking your slaves, white America; separate them into a good place on some of this soil, that you robbed our people of, with superior weapons and supply them with that which is necessary to get started for self.

Then, maybe your doom will be delayed a while. Otherwise, Allah will do it and will not leave a place for you anywhere on the planet.

It is not the evil done to others by the white race of America, it is the unjustified evils done to the helpless black slaves of America. Allah wishes to make America an example of His judgment that both Europe and Asia may know that He alone is God and has redeemed the helpless black slaves from their merciless enemies. I have warned you! Take it or leave it!

Free Slave? - Free Master?

In unity, we can accomplish much. Think of the twenty million of your and my kind putting one dollar a year aside for ourselves in a national treasury towards the day of want. Suppose we laid aside one dollar every month against the day of want. Look at the millions that we could build up for ourselves within a few years. Suppose all of you who are wealthy would spend your wealth to build up a better and more sound economic system among your own people. It would do much to aid our people. Do not put your wealth in the taverns gambling houses, on race horses and other sports. Then you would not be so easy to push over when the day of want arrives.

There is no need for us, millions and millions throughout the country, spending our money to the joy and happiness of others. As a result, as soon as they throw us out of a job, we are back at their doors begging for bread and soup. How many clothing shops do we operate in the country? Yet, all of us wear clothes. Who made our clothes for us? Who sold them to us? We have thousands of grocery stores? But what about our naked bodies? Should not we have stores to sell our people everything they want or need? But no!

We give all the money out of our pockets over to the slave-master. We are satisfied in doing so. There are millions of us. We don't have a factory to weave clothes for our people here in America. Think over that. Where is our shoe factory? Where are our cattle that we are skinning the hides off to make shoes for our people? These are small things - but we want equality with a nation that is doing these things.

We boast that we should be recognized as equals with the master until we own what the master owns. We cannot be equal with the master until we have the freedom the master enjoys. We cannot be equal with master until we have the education the master has. Then, we can say, "master, recognize me as your equal."

Today, you are begging the master, the slave-master's children for what? You are begging them for a job. You are begging for complete recognition as their equal. Let us be honest with ourselves. According to history, we cannot find where the master made his slave equal until the slave made himself worthy of equality.

I am with you to go on top. We cannot go on with weight that is hanging on us. We cannot charge the white man with our faults. We are supposed to be, according to his own teachings, free. We are supposed to have been freed from him approximately one hundred years ago. Have we exercised that freedom? We must answer that we have not availed ourselves of that freedom. If we have not availed ourselves of that freedom which he says he gave us, why should we think hard of him about the way he treats us. This may be a little hard to swallow.

Our fathers, in the days they were set free by the slave-masters, had no knowledge of how to go for self. They had been made blind, deaf and dumb to the knowledge of their own.
Today, you are educated. You claim that you have equal education. Then, why don't you take a walk?

Before we can be justified in accusing the other man, let us examine ourselves first. I don't say that our fathers are the ones to blame for their ignorance and neither are you. They nor you are at fault. The root of the cause can be placed back into the laps of the slave-master. When the slave-master says we are free and continues to say that we are free, should we not take a free step? We charge the slave- master's children with mistreating us.

Suppose you tell a man that he is free. "Get out of our house and go into your own," but the freed slave says, "No no, I"ll work for you. I"ll serve you as a servant if you will allow me to remain in your house." The man of the house tells you, "I won't give you a new suit this year. I"ll not pay you today for any work. Go home and sit down."

Why should you say that man is not treating you right? Why say to that man, "I have to have a job the same as you." Has not he offered the door to you?

If the slave-master did not mean that you and I were free, we should have them to admit it. You remain as a free slave to your slave-master. You demand that he recognize you as his equal. You are making yourself look small in the eyes of the world. If every so-called Negro were fired, what would you do? Would you unite and go to Washington and demand the government to give you a job? You would be foolish enough to do that! If they beat you by the thousands, what right have you to say that he should not lash you? You have made yourself his slave. You continue to preach a doctrine of remaining with the slave-master.

You are still called by your slave-masters' names. By rights, by international rights, you belong to the white man of America. He knows that. You have never gotten out of the shackles of slavery. You are still in them. You are still in authority over your wife as long as she goes in your name, regardless of her separating herself from you. If she has not gotten a legal divorce and freed herself from your name, you are still in authority over her by law. Likewise, you are still under authority of the chains of your slave-masters. You have not tried to free yourself from them. You have not exercised the freedom that they claim to [have given you].

Today is "The Day of Decision." We have lived here more than four hundred years. That you know, according to prophecy, is the prediction of our stay among these people. That time has expired. The time is up. The decision is being made for your and my departure. It is most important to God Almighty, whose proper name is Allah, that I speak to you according to the time that we are living now. Today, you are standing face to face with the alternative of accepting your own or forever be erased from the earth as a people. No one is trying to make you see this importance but your own. Why don't you see? You are blindly looking toward the slave-master to tell you this. How can the master tell the slave, "Look slave, your day has arrived. You should sit in this seat of authority." We cannot build a future on a job that was given to us by the slave-master four hundred years ago. The day has arrived. He has no more work for us to do. He is not willing to tell us that. The time has arrived when deeply within his own heart, he desires that you go out and find a job for yourself. He will forever be burdened. The burden will get greater and greater, as long as he tries to carry you and I. It is time for a separation of the two, black and white. Allah, God, is calling for a SEPARATION.

I am with you to go on top. We cannot go on with weight that is hanging on us. We cannot charge the white man with our faults. We are supposed to be according to his own teachings, free. We are supposed to have been freed from him approximately one hundred years ago. Have we exercised that freedom? We must answer that we have not availed ourselves of that freedom. If we have not availed ourselves of that freedom which he says he gave us, why should we think hard of him about the way he treats us? This may be a little hard to swallow.

Our fathers, in the days they were set free by the slave-master, had no knowledge of how to go for self. They had been made blind, deaf and dumb.

.

ALLAH OFFERS YOU A FUTURE

You and I, the so-called American Negro, are helpless without Allah (God) and Islam, which is the religion of God, His prophets, and our people. We are at the mercy of the Christian World. What has the Christian World done for you and me? Why should we want to remain in it? Have not they continued to segregate you, line you up and burn you, don't they continue to beat your heads and your brains burst out over your ears and eyes? They have done these things to us. They did these things even as you called yourself a Christian. They have shown that they don't recognize you as their equal. Why don't you exercise that freedom which they offer you and go back to your own?

If our share of this earth is not in this Western Hemisphere, then we must look for it in the East. However, 25,000,000 so- called Negroes who have been lost from their own people for 400 years must have a home on this earth that they can call their own. Allah the Great, God of the Universe, will give us the whole earth if we submit to Him and have patience to wait on Him. Regardless of the cost, we must have some earth of our own. Let not the false show and promises of this world deceive you so that you be the loser.

You make yourself a despised people in the eyes of the civilized world by hating yourself and loving the enemy devil. The Original man, Allah has declared, is none other than the black man. He is the first and last, maker and owner of the Universe. The brown, yellow, red and white

55

all came from the black man. The black man used a special method of birth control law to produce the white race.

The true knowledge of black and white mankind should be enough to awaken the so-called Negroes, put them on their feet and on the road to self independence. You my people are so afraid of the slave-master, that you even love them to the point of your own destruction. You wish the bearer of truth would not tell the truth even if he knows it. You hate a leader that tries to unite you to your own kind. Allah offers you a future, an eternal future. This world has no future. It was doomed when it was created. I speak and write what has been given to me from Allah (God) to Whom praise is due. I am not here to excite you for wealth or praise. I don't want your wealth. I don't want your praise. I want for you the thing which will produce unity of self and our kind. I want you safe. The world knows that I want you safe. What I preach is for our own life and the life of our children.

It is Allah's will and purpose that we shall know ourselves. He came Himself to teach us the knowledge of self. How else may you account for the success of my followers and myself? Who is better knowing of who we are than God Himself? All praise is due to the Great Mahdi (Allah in Person), Who was to come and has come. He is the Sole Master of the Worlds. I ask myself at times, "What can I do to repay Allah, (the Great Mahdi, Fard Muhammad) for His coming, wisdom, knowledge and understanding?

My followers and I have and are still spending much time and money to awaken our people to the knowledge of self.

We are suffering much persecution and ridicule to awaken our people to the knowledge of their own salvation. Our present suffering is nothing compared to the joy that awaits us as a people united for one common cause serving Allah, The God of Abraham, Moses, Jesus and our forefathers. Allah has declared that we must know ourselves and unite to our own kind or suffer the consequences. The new government controlled by the Roman Catholics, will stop at nothing in their effort to win the black people of America to them, but the Negroes must know that this world's end is near.

GET KNOWLEDGE TO BENEFIT SELF

I am for the acquiring of knowledge or the accumulating of knowledge, as we now call it in education. First, my people must be taught the knowledge of self. Then and only then will they be able to understand others and that which surrounds them. Anyone who do not have a knowledge of self is considered a victim of amnesia or either unconsciousness and they are not very competent. The lack of knowledge of self is a prevailing condition among my people here in America. Gaining the knowledge of self makes us unite and put us into a great unity. Knowledge of self makes you take on the great virtue of learning.

Many people have attempted to be-little or degrade my followers by referring to them as unlettered or unschooled. They do this to imply that the believers in Islam are ignorant. If such a claim were so, then all the more credit should be given for our striving for self-elevation with so little. But truth represents itself and stands by itself. No followers, or any people are more zealous about the acquiring of knowledge than my followers. Throughout the Holy Qur'an, the duty of a Muslim to acquire knowledge is spelled out.

My people should get an education which will benefit their own people and not an education adding to the "store house" of their teacher. We need education, but get an education which removes us from the shackles of slavery and servitude. Get an education, but not an education at the sacrifice of not learning the knowledge of self. Get an education, but not an education which leaves us in and inferior position and without a future. Get an education but not an education that leaves us looking to the slave-master for a job.

Education for my people should be where our children are off to themselves for the first fifteen or sixteen years in classes separated by the sex. Then they could and should seek higher education without losing respect for self or seeking to lose their identity. No people strives to lose themselves among other people except the so-called American Negro. This they do because of their lack of knowledge of self.

We should acquire an education where our people will become better students than their teachers. Get an education which will make our people put to better use the knowledge they acquire that will make our people produce jobs for self and will make our people willing and able to go do for self. Is this not the goal and aim of the many foreign students who are studying in this country? Don't these students return to their own nations and give their people the benefit of their learning? Did not Dr. Nkrumah return to Ghana to lead his people to independence with the benefit of learning he acquired here in America and elsewhere? Did not Dr. Hastings Banda return to give the benefit of his education to his people, who are striving towards freedom and independence, in Nyasaland? Did not Dr. Azikqe Abubkar of Nigeria give the benefit of his education to the upliftment and independence of his people? Does not America offer exchange scholarships to smaller, weaker and dependent foreign governments so their students will acquire knowledge to aid the people of those countries? Then why shouldn't the goal in education be the same for you and me? Why is scorn and abuse directed towards my followers and myself when we say our people should get an education which will aid, benefit and uplift our people? Any other people would consider it a lasting insult, of the worst type, to ask them to refrain from helping their people to be independent by contributing the benefit for their knowledge.

Get an education, but one which will instill the idea and desire to get something of your own, a country of your own and jobs of your own.

I recall in 1922 or 23, when a debate was taking place in Congress concerning appropriation of funds for Howard University, a school set aside to train my people in the Nation's Capital, a senator said, it is in the records to be examined in effect, what would be the need of the government appropriating money to educate Negroes? He said they would not teach our people the science of modern warfare (defense), birth control or Chemistry. He knew those were things free people must know in order to protect, preserve and advance themselves. We have not been able to protect, preserve and advance ourselves. This shows the slave-master has been successful in dominating us with and education beneficial to him. There is a saying among us: "Mother may have, father may have, but God blesses the child who has its own." It is time we have our own!

I want an education for my people that will let them exercise the right of freedom. We are 100 years up from slavery. We are constantly told that we are free. Why can't we take advantage of that freedom? I want an education for my people that will elevate them. Why should we always be lying at the gate begging for bread, shelter, clothing and jobs if we are free and educated? Do not get an education just to set some useless symbolic monument to the black man in the Western Hemisphere. We need an education that eliminates division among us. Acquire an education that creates unity and makes us desire to be with our own.

The acquiring of knowledge for our children and ourselves must not be limited to the "three R's" (reading, riting and rithmetic). It should instead, include the history of the black nation, the knowledge of civilization of man and the universe and all the sciences. It will make us a greater people of tomorrow.

We must instill within our people the desire to learn and then use that learning for self. We must be obsessed with getting the type of education we may use towards the elevation and benefit of our people - when we have such people among us, we must make it possible for them to acquire this wealth which will be beneficial and useful to us.

One of the attributes of Allah, The All Wise God, Who is The Supreme Being, is knowledge. Knowledge is the result of learning and is a force or energy that makes its bearer or a people accomplish or overcome obstacles, barriers and resistance. In fact, God means possessor of power and force. The education my people need is that knowledge, the attribute of God, which creates power to accomplish and make progress in the good things of the righteous things. We have tried other means and ways and we have failed. Why not try Islam? It is our only salvation. It is the religion of Allah, His prophets and our forefathers. Islam will let you take that step for self.

A GOOD NAME BETTER THAN GOLD

One of the first and most important truths that must be established in this day is our identity. This is what our God, whose proper Name is Allah, is guiding me to point out to you, many people who are members of the Lost and Found Nation of Islam in North America.

You my people, who have been robbed of your complete identity for over 400 years. Is it not time for you to know who you are after 400 years of submission to the white slave masters of America and their false religion of Christianity?

Death for Our Redemption In Christianity

Our true God is not like the "Spook God" of Christianity who demands death for our salvation and redemption. He is offering us Freedom, Liberty and the Pursuit of Happiness on this earth while we live. First, you must be given the names of your forefathers, whose names are the most Holy and Righteous Name Of Allah.

Again, I repeat, that restoring to you your identity is one of the first and most important truths to be established by God, Himself. All nations of the earth are recognized by the name by which they are called. By stating one's name, one is able to associate an entire order of a particular civilization simply by the name alone. For example, If you take the name "Lu Chin," we know immediately that this is a Chinese name, whose land of origin is China, a country that operates on an independent basis and is recognized throughout the world as a nation and her people demand respect.

We know this and more from the name Lu Chin. If we search among the peoples and the nations of the earth, we discover that this is an established truth from continent to continent.

20,000,000 Called By The Devil's Names

It is only when we come to America and learn the nations that names our people are now going in that we discover that a whole nation of 20,000,000 black people are going in the names of white people. How can a so-called Negro say that his name is "Sam Jones;" a white man's name whose roots are in Europe and "Sam Jones" (black men) comes from Africa or Asia?

My poor blind, deaf and dumb people are going in the wrong names and until you accept the names of your people and nation, we will never be respected because of the is alone. This is one of the reasons Almighty Allah has come amongst us, that is to give us His Names, the Most Holy and Righteous Names of the Planet Earth.

Allah Gives Names To Muhammad

It is Allah who gave me my name, "Muhammad." From this name, alone, our open enemies (the white race) know that the True and Light God has come into our midst and is doing a Divine Work amongst the so-called Negroes of America. The white men knows that Islam was our religion, our civilization and our way of life before he made us blind, deaf and dumb to this knowledge.

It has never been the white man's intention to restore to us this knowledge. Now that he sees his formerly dead ex-slaves returning to their own religion (Islam) and worshipping their own God (Allah) and awakening to the truth of their true identity, he knows that God, alone is bringing this change about.

Soon All Will Accept Truth

The white race knows and admits that it is only a matter of time when all the truth will be accepted by our people to his deepest regret. I warn you, my people, God said this from His Own Mouth!

A good name is indeed, better than gold. I am naught but a Warner and a Messenger to you, my people, not self sent, but directly from Almighty God (Allah).

HAVE WE QUALIFIED MAN AND WOMEN FOR SELF GOVERNMENT? PART I

The answer to this question is YES. We do not have to be equal in knowledge with every nation to be successful in operating our own government. Were those Israelites 4,000 years ago the Egyptians equals? Were those whites who first came to this country seeking self government equal to England's Parliamentary Lords?

There are probably many independent people who do not have as many with the "know-how" of the American educated class of so- called Negroes.

We have enough technicians such as mathematicians, construction engineers, civil engineers, mechanical engineers, physicists, chemists, educators, agriculturists, navigators, and aeronauts, among the 20 million or more of us.

Plenty of Scholars, Scientists

You will find scholars or scientists we can use in every branch of government; then, there are our own independent people outside of this country who would be glad to help us get going in a country or state to ourselves. We do not expect or desire to build a government patterned after that of the white man.

Naturally, we would need help for the next 20 or 25 years; after that, we would be self-supporting! The spirit of "doing for self" is now fast coming into our people. They need a new education of self and others.

United under the crescent of Islam is all that is necessary for you and me to become the world's greatest people. The lying and slavery teachings of the white man's Christianity that has crucified our people over the earth must be given up! We must accept the true religion (Islam) of Jesus and the Prophets before and after him before we can be successful in doing anything.

We Have No Future

Let the foolish educators and teachers think not that we have a future in white America's promises. For they themselves do not have a future unless they are willing to divide this country between our people (so-called Negroes) and the Indians whom they robbed nearly 500 years ago. However, we must have some of this earth that we can call our own - and soon.

We and also the Indians, deserve justice in this matter! We can no longer think in the slavery time terms that we used to think. The preachers need and must be taught the true religion of God and stop enslaving our people into that lying and slavery- teaching of the devils (white race).

Believe it or not, we have been serving and worshipping the REAL DEVILS! STOP preaching that old lie that God loves all human beings. He most certainly does NOT love the devils (the white race). He set a day for their doom the day they were grafted and given 6,000 years to rule us. A rule of lying and murdering us day and night and deceiving nearly the entire nation of Black, Brown, Yellow and Red people.

I possess a letter that is supposed to be authentic on how the devils boast of how they have murdered (killed) 100,000,000 black Africans since they have contacted them with their lying Christianity. Do we not love our black brothers' blood regardless to where spilled?

List of Murders

In 1898, a devil by the name of Lacroix, representing Belgium's "big business," admitted he had murdered 160 so-called Negro men , women and children. He also admitted he had tortured some and crucified women and children.

THE CONGO: In 1880, Belgium estimated a population of 80,000,000. By 1911, the population was reduced to 20,000,000 by 1960 the population was 13,000,000.

In 1894 an English traveler, E.J. Glave reported: "Twenty-one heads of black men were brought to Stanley Falls and used as decorations around a flower bed in one of the home of a high- ranking army officer. Missionaries reported that white Christians forced the Negroes into slavery producing rubber."

And if the rubber was of bad quality, the poor black slaves were made to eat it. And you are fools enough to preach their deadly- poisoned religion, Christianity, to the suffering of self and kind. Are you in love with your open enemies, and murderers of all black people, God and His Prophets? Then stick around and see where you will end up!

HAVE WE QUALIFIED MEN AND WOMEN FOR SELF GOVERNMENT? PART II

"And when the devil will say when the matter is decided: Surely Allah promised you a promise of truth and I promised you then failed you. And I had no authority over you, except that I called you and you obeyed me. So blame me not but blame yourselves. I cannot come to your help, nor can you came to my help. I deny your associating with Allah before." (Holy Qur'an 14:22.

The above verse is now being fulfilled. The false leadership of the lost-found members of the Asiatic Nation from the Tribe of Shabazz, so-called Negroes, sincerely loves and worships the devils (white race) in such manner that should be due only to Allah (God).

The devils know that the so-called Negroes are fools for worshipping them as if they were equal to Allah. But the devils will not admit this until the truth forces them to admit that they are not equal to Allah. They will also admit that Allah's promise is true, but their promise is false. The devils did not intend to live up to the truth of their promise even when they made it! But knowing that their followers (so-called Negroes) were blind, deaf and dumb to the knowledge and the truth of them, they could, therefore make false promises, and the blind, deaf and dumb would believe them.

Want To "Socialize"

So it is today, the so-called Negro leadership is so desirous to socialize with the devils under the present act of "integration" that they forsake Allah (God) and His promise of truth -"of setting them in heaven at once!"

The so-called Negro seeks to hasten the devils to fulfill their promise of integration by telling the devils:

"If you don't hurry and fulfill that which you promised us, the Muslims will take all of us." In other words, they are saying this:

"If you will do better by us than you have done in the past, then we will not accept Allah (God) and His Messenger, Elijah Muhammad. We love you and this world's life and will not follow anyone who does not love and follow you." But the devils will admit, after the truth is confirmed, that they have no authority over them, the so-called Negroes, (keeping them from believing in Allah, following His Messenger and the Teachings of Allah's religion, Islam) except that they (devils) called you (so-called Negroes) and you obeyed them.

Afraid To Disobey

The poor, fearful, disbelieving so-called Negroes are too afraid to disobey their known murderers (white Americans). But today, it is different. Obey the call of Allah and disobey the devils who have no power over you if you submit to Allah. The day is very near when you and the devils whom you take for friends will not be able to help each other against Allah.

In fact, and you see it today, any opposition to the teaching of Islam is not prosperous. It is the aim of Almighty Allah (God) to make His religion of TRUTH to triumph over all other religions, even though the believers of other religions may be against it (Islam). See Holy Qur'an 61:8,9,

Watch Your "Friends"

The Holy Qur'an Chapter 9:23,24, warns the Muslims of taking even their disbeliever parents for friends in these words:

> *"O you who believe, take not your fathers and your brothers for friends if they love disbelief above faith, and whoever of you takes them for friends, such are the wrong doers.*

> *"If your fathers and your sons and your brethren and your wives and your kinsfolk and the wealth you have acquired and trade whose dullness you fear, and dwellings you love are dearer to you than Allah and His Messenger and striving in His way, then wait until Allah brings His command to pass."*

There are many who would believe the truth (Islam), but their love for their disbelieving near of kin and friends are greater than their love for Allah and the truth. This lack of love for Almighty Allah (God) will cause them to go to hell with the disbelievers.

HELP SELF BEFORE HELPING OTHERS - PART I

Do you have a name of Allah (God)? There are 99 names of Allah, and "Allah" makes the 100th. You owe it to yourself and your future to be called by one of Allah's names. So-called Negroes, who are the lost-founds members of the Tribe of Shabazz, belong in one of these 100 names of Allah; and they owe it to themselves to hurry and get in His Name. The Bible makes this abundantly clear that those who are without the Name of Allah (God) will be the losers on the Day of Judgment (Isa. 65:15; Rev. 14:9,10).

There are many who think a name means nothing. Those who believe a name means nothing are in great need of teaching. The first thing that is asked into getting acquainted with people is: "What is your name?" We are absolutely judged according to the value of our names. We have been the property of strange and wicked masters and they have called us by their names, which are not Divine Names. Their names are Worthless, and are not deem human names; for example: fish, bird, wood, tree, roundtree, sawyer, rivers, waters, and many others. There will be no one in His Hereafter who does not have a Name of Allah. As Allah's (God's) name is eternal, so must we who are lucky to see the Hereafter, have a name that will live forever.

The present names of the Muslims are names of Allah some use His name "Allah." The names of this wicked race of devils are to be destroyed with them. (Isa. 65:15,

Rev. 14:11). There are many prophecies in the Bible on the total destruction this wicked world as you and I know it to be. So be not too proud to seek a good name that will live forever - a Name of Allah's. Never forget that the Nation of Islam is infinite, the religion of Islam is the only religion accepted by God. Islam means entire submission to the will of Allah. Therefore, those who submit to Allah are called by His name, and will live forever with Allah.

[Those of my] followers going to the white courts to get permits to be called one of the Names of Allah (attributes), this is by no means necessary! There is no price on a good name from Allah. Allah - (God) wants to give you one of His eternal names if you will accept and submit to Him.

These present names you are being called in, are not your names at all! They are the white devil's names. They call you after their names as their fathers did when you were their personal property (slave); but remember, you are not their personal property today! The coming of Allah has redeemed us; by nature you are not a member of the devil's race. But they wish to keep you in their worthless names because they know their race and names are limited on the earth, and your nation and Allah's names are unlimited. We are the real owners of the heavens and earth. It was our fathers who created it, not a white man.

You will soon come to know that we should be ashamed, after having the knowledge to be called after the names of our white slave masters; our open enemies of Allah and the righteous black people whose future was limited to rule for 6,000 years. This time ended in 1914. The white race cannot help from doing evil, killing and doing injustices to each other - let alone you and me!

Be happy that the day is here that their evil doings shall be put to an end. The few ignorant (having not knowledge) Muslims who think that they (white race) are the people of Allah shall soon be made ashamed. The entire white race are the real devils by nature. If you are wise or would like to be made wise, get out of their names into one that shall live forever.

HELP SELF BEFORE HELPING OTHERS - PART II

Many of my people, the so-called Negroes, say we should help the victims of Africa which are awakening. This has been said, as if we owned America. We are so foolish! What part of America do you have that you can offer towards helping Africa? Who is independent, the nation of Africa or we? The best act would be to request the independent governments of Africa and Asia to help us. We are the ones who need help. We have little or nothing to offer as help to others. We should begin to help at home first.

We are twenty million strong. Many of the nations today that have their independence and those who are getting their independence, are smaller in number than my people here in America. Just South of America is Cuba, which has a little over six and one-half million people. They are independent. We are more than three times their number and are not yet exercising the steps of freedom. We are dependent on the slave-master. We do not have two feet of earth for our people. They also have independence. Remember, that we are numbering over twenty million and we have nothing!

Peru has close to ten million people and they have independence. Sudan has a little over ten million; Liberia has about ten million; the Congo has about twelve million; Tunisia has about four million and Afghanistan has about twelve million people and all are independent. Even in

81

this hemisphere, the West Indies, with close to three and one-half million people, have gained their independence.

You and I, here in America, are licking the boots of the slave- master, begging him for rights of independent people. Yes! We are licking his boots. `Sir, let me shine your shoes?' You have been doing that for approximately four hundred years. Today, if one rises up in your midst and says, "We should not lick the slave-masters' boots, we should lick our own boots," you say, "He should be killed because he is teaching us to hate." My people, you are in a dangerous position. Get out of your fear and stand up for your people! Who are you not to die for your people? Who am I not to die for my people? If I am shot down or cut down today, who is little Elijah Muhammad to twenty million of you? If a million of us throw ourselves in the fire for the benefit of the twenty million, the loss would be small compared to the great gain our people would make as a result of that sacrifice. Hundreds of thousands of Muslims gave their lives in Pakistan to get independence....They were successful. The black man in Africa is fighting and dying, today in unity for their independence.

We sit here like pampered babies. We cannot even stand up on the floor; not to think about taking a chance of crawling out of the door. We are too careful of shedding blood for ourselves. We are willing to shed all of it for the benefit of others. I am not trying to get you to fight. That is not even necessary, our unity will win the battle. Not one of us will have to raise a sword. Not one gun would we need to fire. The great cannon that will be fired is our unity. Our unity is more powerful than any atomic weapon or hydrogen bomb. All we have to is unite. Our unity is the best. Why are you afraid to accept Allah and Islam? It is only because the slave-master did not teach you of this! We must unite as a nation of people!

Separation of the so-called Negroes from their slave-master's children is a must. It is the only solution to our problems. It is the only solution, according to the Bible, for Israel and the Egyptians. Separation will prove to be the only solution for America and her slaves, whom she mockingly calls her citizens, without granting citizenship. We must bear in mind, at all times, that we are being mocked.

You must know that this is the time of our separation and the judgment of this world (the Caucasian), which you and I have known. Therefore, Allah (God), has said to me that the time is ripe for you and me to accept our own, the whole planet earth. Are you waiting for the Divine Destruction? Come! Let us reason together. First, in order for us to reason, you must have a thorough knowledge of self. Who is going to teach you the knowledge of self; surely, not your slave-master who blinded you to that knowledge? The Slave-master, will not teach you the knowledge of self, as there would not be a master-slave relationship any longer.

Today, for the first time in our history, we have that True Friend in Allah (Whom came in the person of Master Fard Muhammad) and the Nation of Islam. We have only to submit and accept Him. Allah (God) to Whom praises due, is here to give you and me a superior knowledge of things and a country of ourselves.

THE HOPEFUL AND THE HOPELESS

We must have faith in the truth when it comes to us. We (so- called Negroes) today, are divided into two classes: the hopeful and the hopeless. The two classes confuse each other. The poor, uneducated, under privileged, the victims of the lawless brute force of our enemies are the hopeful, and they gladly bare the truth as it is written in Mark 12:37.

The intellectuals, the rich, the religious leaders and teachers of the old order are always the "die hards" with the rulers of the people (the poor so-called Negroes, the Lost-found members of the tribe of Shabazz). Allah (God) is now opening their hearts for the acceptance of the truth; the knowledge of self and others, the true religion, Islam; the religion in which the Believers are rightly guided, backed and protected by the Author, Allah (God). The Truth (Islam) inspires hope in them for a better future in a better world where freedom, justice and equality is the nature and rule of the people - where hypocrites and murderers will not be tolerated. A future where every Believer is the brother of the Believers, and is carried into practice every minute of the hour.

The poor wants freedom indeed! He wants equal justice, equal opportunity, and an equal chance to bring into practice every good faculty that is latent in him. He wants to live under a government of righteousness and where unjust judges and rulers will not exist; where the poor enjoys peace and security equally with the rich and the rulers of the land.

Allah, through their belief is Islam, makes the once slaves to lift up their heads in pride, honor and respect. The once slaves are made to feel equal with their masters and is fired with the spirit or doing for self. He will want to be a servant for no one except Allah, to whom his life becomes dedicated. He now, for the first time, feels like a man with a true sense of self- pride. He now has hope and is hopeful of his future. Now, as all other independent people, he wants some of this earth he can call his own, wherein he (and his people) can set up a government of his choice. This is the effect Islam has upon the Believers.

The hopeless are the rich and wealthy; teachers, educators, religious leaders and politicians lovers, the friends of the enemies of the poor. They have no hope in self, nor in their nation. Their hopes are in the robbers of their people (the white slave masters). They are qualified to start self-government, except for having the knowledge of self. Many of them are experts in every avenue of the political sciences in government; were given the chance to study and learn from the slave masters. But they just feel and believe that to try leaving their old slave masters and teachers, will cause them to go to the bread line. They are hopeless. They would rather lick the boots of their masters than to leave their masters and demand some of this earth they can call their own wherein they can set up their own government to their own likeness.

We (20,000,000 so-called Negroes) cannot forever depend on the white race to make jobs for us and our children. We must prepare and qualify men of our own race to help lead and put our people in the paradise of self-rulership.

We have in you, and in us - if united - the know-how to create and make jobs for ourselves and people; why do we not do it? It is because of the enemy of <u>hopelessness</u> in the ability of self to do something for self! For too long we have been dependent upon the slave masters. Let us stand up as men and demand OR TAKE some of this earth for our 20,000,000 homeless whether the world like it or not! We must have a home on some of this earth we can call our own AND AT ANY PRICE.

WE MUST HAVE MORE THAN A JOB!

The condition and history of my people,(the so-called Negro in America), is pitiful and a disgrace before civilized people of the earth. We have nothing of our own! We can only say we have what the slave-master and his children have given us. It is a foolish idea to depend on the white man to care for us and our ever increasing population. The leader of the Nation of the black man in America must get this foolish idea out of their heads and quick!

I think the American white man has done a good job in a manner of speaking in caring for us one hundred years, after he has said to our fathers that we were free. We have not exercised that freedom nor have we asked the rulers of the land to let us go for ourselves. We have not said to the slave-master, "Take that which belongs to you and let us have that which you have taken from us." Instead, we have acted as a lazy man.

My people have constantly asked the white man to give, give, give. Their cry has been of pleading and begging. To the slave-master have been said, "I want the love and friendship of you who have enslaved my fathers, not the love of my own kind." This is the prevailing idea of the leadership of the so-called American Negro. Their craving is to be made like their slave-master and his children. "Let me be like them. Let me be the brother or sister of white America." They ask this before they even love their own kind. We have been craving for the love of other than our own kind. It is an act of which we should be ashamed. It is an act of craving that is disgracing you and your children. It is an act that keeps you a slave and causes criticism by the civilized nations of the earth.

I desire that you think along the terms of Elijah Muhammad. The so-called Negro must be separated from his slave-master and his children. He must be given the chance to build a nation for himself. He must be given the chance to go for self. The so-called Negro is four hundred years behind with a history in the Western Hemisphere written in hard labor, injustice and blood. We have always been ready to jump to our feet and defend the slave-master against his enemies.

For those lost lives and efforts, we have nothing today. My people have become a nation of beggars. We only beg the master for a job. We want sport and play on an equal basis with the rich white man of America. The country belongs to the white man who took it from the red Indian. All we have asked for is a job. Then we give the paycheck back to the white paymaster. We keep five dollars to sit in a show or a game of sport and play. The Bible states we are a foolish people. You must get out of such foolish acts! You must unite and help me. Regardless of your fear of the slave-master and his children, you must unite with me. We have before us a job that must be done! We must care for and deliver our people. Our people are crying for freedom, moaning for justice and calling for equality to be free to integrate, intermarry or mix the blood as this is already going on. It is a disgrace before the nations of the earth.

Almighty God, Allah is in our midst today to bring the so-called American Negro out of the hands of the slave-master just as He delivered Moses and his people out of the hands of Pharaoh from a four-hundred year period of bondage.

KNOW THYSELF PART I

There is now an effort to celebrate a so-called "Negro History Week" beginning February 12, and some of my people will participate. The planning of that week, to teach the slave a knowledge of his past is not complete, sufficient nor comprehensive enough to enable my people to learn the true knowledge of themselves. It is important that my people learn the true knowledge of self as it means their salvation.

We are not Negroes because God, Whose proper name is Allah, has taught me who we are. We are not "Colored" people because God has taught me who we are and He has taught me who the "Colored" people are. The poor so-called American Negro is without a knowledge of self. You are a so-called Negro because you are not a Negro. Allah (God) has given to me our proper names, the people from which we were taken and brought here to the shores of North America and the history of our forefathers. Allah has taught me and today I do not fear to tell you, that you can discard that name "Negro." We are not Colored! Those are some of the main things which we should remember.

We must become aware of the knowledge of self and the time in which we are living. You must know these things whether you agree that Elijah Muhammad is on time or out of time. If what I say is out of season it goes for nothing. If I am on time or in season, then all I say will bear fruit. There is much misunderstanding among us because of our inferior knowledge of self. We have been to schools where they do not teach us the knowledge of self. We have been to the schools of our slave- masters children. We have been to their schools and gone as far as they allowed us to go. That was not far enough for us to learn a knowledge of self. The lack of knowledge of self is one of our main handicaps. It blocks us throughout the world. If you were the world, and you are a part of the world, you would also turn a man down if he didn't know who he actually was. If we, the so-called Negroes, don't know ourselves, how can we be accepted by a people who have a knowledge of self?

If we are representing ourselves as Negroes and "Colored" people, how did we get these names? Where do we find the age or the record of Negroes and "Colored" people in the ancient history of black man? Your search of the ancient history of the black man of the Earth will prove that not once in time were Negroes or "Colored" people living in Asia or Africa. How did we come by those names? The names are from the slave-masters. They have called us by their names and the nick-names used among themselves. It even seems that we like being called by the slave-masters names. After nearly a hundred years of freedom, we are still representing ourselves by the names our slave-master called us! We must learn that the slave-masters names are not accepted by God nor by the righteous people of God.

It is time for us to learn who we really are, and it is time for us to understand ourselves. That true knowledge is here for your today whether you accept it or reject it. God has said that we are members of the original people or black nation of the Earth. Original means first. Historian

J.A. Rogers points out in his books that beyond the cotton fields of the south and long before the white man himself was a part of our planet, we were the original people ruling the Earth and according to The Holy Qur'an, we had governments superior than any we are experiencing today. Trace over the Earth. Check back five, ten or twenty thousand years ago. Look at history who were those people? They were our people! Today, we are confronted with proof of who the original people are and who shall live on this Earth and call it their own.

KNOW THYSELF - PART II

The first shall be the last! If we are the first people, and that is an undeniable fact, we shall be the last! We cannot find a people who were before the black man. Beyond a shadow of doubt, the black man was the first man in the sun. If we preach a doctrine today that a the black man will be the last and that he will come into power today, why should you be surprised? Should you be surprised to learn that the so-called American Negro is a member of that nation which was here trillions of years before the white race? Should you be surprised that we preach the black man will be here after others are gone? The original tree is stronger than its branches. We have been robbed, spoiled and buried under the rubbish heap. Allah has told me that we are the original people - we are the father of all races. If truth is called teaching supremacy, then it will have to stand! An examination will prove to the contrary. You will find white supremacy is taught to us in the North, South, East and West of America. It is a shame! The white race's achievements, history, inventions, discoveries, ownership, progressiveness and godliness are from us, the original nation.

Some scholars say that we have come to the crossroads. They say that we have met on the "field of decision." I don't condemn them. I say, the so-called Negro has arrived at the day in which we must make our minds up to take our place alongside our own kind. We are in a day that we have no time for sport and play. Nor are we in a day that we should sit down, sing love songs or play games of chance. We are in a serious time! A time when the old world is going out and a new world is coming in.

The solution to our problem is separation from the white world. Some of us think that we cannot solve our problems unless we have it dictated by our slave-master's children. Those are the thoughts of you who have lost your heads. It is time that you know self, and know that Allah (God) is in our midst, manifesting the time. You will soon come to know that there is no God but Allah and I am His servant. Be yourself - Allah has said that you are the best, the powerful.

WE MUST HAVE LAND AS OTHER NATIONS

YOU SAY, BUT, I don't want the white man to carry us. Just give us an equal chance," What kind of equal chance? What do twenty million people look like milling around in a factory of white people all the days of their lives and their children's lives, looking for a job? We need to look for some land. Who will recognize millions and millions of people who will not protest their condition? Yours and my condition here in America is the worst of any people on earth - it is unequalled, and we are without one tiny state in the union. We are still demanding equality. The white man will not accept you as his equal because he knows his slave is not his equal. He does not want you to marry his daughter. He does not want you as his son or his son- in-law even though you greedily desire to be. You are most eager for integration so you may have a chance of inter-mixing and inter-marrying with them than you are for justice for your people and getting some land - land for you and your children on this earth.

IF I AM YOUR equal as you are a citizen, then prove that I am a citizen of America by giving to me some earth like that which you own. The so-called American Negroes can never have a successful future in America as long as they do not own some earth. You are a nation within a nation. You have been carried by another nation all your life, here in America for more than four hundred years. Today you continue to beg them to carry you and recognize you as their equal without even asking them for something. You are not asking them for anything worth-while. Why don't

99

you unite as leaders and go down to Washington and tell the Washington leaders, "We don't want to sit in your schools beside you. What we really want from you, if you don't want to let us go, is a place for our people in this country. You have said that we are free. Let us go! If we are not going and you will not help us to go, then give us a chance to live to ourselves here. We don't want to force our presence on you and upon your children. If you will not let us go and seek earth somewhere else other than America, then set aside some of these states for us."

THE SO-CALLED AMERICAN Negroes say they don't want to be separated and that is because of their inferior knowledge of their own kind and the white race. If you had a thorough of yourself and a thorough knowledge of the white race, you would desire to be separated. What have the slave-masters done in the way of justice that we should want to live with them? What have they done in the way of justice that we should want to eat with them, drink with them, walk with them or marry them? What have they done for us that make the so-called Negroes desire them? It appears to be their greatest desire to make unity and love to the slave-masters children. You should first make unity and love among yourselves and your own kind. I think white people would be foolish to accept a so-called Negro as a friend or as a neighbor of theirs, when he is not a friend or neighbor to himself. We are divided. There is no unity among us. We have allowed the slave-master's religion to divide us one hundred percent. We do not have a knowledge of the Whiteman or ourselves. I have told you the truth.

Some of you say and write that, "Elijah is teaching hate." What is there in the teachings of Elijah Muhammad that you can single out as "hate teaching?" What part or the whole of this teaching do you construe as hate? If I say that you should love yourself as a black man, is that hate? I say that black mankind are the people from whom you were taken. Is that hate? I say the white race came after the black and is a grafted race from the black man. Is that hate? I am not telling you to hate white people. I am only telling you who they are. We are very quick to single out one of our own as an enemy, when he speaks up for the good of black mankind. I am for the black man!

SOME OF YOU may not like me because I love my own kind. Any man that is brown, yellow, red or coal black is a member of the black nation. Any man who has not accepted self or speak and love others more than his own kind, cannot be trusted. The time has arrived for the truth. You should know exactly where you stand. There are no people more blessed this day than the so-called American Negroes, who have been chosen by Allah Himself, The God of The Universe. You and I should be happy to know today that we have on our side a God who defends and guides us. You may believe in that which the slave-master gave to you for a religion. But you must prove to me that it was the religion of the prophets. You may say, "the Negro is not mentioned in the Bible or any Holy Book." If you don't see where you are mentioned by the name, "Negro," it is only right that you should discard the name. Then see if you can find yourself under some other name. Almighty God, Allah, has taught me the truth to teach to you. I must deliver it to you whether you accept it or not. It is not my fault if you reject it after I offer the truth to you. It is my fault if I don't offer to you the truth God gave to me.

WHAT DAY ARE we living in. We are living in the day of judgment of the Caucasian World. We are living in the day in which we should separate. You must know this even though your minds are filled with wealth, sport and play. It is the time of judgment of this world as you and I have known it. There are scholars who think this is the time of their judgment. Who is going to tell you, if one of your own kind does not? Are you looking again for a spirit God.

MR. MUHAMMAD SPEAKS

The Monroe, Louisiana, southern courts with their southern judges of hatred and attorneys of hatred and are Negro-blood thirsty take their own law of justice, twist it up and throw it back up on the shelf. And when they look and see a poor, innocent so- called Negro begging for justice as his grand-parents before their grandparents as far back as 400 years ago, they receive nothing but the spitting of anger and threats of murder from the Judge throughout the courts of America. Just to mention `justice' for a so-called Negro in the south is an insult to the judge who is supposed to be the judge of right and wrong between the state and opposing attorneys. He becomes more a vicious enemy against the poor so-called Negro than even the prosecuting attorney when he sees a so-called Negro before him.

The so-called Negroes have no justice under the law, not only in the south, but nowhere in America. As I plainly stated this in Washington D.C., in 1959 in the Uline Arena before 10,000,000 people that everything has failed us as far as justice is concerned the Justice Department in Washington, the churches, the priests, and the preachers have all failed the so-called Negroes when it comes to justice.

By the help of Allah, and by the blood of the original man whose father is the originator, I Elijah Muhammad, will fight for this cause to get our people justice in America. And by the help and power of Allah and the power of the universe, and the power that is in the Nation of Islam, and the power of every atom that is bound in the planet earth and that is bound in other planets.

What angers America is just the idea of her 400-year old slaves now wanting to go over to the paradise of freedom, justice and equality under the crescent of the divine religion of Islam where they will have sincere brotherhood and friends throughout the civilized world.

America knows that under her flag we have received nothing but hell; beatings and killings without due process of law day and night - not in the past only, but the present. She wants to make some so-called Negroes believe that the religion of Islam can be thrown out the window by turning hypocrites themselves in trying to make democracy work. This is done just to deceive the so-called American Negroes.

But I say to everyone who reads this paper that Islam is here among these black people to stay as long as there is life in their bodies. The God of Islam (Allah) is with me and will back me and others up who are working hard to deliver our people from such an evil and merciless race of devils. What glory and honor does a so-called Negro get under the stars and stripes? No honor, no glory - only hell. We have proof of this by their so-called courts and justice. There is no justice for us; and this America knows. She would like to hurt everyone of you and make you like it; it pleases America to do you evil. But not we Muslims; we will declare the truth and die for it! Thanks to Allah for removing fear from us, and I pray he puts it in them that they may fear and tremble every day until they be taken out of the way!

MUSHROOM GROWTH OF NEGRO MUSLIM MOVEMENT BARED

The Negro Muslim movement, whose California headquarters are in Los Angeles, came under investigation more than two years ago, the State Senate Fact-Finding Subcommittee on Un-American Activities disclosed Monday.

"Since that time the movement has grown at an amazing pace," the committee reported.

The movement, which is sometimes referred to by its officers as the "Lost-Found Nation of Islam in North America," is " competing with the Communists for the Negro minority," the report said.

"It, too, is based on force and violence and class hatred. It, too, operates in secrecy and is based on a fanatic adherence to a potent ideology. It, too, advocates the forcible overthrow of our government - indeed, of the entire white race."

Estimating that Muslim members number 70,000 in the country, the committee declared:

"Every real or fancied act of discrimination drives more Negroes into Muslim ranks... "Prominent Negro leaders throughout the country have unanimously condemned the Muslim movement.

"But virtually all of them concede that it has exerted a great appeal to many Negroes, it has given them a purpose, a hope, something to work for. It has bound them together with ties of religious and anti-white fanaticism, and although members declare they are conscientious objectors they would at the same time eagerly rise in violence against the white man.

The report said Muslims advocate separation from the white "slave master" and building a social and economic system "for the deliverance and salvation of the Negro people."

Muslims in prisons, the report pointed out, have been causing trouble by demanding "complete segregation from white inmates" and the right to practice their rights.

The movement was found in 1933 by Wallace Fard in Detroit, and for the last 15 years has been headed by Elijah Poole calls Muhammad, the Messenger of Allah.
The main office of the California Muslims is at Washington Blvd. and Figueroa St.

Muslims, the report said, "are required to follow many of the dictates" of the Moslem religion. This includes praying five times a day facing toward Mecca.

The committee wondered whether the Smith Act, "Which resulted in the conviction of so many Communist leaders in this country," might not be applied to the Muslims.

A NATION IN A NATION

We, the once slaves have grown to be a nation of twenty million or more in a nation that enslaved our fathers, and to this day has deprived us of equal justice under their own laws. No equal civil right - most of us are treated by white citizens of America as animals. It is common to see and hear of white mobs attacking, beating and shooting down poor blacks, whose fathers and mothers labor, sweat and blood helped make America the richest government on earth; nevertheless, we are yet the most hated and mistreated people.

Allah (God) wants to make a great nation out of us (so-called Negroes). But if we desire to remain the slave or servants for our slave masters, it is all right with Allah. Do we love ourselves and our children? If so, why not we build a future for ourselves rather than beg the same slave masters for jobs, and equal shares in whatever they have - even to equal membership in their society and families (inter-marriage).

This is definitely not a wise thing to do, but a very foolish and destructive thing for the once slave and his master to do. By the help and guidance of Allah (God), I have put before you the wise and best thing for your future.

Firstly, some of this earth that we can call our own. Without some of this earth that we can call our own, we cannot hope to even become a free nation out of the nation of the slave master. IT IS FAR MORE IMPORTANT TO TEACH SEPARATION OF THE BLACKS AND

WHITES IN AMERICA THAN PRAYER. Teach and train the blacks to do something for self in the way of uniting and seeking a home on this earth that they can call their own!

There is no such thing as living in peace with white Americans. You and I have tried without success. Look what white Americans did to my followers in Los Angeles, California on April 27, 1962. They know that we, the Muslims, are a peaceful people and do not carry arms, but the heartless enemy devils care not for peace, they were created and made to hate peace. Night and day they are out seeking a chance to beat and kill you while at the same time you are out seeking to show them HOW MUCH YOU LOVE THEM. A very foolish people you are. How can anyone other than you (so-called Negroes) love an open enemy?

It is the right time that we [seek] INDEPENDENCE for our nation from the evils of our open enemies, and not the foolish things other organizations are doing. They want our people integrated into our open enemies, to be destroyed as a people. They seek that (recognition) which means better qualifications, education, knowledge of self and others, manners and self-respect and the respect of others. But our people just do not have these qualifications until they first come to Islam and bear witness to what Allah (God) has revealed to me. No intelligent and refined society will accept us until we have the above stated qualifications.

We just cannot complete with them in business unless we unite and get some of this earth that we can produce our own people's needs. For example, here in Chicago, Illinois, the black man is robbed on the Southside of the city through giant cut-rate stores owned by the white man, who makes it almost impossible for black peoples independent stores to survive. But with the right understanding and business unity among us, we could turn this great flow of millions of dollars from going to the North side's White businessmen back into the pockets of the poor Blackman on the Southside. ASK ME HOW YOU CAN DO IT?

We must stop being foolish as to spend our few hard earned dollars with the rich of the land. You who are wealthy or rich among us should help set up independent businesses that your people demand which would add wealth to your people and also yourself through lower prices. This would also give employment to our people. But to be successful, WE MUST HAVE SOME OF THIS EARTH TO PRODUCE OUR PEOPLE NEEDS.

SO-CALLED NEGRO LEADERSHIP - PART I

The leadership of my people, the so-called American Negro, has absolutely aided the slave-master in keeping us a subjected people. The leadership continues to make a cry for social equality with white people. What intelligent people would want to fraternize, intermingle, integrate, sweetheart and marry the kidnappers, murderers, enslavers and burners of their people? Only a people such as my people with blind leadership would ever desire or strive for such a lowly disgraceful act! The blind cannot lead the blind. The leaders of my people want and show great favor with the slave-master against the good of their own people.

The so-called Negro editors, preachers, lawyers and other professional leaders of our people continue to lead the fight in begging the white man for civil rights. History shows we have been in this part of the world for more than four hundred years. We served more than three hundred of those years in servitude slavery. We have been so-called free for one hundred years since we were freed, we have been called citizens of America. Why then are we seeking civil rights if we are citizens of America? Why should the leaders of our people continue to beg the government to grant us civil rights? We don't have to beg the government to give us those glorious benefits that are laid down in the Constitution in the 13th and 14th Amendments. If we are citizens, we should be enjoying them without asking for them! Yet, we are still begging for justice! You need a better leadership.

The preacher leadership of my people are in the most ignorant class. They knowingly lead our people to a path of destruction and disaster because of their love of and fear of the enslavers of their people. We have records of several so-called Negro preachers who have made attempts o attack and destroy the Muslims and myself, The Messenger of Allah.

Reverend Borders of Atlanta, Georgia, on April 9, went on the air and stated to a radio audience that he would drive the Muslims from the city of Atlanta if he had the people with him. Reverend Borders would have an easier task of trying to dry the oceans up rather than direct his slave-masters slave-keeping attacks at us. Another preacher in Monroe, Louisiana, said the white officers who broke into our religious service March 5, on an un-armed people, should have killed us! This ignorant preacher, eager to show his slave-master that he is not with us, calls for the defeat of his own people. Reverend Gardner C. Taylor, who is warring with Reverend Jackson for control in the white man's Baptist religion, chose the occasion again to denounce the Muslims who practice Islam, the religion of Almighty God Allah. The preachers claim that they are men of God. Where is their proof? It was the preachers who condemned Jesus to his death! It was the elders who opposed Moses! It has always been the clergy class who opposed the prophets of God. Yes, the scribes and Pharisees as they are referred to in the scriptures, have always opposed the righteous men of Allah. They oppose me today. The religious leaders of our people will soon learn they cannot overcome the purpose of God. In the 61st Sura of the Holy Qur'an, it states that they desire to put out the word of Allah with their mouth.

The so-called Negro leadership does not care to give their own people justice as long as the white man does not. The Negro leadership and the slave-masters are as two murderers and thieves of my people. The white man murders us as the Negro leaders rob us. In fact, both will rob us.

Since our being kidnapped and brought to America, we have received nothing but promises. It is promises which today satisfy the leaders of my people. There is the promise of fair employment and integration or social mixing. The devil is full of tricks and we cannot put any confidence in him.

The leaders of my people must remember that we are all black people of the black nation. The hurt of one member should be the hurt of all of us. Regardless of the type of leader for my people, he should not be afraid to speak for his brother. Regardless to where he may be, the leader should be for his brother. He should not flinch. My people must wake up and know their present leaders have failed them. Such leadership should and must be discarded!

The religion of Islam has powerful life-giving effects on the believers. Islam makes the believer feel that he should get up and begin doing something for self. Islam makes you and I see each other as brothers. Islam arouses the old love for each other that was put asleep in us by the slave-master. I represent Islam as a religion to you. I want you to know the power and effect of that religion on us. If you ever accept Islam, you will stand up as one people and a nation. You will not lay as a race of slaves! We have a God with us! He is not to come because He is already here. Many Christians will admit that God must be present among us. Some of us today in this vast, moving world do not even take a moment of time to think or even check to see if this is the day of God's visit to a people or if it is the day of the devil's visit.

I have been sent directly from Almighty God, whose proper Name is Allah. He has given me that which the prophets wrote of, which will give my people life. It will bring light to you and your understanding will return. The leadership of my people would be wise in joining with me in this Divine awakening of our people. Their interference will lead only to their destruction in a lake of fire with the enemy of their people.

SO-CALLED NEGRO LEADERSHIP PART II

Why do you oppose Freedom, Justice and Equality for your people and self? Freedom, indeed has not been given to you in America; no equal justice has come to you, nor equal opportunity. Should not the Leadership seek good for his people, even at the cost of his life? What future do we have in being integrated in the white race who are the children of those who enslaved our fathers and mothers? Daily, we live under the very shadow of death at the hands of their children.

We want for our 20 million people here in America, what White America has for herself. You are a Nation within a Nation, depending on White America for sole existence - without trying, or even seeking a chance to try and do something for self - other than to beg for that which belongs to White America. You beg as though you are too lazy to work and build a future for self. What future does 20 million no-whites have [among] their slave-masters? Is not it clear to you that your hopes of existence depend only on whatever type of labor the white man will offer you? Can you hope to continue seeking employment for your 20 million people in the factories and offices of the white man, while he already has unemployment among his own which is increasing daily?

The ever-changing map of the white world is increasing their own problem of existence. You may be unable to see and foresee this, this is why we would like to help you see. Twenty million ex- slaves falling or refusing to see and go for self today, will prove to be fatal for them in the near future. If the blind cannot see his own way and refuses to be led by the hand of the seeing one, who can be sorry for his stumbles and falls?

Allah (God) is with us to do something for self, but you are opposed to doing something for self and choose to beg for the crumbs, while there are clear signs that soon there will be no crumbs for you. Judge between you and me in what I am seeking for our people and what you are seeking for them. I am seeking a permanent home for my people where they can be free to build a future for themselves. If you were only wise enough to come and confer with us, the picture would be a different one.

Gone forever is the Negro mule and plow. The white man is ever advancing in the science of machinery (mechanical devices) and is rapidly putting our people in the bread lines. Something must be done by us to check the spread of poverty, suffering and want of our people! We do not have to seek the solution. God has given it Himself. Submit to Allah, unite and let us go for self on some of this good earth.

You, as religious leaders of the people, are doing your people more harm than good in seeking to integrate them with the slave- master for total destruction. We must be separated from those who have enslaved us and are not willing to do Justice, nor grant us equal opportunity. WE MUST UNITE AND SEEK THESE THINGS FOR OURSELVES!

No Justice for So-Called Negroes Part I

The so-called Negroes of America will soon learn that there is NO justice under the Flag of America for them. You will soon bear witness that the white race of America is none other than the real devils in person. As Allah has said, if you will only think how they have mistreated you and I for the past four hundred years and the things that they have planned against the so-called Negroes, you would say to Allah and His Messenger that you bear witness there is no God but Allah Who has revealed to us the truth and pointed out to us our open enemies (the devils) who have been concealed from our knowledge.

They hate God for making them manifest and they curse the name of Allah (God) in the presence of the Muslims. They have been persecuting us ever since 1932, without a just cause. Many times we have been attacked by them with intentions of crushing us to keep you from hearing the truth of them that God has revealed. They have not and cannot deny the fact that they are the real devils. This truth of them they call "hate teachings," for they know you would not like them if their true self was revealed to you. All one has to do is to read the past history of the white race, and you will find that they have filled the world with evil and bloodshed since the day they were grafted and given the power to rule. (That power is now being taken from them). They do not love peace. They hate the black people and cannot and do not try to hide it. They will make false charges against you, hire false witnesses to testify against you - even among your own black people and say that you are planning evil and take you into their

117

courts before their unjust judges and juries and give life imprisonment for nothing. When you hire a lawyer, he has to argue your case with both the prosecutor and judge, who are supposed to listed and judge the justice of the argument made between the opposing and defense lawyers according to the evidence of the case. In [our] case, we the poor black people of America, especially if he or she is a Muslim and follower of Elijah Muhammad, you will see the Judge fighting the defense as much as the prosecutor. It is almost useless to hire a lawyer of your color or kind, because they don't give him any respect, regardless to how much he knows about the law. The black lawyers know this; [consequently], he is really afraid to use that part of the law that would help their clients, or prove to the world that there is no justice in the "lily white courts" of America that the white man is bound to respect, when it comes to the so-called Negroes; unless, the Negro is an "Uncle Tom." or a "stool pigeon," who is as poisonous against his or her own kind as the devils themselves.

A couple of weeks ago, in Monroe, Louisiana, the Chief and Commissioner of the Police Force went to a peaceful assembly of my followers where they were praising Allah (God) and teaching others of their kind to do like-wise behind closed doors. The Chief and Commissioner, without any warrant or protest from the people, or any disturbance of the peace, goes and break the door in with their other officers and start beating the heads of the peacefully-assembled people and hauls them to jail; put false charges against them and set their bonds from $1500 to $2500; within one week, they were ready to rail-road them to prison for long terms for NOTHING, but to try to hide their own evil done against a peaceful people, if we had not been present with a lawyer of their kind and the cash for bond.

NO JUSTICE FOR SO-CALLED NEGROES PART II

We await the day of April 18th when Judge W.M. Harper sentences eight Muslims whom Monroe police beat and brutally assaulted for worshipping in the religion of Islam. The police placed false charges against the Muslims to cover up their own disregard of the laws. It is stated in the U.S. Constitution that a person may practice any religion of his choosing, has the right of free speech and peaceful assembly without sanction by government authorities. Police Chief James Kelly stated to several of the Muslims during investigation of the religion of Islam that he would not tolerate the religion of Islam in Monroe. The Muslims face one year compulsory jail sentences and $500 fines each. Faced with the sentence, Islamic Teacher Troy X said, "There is no God but Allah and Muhammad is His Apostle."

The city officials of Monroe made an all out effort to break the Muslim's spirit and means and ways for obtaining defense counsel. The Muslims were attacked in their Mosque, a religious place of worship in Islam, by the police armed with machine guns, tear gas and heavy caveman-like clubs. The unarmed Muslims were beaten, arrested and placed under false charges of assaulting police officers on Sunday, March 5th. Included among arrested were children and the four months pregnant Muslim wife of the Islamic teacher. The Muslims were unable to get attorneys in Monroe to defend them in court as the local authorities brought political pressure on the attorneys. Every bonding company in Louisiana refused bonds to release the Muslims who were held in jail ten days. Muhammad's Mosque Headquarters in Chicago secured the services of Attorney James R. Venerable of Atlanta, Georgia. The Headquarters' Mosque placed $1,500.00 each as bail for the release of the Muslims. Attorney Venerable was arrested after the trial for auto theft even though he is numbered among the wealthiest white men of Georgia. Veteran observers said these false charges against the attorney were further intimidations to prevent the Muslims right to counsel. For four hundred years we have been deprived of equal justice.

Mr. Patrick M. Malin, Executive Director, American Civil Liberties Union, wrote Attorney General Robert F. Kennedy to intervene. Mr. Malin stated, "If the facts as presented to us by the Muslim Group are correct, a violation of federal civil rights seem to have occurred."...

Many legal experts doubted that the Justice Department would take serious note of the violations of the freedoms of religion provision in the U.S. Constitution. Attorney General Kennedy had information on the Muslims before the trial and failed to guarantee civil rights. All this is to prove that we have no justice under the American Flag.

NO JUSTICE FOR US IN USA

We have wondered why white people hate and mistreat us after we have been so obedient, so submissive, with "hat in hand" and a scared smile or grin on our faces from ear to ear.

We have killed their enemies for them, and sometimes those whom they called their enemies were our own people. For 400 years, we've tried to understand why the white race here in America hate, beat and kill their helpless free slaves, and yet preach Jesus Christ and God's love and justice; but even those white preachers and priests, the Pope (Father of the Church) have never united and protested to the government against the lawless, out-right beating and killing of us, the so-called American Negroes. (Members of the Tribe of Shabazz).

Injustice Increased

Even today, while the government is offering integration, (which will not solve our problem, but make it harder to solve) injustice to us have increased!

And the so-called `God-sent' white and black preachers of Christianity are not using their churches and followers to protest against these injustices. We are witnesses them, into a lake of fire. (The lake is none other than the entire continent of North against them, even by the recent police brutality and murder of our people in Los Angeles, April 27, 1962.

We do not have united Christian preachers nor priests of the churches protesting against such unprovoked, lawless, outright murder of our people. Even, according to the Los Angeles Times and the Herald-Examiner newspapers, the black preachers spoke in sympathy with that ungodly, merciless, brute police force headed by the worst hater (William Parker) of the black people in this unjust government of America. Today, Allah is making them manifest to the world as a race of devils, made to be our enemies and murderers until the day of their doom (which is very near).

Hits "Free Devil Murders"

Here in North America will the fire of hell take place first on those who sit and rejoice to see poor, innocent black men burned to ashes, at the hands of the free devil murderers of our people.

The black people of America must be given the knowledge of self and of these open heartless devils whose aims today are to take the poor black people to hell with them, while at the same time give you as much death and hell at their hands before Allah takes them into a lake of fire. (The lake is none other than the entire continent of North America).

They teach love, but this does not mean that they love you because of your belief in Christianity. NO! But rather that you love them - this will make you an enemy of God. I have warned you the white race's name alone will get you hell from God. They would like that you believe as you have always in that which they taught you - Christianity!

They call the Truth that I have received from Allah "hate teachings" because it makes them manifest. Who could love the devils after having the knowledge of them?

Deliver Poor And Needy

Read the following chapters and verses from your Bible which refers to you and them: Psalms 82:3,4. "Do justice to the afflicted; deliver the poor and needy; rid them out of the hands of the wicked (the white devils of the U.S.A.) They (the black people of America) know not, neither will they understand, they walk on into darkness.

All the foundation of the earth is out of course. (Not the earth itself, but the governments of the wicked is out of a wise course.) Justice standeth afar off (for the so-called Negroes.) Truth is fallen in the streets (is not accepted.)

"None calleth for justice (when it is for so-called Negroes, nor any pleadeth for the Truth; (They trust the devil's lies) the devils feet run to do evil, they make haste to shed innocent blood. (Kill a so-called Negro.) Their thoughts are evil, wasting and destruction." (Isa. 59:4,9,14)

Let us unite and seek some of this good earth for a home that we can call our own! Leave a people who are daily bent upon your destruction, your disgrace and shame alone!

SOME EARTH THAT WE CAN CALL OUR OWN

Stop wasting your money! Your money was not given to you - it came the hard way, so why should you give it away for that which you can do without? If you and I would do just that, we could save millions of dollars which we could put into education, the purchasing of land, machines, poultry, milk cows, beef cattle, sheep, machines to cultivate the land to cut and saw timber to build homes for ourselves. We should dig for mud to mold and burn into bricks for our own homes and factories and grow our own cotton to make the clothes which we wear. We should feed our own stomach and hire our own scientists from among ourselves. Produce our own needs, and capture our own market before it is too late.

How can we begin? Stop spending money for tobacco, dope, cigarettes, whiskey, wine, beer, fine clothes, fine automobiles, fine furniture, expensive rugs and carpets, gambling, prostitution, idleness, sport and play, games of chance and horse racing. Stop careless spending of money, credits, loans at a high interest, which means selling yourselves to slave for the "loan sharks." Stop going into stores seeking the highest priced merchandise to purchase. Buy according to your means (your income). If your income is only $75.00 or $100.00 per week, and your rent is about the same every month, and food about the same price; and you have clothes, transportation and other little bills to pay, can you then afford a high-priced care note of $100 to $145 per month? If you must have a car, buy the low-priced car, or a rich man's used car; and not his used Cadillacs and Rolls Royces. I hope that you will begin leaving off the use of these things which you do not need to buy.

For your health's sake, stop eating the swine's flesh (the animal that was grafted from cat, rat and dog for medical purposes, and sold to be nine hundred and ninety-nine percent poison)! Live and act as a civilized person and we will soon be able to say that we are living like civilized people, along with love and unity in the Name of your God and religion, Islam.

If you will write to The Public Relations Department, Muhammad's Mosque No. 2, Chicago, Illinois, we will send you information on how we can help build a great future for the so-called Negroes in America by just sacrificing the money that we throw away to destroy our health in cigarettes, beer, wine, hog and whiskey for one week out of each month!

Allah (God) does not like for us to break His law by eating the swine's flesh, drinking intoxicating drinks and using the poison tobacco weed. We must make a better future for ourselves and our children. Stop wasting and spending our money with the rich and spend it among ourselves, for we are the poor. Stop walking passed your own black brother's business to buy the merchandise of the rich just because the rich can sell at a lower price than your poor brother. Trade with you own kind until you are able to compete in prices.

PEACE PART I

Can there be any peace for the peace breaker? Allah told me that six thousand years ago, this same people's fathers (white race) broke the peace of the righteous in the gardens of Eden (the place that is known as old Persia). They called the truth of God a lie and made lies the truth.

They said to the people of the Garden, according to the Bible (Gen. 3:4-6),

> *"And the serpent (a name used according to the evil, deceiving characteristics of the Caucasian race) said unto the woman, you shall not surely die; for God doth know that in the day you eat thereof, then your eyes shall be opened, and you shall be as gods..."*

The serpent lied, because they did die. And the deceiver (serpent) was driven out of the garden into the wilderness of the earth to build a wicked kingdom of evil to be destroyed on the coming of God.

They (the white race) are playing the same trick on the black nation today as they did in the days of Adam. They shall suffer eternal expulsion from this earth in a lake of fire (Rev. 20:10). Can they enjoy peace? After they were cast out of the garden, according to the Holy Qur'an; 7:16, "because thou hast thrown me out of the way, Lo, I will lie in wait for them on the straight way." As he had deceived Adam and his wife, he now declares that he will deceive the righteous in their straight path in the days of the resurrection and judgment of his evil world. He swore to them in another place that he would lead them to a tree of immorality and a kingdom that decays not. This kind of teaching is found in the teachings of Christianity. It is a very clever way of deceiving the black people of America,

129

for here, Satan represents himself as an angel of light. They paint a picture of lies of "beyond the grave," when they know there is no life or communication with the dead. All ceases to be life after death. This is universally known. Can they have peace? When they were created to destroy the peace of the righteous, as it is written,

"Destruction cometh; and they shall seek peace, and there shall be none, mischief shall come upon mischief and rumor shall be upon rumor," (Ezekiel 7:25).

They wrongfully represent themselves as peace-makers and lovers of peace and freedom (but only for themselves). This kind of talk deceives the nations while at the same time they are the troublemakers. As it is written;

"but the wicked are like the troubled sea when it cannot rest, whose waters cast up mire and dirt."

So it is with this wicked race, whom God has permitted to become the richest and most progressed people of earth. The more they increase in riches and power, the more they seek to trouble those that are at peace with them. They envy the peace and progress of others and are never satisfied, though they have the world bowing at their feet. They are forever deceiving the poor so-called Negroes with false promises and the so-called Negroes seem to love it. There is no peace for the wicked saith the God of peace (Isa. 57;20,21) The only peace today is with Allah and in His religion of peace, Islam. Believe it or leave it! Hurry and join onto your own kind. The time of this world is at hand.

PEACE PART II

Islam, the religion of entire submission to the Will of Allah (God). "Nay, whoever submits his whole self to Allah and is a doer of good, - he will get his reward with his Lord; on such shall be no fear, nor shall they grieve." (Holy Qur'an 2:112)

That and that alone is Salvation according to the Holy Qur'an. Fear is the number one (1) enemy that is blocking progress and success from coming to the so-called Negroes of America. This fear causes them to grieve. The world knows the poor so-called Negroes of America have and still suffers more grief and sorrow than any people on earth. This fear is the fear of the slave- masters (white men) and what the slave-masters dislike.

Let the so-called Negroes submit to Allah (God), and they will not fear anymore, nor will they grieve anymore. As it is written: *"The fear of man bringeth a snare." (Proverbs 29:25)* This fear has surely snared the poor so-called Negroes.

The Lord of the world's the Finder of we the lost members of the Asiatic Black Nation for four hundred (400) years said, the slave-masters put fear in our Fathers when they were babies. Allah is the only one that can remove this fear from us, but He will not remove it from us until we submit to His will and not our will and fear Him, and Him alone. Then, as it is written:

> *"And it shall come to pass in the day that the Lord shall grieve thee rest from sorrow, and from they fear, and from the hard bondage wherein thou wast made to serve." (Bible: Isaiah 14:3).*

There are so many places that I could point out in the Bible and Holy Qur'an that warns us of fearing our enemies above or equal to the fear of Allah (God). It is a fool that has greater fear of the devils than Allah, who has the power to destroy the devils and their followers. (Bible: Rev. 21:8 - Holy Qur'an 7:18 and 15:43).

We must remember that if Islam means entire submission to the will of Allah, that and that alone is the True religion of Allah. Do not you and your religious teachers, and the Prophets of old teach that the only way to receive God's help or Guidance is to submit to His will, - then WHY NOT ISLAM! It (Islam) is the True religion and the only way to success.

AMERICA PERSECUTES THE MUSLIMS

The Monroe Louisiana City police made a wanton lawless brutal beastly attack on the peaceful religious meeting of my followers Sunday, March 5, 1961. [Afterwards], these law-breaking police officers placed false charges on my followers to cover up their law- breaking crimes and complete disregard of protection-provisions in the United States Constitution.

My people, the so-called American Negroes, have long been the victims of attacks by their slave-masters. The enemy always go free after doing these unjust things to our people. The history and record is filled with the facts of how the slave-master fails to bring his own to trial for breaking their own laws in mistreating us and denying us justice.

America tells the Negro he is an equal citizen and must fight for America, but America denies him justice. The so-called Negro has been declared an equal citizen. Where is this equal citizenship? It is only in words! It has not been in deeds! The so-called Negro does not have freedom in liberties of government that the slave-master enjoys, yet America refers to him as a citizen on an equal basis with the slave-master. The U.S. Constitution declares equal justice for all. This equal justice is never practiced on the so-called Negro. Since America cannot follow their own laws of the country, not to mention the laws of nature, why not separate the so-called Negro? By so doing, America would not be charged with injustice to her former slave. The so-called Negro in America has never had the opportunity to go for self.

If the slave-master said to his slave 100 years ago, "You are free," why didn't the slave-master send the so-called Negro back to where he came from, on his own land? Then say to his people" "Here is your brother that we kidnapped three hundred and ten years ago." No! The slave-master kept him caged in. If you take a wild bird and cage him, you are responsible for his well- being, treatment and protection - but no, you killed and burned the bird. If you let the bird out of the cage, giving him the opportunity to return among his own flock, the bird is then free to fly where is pleases.

The so-called Negro is here in your midst as you kidnapped and brought him here, more than 400 years ago. You have now set up an invisible chain and an invisible wall of limitations about him. Under your religious and political system, you are always promising him that you will do better. You never do! Since you can't follow your own laws of justice and protection towards your servant, the so-called Negro, let him go! You then can represent America as a place of equal justice for all or separate them here into a place to themselves. Let them live in peace and God will let you live in peace.

It was terrible the way Police Chief Kelly of Monroe broke and forced his way into a peaceful assembly of people gathered to worship Allah, the God of their forefathers, the prophets and of their choosing. He even warned some of the followers the night before that he would break up their meeting if they attempted to hold a religious service devoted to the religion of Islam. The Monroe police armed with weapons, broke down the doors to the Mosque. They broke in on unarmed people with heavy billet clubs, brass knuckles and drawn pistols. Among the people gathered to worship were women and children with the wife of the minister present who is four months pregnant. The police started beating on them. The police in beating did not use ordinary police sticks, but the big heavy sticks similar to the kind their ancestors used in the caves and hillsides of Europe to guard themselves at night against attacks by beasts.

This Police Chief, Kelly, said in court - it's in the record to be examined if they have not tried to cover it up, too - that he went to Muhammad's Mosque religious service, because he had a suspicion that this religion was subversive from what he had read and heard! Yet he did not place this charge of subversion against my followers to bring them to court! If we are subversive and are trying to overthrow the government of America by force, let him or any other who say so, carry us into the Federal courts of justice and prove it!

Are not Police Chief Kelly and judge W.M. Harper acquainted with the provision of the United States Constitution which states that shall be no law respecting an establishment of religion, or prohibiting the free exercise thereof; or abridging the freedom of speech; or the right of the people peaceably to assemble? Is this provision only meant to apply to white people? Why continue to persecute my followers under Police Chief Kelly's false charges?

If there was ever a time that we should be united regardless of religious beliefs, it is now! Why can't we unite? Is it not due to fear of not pleasing the slave-masters? We must build a future for our children. Not the future that the white race has built for us, which is nothing but slavery, begging, suffering, injustice, disgrace, and murder at their hands. The Negro leadership should take examples from our people in Africa and Asia, who also were deceived, robbed, and enslaved by the white race of Europe and America, under the white man's slavery teachings of Christianity. Now, Africa and Asia have awakened to the knowledge of the deceivers, and are throwing them and their damnable teaching out. Africa and Asia are now returning to the true religion of God (Allah), the same as I am teaching here and have been for 30 years, and they are on the road to success.

Why do you feel proud here over what belongs to the white man? You own nothing here but the freedom to be a fool for white America. The college-trained Negro clergy politician and educator knows that there is no future for them under white Christianity. They have neither a country nor a chance to build a civilization for their own people but yet they refuse to take part with me in the sure program of God for our people even after watching our success daily. Soon we will strip them of their followers and then we will see if their beloved white friends will be their followers, whom they now are greatly admiring to the destruction of their own people who are now in the mud. Why shouldn't you and I work together for the common good of our people in America?

AMERICANS PERSECUTE THE MUSLIM, PART II WHAT WILL BE HER END?

"And they cried with a loud voice, saying, How long O Lord, Holy and true, dost thou not judge and avenge our blood on them that dwell on the earth?

The above verse is a prophecy of the lost and found people of the Black Nation of Islam called "Negroes" by their enemies (the American white devils) who have persecuted and killed black people for the past 400 years. Some think this verse might refer to some of the Muslims who came here some years ago and were persecuted by these same devils and are now in jails here in the U.S.A. Some of them have been held here in prison for 40 years (so Allah (God) told me). They also were persecuted for trying to teach our people here in America the true religion, called Islam. It can be understood clearly in these words: "How long O Lord, Holy and true, dost Thou not judge and avenge our blood on them that dwell on the earth? We all dwell on the earth, but why the "earth" is really used here (this verse) is to distinguish between the place where this enemy dwells and the place or country of the Muslims, called the Holy land. Europe and America used to be called the wilderness or home of the exile demons.

The so-called Negroes are the only people whose history shows, have been beaten and killed daily by another people, for the past 400 years. The jails of America are now filled with the poor so- called Negroes mixed with the Muslims. The so-called Negro prisoners are fast becoming converts to Islam. This is Allah's (God's) doings that the scripture may be fulfilled; where in it says:

137

"which executeth Judgement for the oppressed: which giveth food to the hungry, The Lord looseth the prisoners." (Ps. 146:7; Acts 12:17; Rev. 2:10).

The Government of America hates her slaves (so-called Negroes) more than any of her outside enemies. She treats the so-called Negroes as if they were enemies of hers, who once made them prisoners and ruled them under a very wicked hand, whom the Americans finally overcame and now takes revenge on her oppressors for their past evils done to the people of America.

The poor so-called Negroes have never been able to get along with their masters (white race) in peace. This proves to the so- called Negroes that Allah's word is true. "Twelve Leaders" from all over the Planet had a conference in the Holy City Mecca, Arabia, over the lost-Found Nation (the so-called Negroes) in the wilderness (America) who must return to their own. These leaders agreed that the devils (the American white race) are disagreeable to live with in peace and have decided to remove them from the Planet Earth. I will agree with the scientists, for we have tried to live with them in peace, even up to this very minute (400 years) and they yet show the world that they do not want any peace with any black people.

Let us read another prophesy of America's cruel treatment to the so-called Negroes under Allah's deliverance of the enslaved so- called Negroes from her hands in these words: "He who smote the people in wrath with a continual stroke, he that ruled the Nations in anger, is persecuted, and none hindereth."

"That made the whole earth as a wilderness and destroyed the cities thereof; that opened not the house of his prisoners." (Isa. 14:6, 17)

Another true prophecy made by Jesus of the persecution of the Muslims

"But, take heed to yourselves, for they shall deliver you up to councils; and in the synagogues ye shall be beaten, and you shall be brought before rulers and kings for my sake, for a testimony against them." (Mark 13:9).

All so-called Negroes who accept the truth (Islam) many expect such persecution and be hated for accepting the name of Allah or one of the ninety-nine attributes of Allah. "Muhammad" or "Mohammed" is a Name of Allah (God), which means praise and one who is worthy of praise, and is praised much. these are the names prophesied in the Bible: (Chronicles 7:14; Isa. 43:7; 40:26). America would like to frighten the black people away from their salivation in Islam, by persecuting the Believers.

Allah makes the Muslims fearless and will soon put fear and trembling in the hearts of our enemies. Allah will bring upon America that which He has never brought upon people in the past and never will be the like of such judgment anymore. America must pay for her evils done to us. There is no such thing as forgiving! Allah said to me that He would repay her for all that she has and is doing against us.

139

ROBBED AND SPOILED

"They are all of them snared in holes, and they are hid in prison houses: they are for a prey, and none delivereth for a spoil, and none saith restore." (Isaiah 42:22)

If my people's condition, or rather history in America is not the answer to the above saying of Isaiah, then try to find the answer to it elsewhere. Our fathers were brought here as merchandise to be sold on the slave market. Some, according to the white man's own written history of that account, were brought here in physical chains to be chained again mentally for four hundred years and they are still mentally chained. They are still being beaten and killed without any law of Justice for them.

The white murderer's word is heard and believed by his brother murderer in the office and seat of Justice. The poor black man (his master's most loyal and faithful slave), his word is not heard. They are afraid of an arresting officer taking them under arrest for fear of being mercilessly beaten; skull and face bashed in or shot outright, and the white brother says: "What is it to kill a d - Negro?" They are outright murderers clothed with authority to mistreat and kill my poor Black People whom they have been murdering (all of their lives) for the past four hundred years. Even when their own people (Black) are put in authority and arrive on the scene with a gun and club, they will (in many cases) prove to be even worse and quicker to beat and kill their own people than the white officer. This they do to be befriended by the white people.

"Robbed and Spoiled": They are pitiful (robbed by all), no, not even spared by their priest (church preachers) (Luke 10:32) The same robbers rob them of their own

women; disgrace and corrupt them with all kinds of diseases, besides spotting up her children like the animal family. They are robbed so completely that now, after four hundred years they love the robbers of themselves and their kind. After being completely robbed of the knowledge of their God, religion and people, they now are a prey in the hands of all first-rate robbers of all races and people.

Our open enemies, the devils, are now using every tricknowledge on my people, after hearing the Truth (Islam), in order to take them (Black People) to hell with them. There never was and never will be true friendship between White and Black people regardless to what you try doing to bring it about. Nothing will bring peace between the two but SEPARATION of them.

SEPARATION OR DEATH

Let us take a look at some of the disgrace that White America has committed against you, my people, and then let us look at the things they are doing now.

We know that during the Civil War, Negroes went into battle with their slave-masters fighting to keep their south land enslaved. They felt as though they were justified. Their slave-master taught them that he (the slave-master) was fighting for what was right. He still thinks the same today.

Though uneducated, they (slaves) were like machines - controlled by the white man. Now, even though the south lost that war, they continue to control the Negroes. It was through the Negro Congressman, who were elected during the Reconstruction period following the Civil War, who helped pass many of the so-called "Jim Crow" laws.

Today, the south still use these laws against our people. Don't get angry with them, for they thought that by passing those "Jim Crow" laws, they were protecting their people from the white man. But time is a funny thing, for those laws reversed when the white man began to gain political office-by using fear and force on the potential Negro political office seeker. He formed the three "K's" and with that, brought death to our people. You know that through fear, you can gain control over people and that control can be used to a person's advantage.

As the white man gained political control, he constantly passed state laws to make the Negro (even though they were freed by the Federal Government) feel as though they must still depend on the white man. He set up separate schools (but only taught his history). He set up his religious churches (Methodist and Baptist) but they too were still separated.

They taught the Negro their religion (Christianity) so you could look to him for dependence. Now, he is still trying to make you dependent on him by saying, "I will give you Civil Rights," but he is still trying to make you dependent on him by saying, "I will give you Civil Rights," but he thinks you don't realize that he promised you those rights when the 13, 14, and 15th Amendments, for Civil Rights, were passed in 1866. Well, it has been approximately 100 years now and he still says, "We will give you rights, but don't be in such a hurry!"

Brothers and sisters, how much longer do we have to wait - another hundred years? I say, White America doesn't want to give us complete freedom, justice and equality. They don't want to give us a piece of this country where we can have what so many of us died on the battle fields of their country (Civil War) and Europe for; a part of this country where our future kind can enjoy freedom, justice and equality and have an economy of our own; a country where we can worship in the true religion of our forefathers, which is Islam.

Islam is the only true religion of God (Allah). It is the religion of all His prophets, from Adam to Muhammad.

Teach this (Islam) to your brothers and friends, your children and their children's children.

Build your future on freedom, justice and equality. Build it on a part of this good earth that we can call our own! Be "Freedom Riders" on your own soil! Seek to mix with your own black kind keep your identity from being destroyed by the devils (white man). All they want to do is destroy your identity by offering you token integration.

SEPARATION IS A MUST

The poor so-called Negroes (the lost found people of the black nation from the Tribe of Shabazz) in America, brought here by the white man in 1555; said Allah (God in Person) the best Knower that our fathers and mothers were brought in chains at a great loss of life. According to history, we have served them (our slave masters) well for the past four hundred years. According to the Bible's history made by Abraham on receiving the prophecy of our enslavement in a strange land and people to serve for four hundred years.

America was not known to the white Europeans before Columbus discovery of the Western Hemisphere in 1492, four hundred and seventy years ago. Beyond a shadow of doubt, this is the strange land, and the white race, a strange people to the original Indians and our father, who were brought here in 1555, four hundred and seven years ago, did not know either the people (white and Indian) or the country, all were strangers.

If this is not the answer to Abraham's prophecy, then you may tell me. Today our unrest and longing for unity and love of self and kind, and the desire for freedom, justice, and equality; a home on this earth that we can call our own, and the presence of God among us. The giving and calling us after Divine names, is a true sign that we are the people that Abraham saw and prophesied that would be lost and must be found. The prophecy is mentioned in many places throughout the Bible. It ends with the struggle between the symbolic lamb and beast over the

147

delivering of the same people (the so-called Negroes in America) from a wicked merciless murderer like a savage beast over a prey.

It is a must that we be separated from our Slave Master's children, who like their fathers, hate and despise us with murder and slavery in their hearts for us day and night. It is foolish and ignorant to hear any black man or woman praising the offer of integration with a four-hundred-year old enemy of ours, which is inviting death and destruction of both races. Not one offer to give the once slave land to build a government and nation of their own, where they can live without fear of being beaten and killed without justice. Our enemies go in gangs to kill you. They rejoice to do you harm, this you know.

They are not like you and me. Their father was a devil, who created them to be enemies of the black people (the righteous) by the spirit of their father (which was false and murderous) so are they, and today they are deceiving you under false pretenses that they will do good bye you just to keep you here with them to share hell fire with them. My Allah will give us heaven if you will only believe and come follow me. We need a country to ourselves like all other nations, and we will get it soon.

> *"Separate, whereof ye can come out from among them and be ye separate, saith the Lord, and touch not the unclean (the wicked white race) and I will receive you and will be a father unto you, and you shall be my sons and daughters, saith the Lord, Almighty (2 Chor 6:17,18)" And I heard another voice from heaven saying, Come out of her, my people that you be not partakers of her sins and that you receive not of her plagues. Rev.18.4*

SEPARATION OR TROUBLE

Separation of the two (Negro and white) is the only solution to the ever growing problem of "What must be done with the Negroes?" Both the so-called Negroes and their white slave-masters do not seem to want to let go one another. Separation of the two races would be an act of wisdom and justice. Forced integration, which means socializing, inter-marrying of the two races (black and white) [resulting in the eventual swallowing up of the so-called Negroes' race by their white slave-masters and mongrelizing the two races. This will destroy the respect of the society of both, nationally and internationally. Again, integration is against the wishes of the intelligent thinking group of both races - these want to preserve their race and the respect of their society.

The government is trying to enforce this wicked and contrary law to the Divine Law and place of God, which will end in revolution and war, and total destruction of the wealth of America. This integration is not the wise and proper way of solving the so- called Negroes' problem in America, but is an outright deceitful and wicked plan to destroy the Divine Plan of Allah for the future of the so-called Negroes. Both are sure to run into trouble with Allah's chastisement - both Negroes and whites, as it is plainly hinted and written in the Bible and Holy Quran. (I will gladly point it out to the disputer).

The wise white scientists know it as well as I, and hope to prevent it, but they are out-numbered by their wicked wise. God created two kinds of everything, so it is with man. He didn't intend for them (Negro and white) to mix, and has set a day of reckoning for those who willfully, and knowingly break His natural law in which He has created man. It is their purpose to try and make Allah (God) a liar, so as to deceive the blind, deaf, and dumb so-called Negroes, as the devil deceived Adam and Eve in the Garden of Paradise. While knowing full well that they would lose their place with Allah and a peaceful home if they accepted his advice, so it will be with the so-called American Negroes, who after being offered heaven at once by Allah, accepts the wicked advice and the offer of temporary enjoyment with racial inter-marrying and having sexual intercourse with a people with whom Allah is angry.

He will punish both parties as he did Israel and the people whom Jehovah forbid Israel to intercourse with. Israel was punished, and finally lost the goal which Jehovah had set before her and the deceiving enemies of Israel were destroyed. I warn you to let Israel's history from the days of Moses to this day, be a lesson to you. REMEMBER, both Israel and the Christians are on the brink of a pit of fire. The best and only solution of this problem of the so-called Negroes is SEPARATION and give them a start in a territory to themselves, regardless to the ignorant love of the slave for his master.

Take a look at the foolish plan of Martin Luther King for the poor so-called Negroes and how he and his plan were criticized by Mr. James B. Kilpatrick, Saturday, on the Television program. "Nation's Future." There we saw the man, Rev. King, a college man, a Christian Minister and Pastor, with a plan to take our poor people and himself

150

and throw them at the mercy of an angry Negro-hating mob, to be beaten and killed for nothing; only to be accepted as whites accept white in white private-owned places, and finally allow his people to become white, and to mongrelize both races.

What does he think the intelligent white and black people think of his silly plan? What kind of foolish so-called Negro parents will let such foolish preachers use their babies as a test of the mob's fire? What will those children's think of such parents when they grow up and see the light of truth? Mr. Kilpatrick asked Rev. King, "Why do you want to integrate and make your race a coffee color, with complete integration, losing your race identity?" He was telling Martin Luther King, in so many words, that you and your race will not cause the white race to lose their identity, but the Negro will lose his. Such slander and mockery coming to the decent and intelligent so-called Negro by the ignorant love of a so-called religious leader of his people is a disgrace.

Such short-sightedness by Rev. King and the NAACP for the so-called Negroes of America, is making the nations of the earth, both black and white, laugh us to scorn, to see us, a race of lazy beggars great lovers of our enemies, desire to destroy our race to become ONE in our enemies. Why doesn't Mr. King and his NAACP organization join with me on a decent plan; a plan that makes sense and one that will make a future for our people. Ask for separation and some of this good earth that we can call our own, where we can live in peace together, away from those who do not want us. This is the plan of God and it will bring an end to the every growing trouble between the two races. If the white man (some of them) wanted to colonize us in Central American back in 1867, why not a free territory today, for we will not accept colonization.. It is the time of our FREEDOM, and we will not accept anything less!

The NAACP and Mr. King want the freedom of voting, and in this way they think they will be able to gain equal power in a white man's government and country. A Negro will never be the president under the Stars and Stripes of America. If he did, what could he do but to bow to the wishes of the owners of the Stars and Stripes? Let us seek some stars for our own nation and stop begging the white man for that which he has. We are not in such condition as being at the mercy of the white race, as long as we are members of the Asiatic Nation.

SEPARATION

WE MUST make jobs for ourselves. Newspapers and magazines are writing and telling of our people heading the unemployment lines, being fired off their jobs and without the means of finding new gainful employment. No new jobs are being offered our people. Our people here in America number twenty million with more than seven million eligible for gainful employment. Our number in America is the equal or exceeding many independent nations which sit in chambers of counsel. As a nation of people contained and suppressed in America, we must begin to think for ourselves and do the thing which is best for us. Many television news programs show our people in the relief lines and at the employment offices sitting and begging the slave-master for his bread and jobs. We should be seeking something of our own. Our people will always be a nation of beggars until we get something of our own!

I stated at our mass public meeting last Sunday, at the international Amphitheater, that the present administration of the government promised the so-called Negro employment. You do not have it. The so-called Negro put his faith in the promise of the present administration by pooling his votes for it. I stated at the meeting that if they had said they would give us a few states, Elijah would have voted for them. The best thing to do to solve the problem of the so-called Negro is to separate him from the white race.

The work of Allah among the so-called Negro is to separate him from his slave-master and give him something of his own. Also at the meeting in the International Amphitheater, I called again for the separation of the so-called Negro instead of integrating him among the white race. We should be given two or three states so we may have a land of our own. We should be given the proper instruments or tools to sustain and build up our own civilization. We should be given support to last our nation twenty years. After that time if we are not able to go for our self, the slave - master should take his armies and kill us.

Many of the national television companies reported on their TV stations my call for the so-called Negro to be separated into a land of his own. One commentator said many so-called Negro leader do not agree with me. Naturally, the so-called leaders are afraid to ask for anything. The white man speaking for the Negro leader is another indication of their power and control over the ones who are supposed to be guiding and benefiting our people. We cannot depend on the white race for our future, with only a job in view.

We must be separated into a land of our own. Permanent employment lies in our having ownership of land. We can have lasting jobs on our own land but not on the land of others. The jobs of the white man are the ones that he has created and built for his own people.

I am very happy and thankful to Allah (God) for more than 8,000 people who came to our public meeting last Sunday. I am especially thankful for my faithful following who traveled from all parts of North America for our Annual Savior's Day meeting for the commemoration of the birth of our Savior who came in the Person of Master Fard Muhammad.

SEPARATION OR DEATH

What is it today that is pushing and forcing America to pass a law permitting the integration instead of the separation of black and white? Does America see her doom? They understand the time of day while you do not. They know that it is the time of the judgment of Allah: to destroy the power of Satan's rule. The truth of their 6,000 year history has been revealed for the first time. This true knowledge of them is causing trembling and fear. They are today, more than in former days, reminded of the destruction of Noah's people and of the burning fall of Sodom and Gomorrah and of ancient Babylon.

The great destructive force of Allah's force against His enemies is known to the American scientists. My people have not the knowledge of self, kind, God, nor the Devil. They are the ones that the truth must come to. The knowledge of God and the Devil points out to us the ways of escape. The devils could not tell you that they are the made enemies of the black man, the opposers of peace and righteousness, the lovers of evil and haters of good. The secret of this people of actually being the devils was not to be revealed until they had lived their time of 6,000 years, which was up in 1914.

Allah revealed them on His coming. He appeared under the name of Wallace Fard Muhammad in 1930. His work included the redemption of the so-called Negroes who are the Lost and Found members of the Family of God. We are the true owners of the earth which the devil was given the power to rule for the past 6,000 years. It is with praise

155

and gratefulness that we should wait on the judgment of Allah. Once again, we will acquire the freedom to live and worship our Creator without the fear of the interference and disturbance of the devils. We should be thankful that the end of the wicked ruling power of this world is at hand. We must also realize that we too are taking part in the judgment, and we will be judged upon our acceptance of the Truth.

We are today given a choice: all those whose out of their own desire, choose to remain with your and God's open enemy (white man), then let it be written, let it be done. Those who separate from the devils (the Caucasian race) in this day will be among the chosen of God and will inherit the New World, the Kingdom of everlasting life, as we read in the Bible. As we further read in the Holy Qur'an, they will enter gardens beneath which rivers flow and where the greetings therein shall be: Peace! So it come to you as warning of the time in which we now live, separation or death! It will mean death to both black and white to integrate; it will mean death to white America to refuse to give up the Negroes.

The white man, I must repeat is talking integration today instead of separation because he sees "Lazarus" (the Bible's symbolic character of the Negro) running to Abraham's bosom. He knows that he cannot get to a safe place to lay his head. They desire to carry as many of my people into hell fire with them as possible.

SEPARATION SOLVES THE PROBLEM

THERE IS NO DOUBT THAT we are living in the time of universal separation of black and white. Due to your ignorance of the time, and the Divine Plans of Allah (God), you probably would not like to hear or talk about it. The wise and alert people of yours have knowledge of it, but do not like to talk about it because of the love they have for the present world. The poor ignorant ones have no knowledge of it and care less as long as they are given the crumbs. It is not your will or power which is bringing it about, it is the Will and Power of Allah (God) as foretold by His Prophets from Moses to Muhammad.

How many of my people, the lost-found members of the Asiatic Nation (the so-called Negroes) know that this is the Bible's judgment of this world and that the Divine Truth of Allah (God) is that which separates the righteous from the wicked? You may ask, "Who are the wicked?" The wicked are the people who were created wicked by nature (the Caucasian Race) whose limited time was 6,000 years. They have many followers of all races of earth - Black, Brown, Yellow and Red - but this does not mean that the Black Nations are wicked by nature. They are righteous, by nature, who are the real original people and owners of the earth.

The White or Caucasian (European) race is known to God and His Prophets as Satan, the Devil, the Enemy of God, and His people (the Original Nation). Power was given to them to rule with evil and falsehood, the darker Nations for 6,000 years. This they have done, and are now 46

157

years overtime and they know this. It will take a few years to complete the separation but nevertheless, the work is going on now at a very good rate of speed.

Search the history of these people (Black and White). The two have never been able to live in peace together. The white race is as the Bible says of them, under the symbol of a trouble sea (Isa. 57:20), never at peace and is the hater of truth and righteousness. The so-called Negroes know them and their evil doings better than any people, but being without a teacher of their own kind for the past 400 years, they have become such lovers and great admirers of the devils and their evil doings, that they do not want to be separated. That is why the problem is so hard to solve, though the work will be done regardless to whom or what.

We number over seventeen million here in America and are without a home of our won and a true friend unless it is Allah. The wicked must be punished for their wickedness poured upon us without ever being hindered. This country is large enough to separate the two (Black and White). They can live here but that would not be successful. The best solution is for everyone to go to his own people and country. We, the so-called Negroes have both a great nation to go to and a great country. Allah (God) has come for our return. The native home of the white race is Europe. It is up to you and me to obey the Word of Allah (God) or obey our own desire. This is for the sake of saving your own flesh and blood from the destruction of this evil murderous race who is ever seeking an excuse to take your innocent lives, and to cut you off from good. They are ever around and in your homes after your girls and women to make you a disgrace before God and your people. YOU MUST JOIN ONTO YOUR OWN KIND. You may hate me now but one day you will love me.

Think it over: Why should we believe in their religion? Why should we be called by our enemies' names who enslaved our parents and will not give us equal justice, since we are free to choose our own people's names? Why should we continue to make fools of ourselves and our children begging them to accept us as their people when we have a Great nation to turn to?

SEPARATION OR DEATH PART II

Allah (God) offers we the lost-found members of the Nation of Islam (the so-called Negroes) heaven at once, if we would only submit and accept Him. He (Allah) has already accepted us, but due to blindness (mentally), fear and love for the devil slave masters and their children, put in them by the white devil slavemastes over three hundred years ago, the lost found black people of America act like fools, though they may have college and university education.

The white man's education, without the knowledge of him and your own self, will never remove your fear of the devil slave-masters' children nor will it remove your desire and love to be like them (the devils). The evils done to us by these white devils are unforgivable - this the poor black man should know, but he doesn't! They must be taught this vital truth, that there can never be a judgement of this world until this 20 million lost-found people hear the TRUTH (the knowledge of self, God and the devil). The blindness of the black clergy and politicians is pitiful. It is a shame they were made so dumb by the devils, that even today, the day of our salvation, the leaders are just as blind as their followers. Both are following the devils into the lake of fire.

It is very sorrowful to see and know how our people in the south and throughout America are begging the white people (their real open enemies, the devils) to accept them into their social equality, instead of asking for the opportunity to separate from them. The heads of this disgraceful program, seeking love and friendship of the devils, are the so-called leaders; black preachers and black politicians. The NAACP could be made a powerful organization if they would accept Islam, Allah and His Messenger, otherwise, it will soon disintegrate. If the Negro leadership was only wise to the clock of time and the slave master's code of laws for their black slaves, they would be as I - seeking separation and a home of our own somewhere on this Planet Earth which our Father created for us and not for this race of devils.

The type of Christianity that the devils gave my people is taking them to hell instead of heaven. The true religion of God is Islam and others WILL NOT BE ACCEPTED. You must be freed and separated from the slave-masters. The slave code of laws that the devil made for we the lost-found Nation of Islam, makes us a permanent piece of property, belonging to them. No power of self-redemption or change of masters. No access to the judiciary, no honest provision for testing the claims of the enslaved to freedom; rejection of testimony of so-called Negroes (regardless to the nature, true of false), or whether slaves or free. The laws are unequal. Free social worship and religious instruction prohibited.

The legal recognition of the Negroes rights is ignored. Submission is required of all so-called Negroes to all white devils, as written in the slave code of laws, as enforced in many parts of the United States of America over Negroes and Indians, or any people of color. Adequate protection for the lost-founds (so-called Negroes) under the devil's law is almost impossible. All white devils are brothers and friends of each other against the black people.

According to the American Slave Code of Law, by William Goodell - page 301 under the above title, the Negroes may be used as breeders, prostitutes, concubines, pimps, tapsters, attendants at the gambling table and as subjects of medical and surgical experiments for the benefit of science. The evil and worse part of it all is the fact that the devils, white people, destroyed the Negro's love for self and turned the Negro's love for self toward his enemies.

THE BLOOD SHEDDER (REV. 16:)

ACCORDING TO the word of Allah (God) and the history of the world, since the grafting of the Caucasian race six thousand years ago, they have caused more bloodshed than any people known to the black nation. They are born murderers made by nature to murder. The Bible and Holy Qur'an Sharrieff are full of teachings of this race of murderers. They shed the life blood of all the living, even their own. They are scientists at deceiving the black people. They deceive the very people of Paradise (Bible:Genesis 3:13). They kill their own brother (Genesis 4:8). The earth testified against them (Genesis 4:10) and revealed their guilt to its Maker. (Thy brother's blood crieth unto me from the ground). Thy very soil of America is soaked with the innocent blood of my people, the so-called Negroes, shed by this race of murderers, also crieth out to its maker for the burden of the innocent blood of the righteous slain upon her. Let us take a look at the devil's creation from the teachings of the Holy Qur'an.

> *"AND WHEN your Lord said to the angels, I am going to place in the earth One who shall rule, the angels said: What will thou place in it such as shall make mischief in it and shed blood, we celebrate Thy praise and extol Thy holiness."* *(Holy Qur'an Sharrieff 2:30).*

This devil race has and still is doing just that - making mischief and shedding blood. As the Holy Qur'an says, "When your Lord said to the angels: Surely I am going to create a mortal of the essence of black mud fashioned in shape. (Holy Qur'an Sharrieff 15:28). The essence of black mud (the black nation) mentioned is only symbolic which actually means the sperm of the black nation, and they refuse to recognize the black nation as their equal, though they were made from them by one of their black scientists (names Yakub). They can never see their way in submitting to Allah (God). His religion, Islam and His prophets.

THEIR EVERY cry is - beat, kill, kill the so-called Negroes! The day has arrived that Allah will return to our murderers that which they have been so happy to pour on the poor, innocent so- called Negroes, as they love to shed the poor, innocent blood of their Negro slaves, and even plan to kill me for teaching the truth. Allah will give you your own flesh and your own blood to drink like water. Your arms and your allies will not help you against Allah (Rev. 16:6).

The heads and bodies of the so-called Negroes are used to test the power of your club and guns. Yet, the poor, foolish so- called Negroes admire the murderers regardless to how much they are murdered. The day is near, even at your door when you shall receive fully what you have sown. Allah has said it!

THE SO-CALLED NEGRO LEADERSHIP PART III

It is the Divine Will of Almighty God (Allah) that we be separated! It is very foolish on the part of so-called Negro leaders to oppose it! All of your opposition will be brought to naught! I am a man who preaches justice. I am not self-made, politically made, seeking office, nor am I in, a position because wealth. I am Divinely sent! If Almighty God, Allah, were NOT with me, I could NOT get through America teaching, preaching and doing this Divine work. I want my people to be aware of this before the destruction takes place.

We need a place in the sun for the future of our people as other nations have and want. Our past leaders never asked for this. It was the same in the case of Moses. Moses demanded equal justice for Israel. The leaders opposed Moses in seeking freedom, justice and equality for his people. If you study the foolishness of the leaders of our people, you will agree that they are doing nothing but keeping our people bound in chains of slavery as beggars! Why don't the leaders demand something for their people? Why don't you unite and say "Give us some earth!" The black man should be interested in himself as the white man is interested in himself.

The leaders of my people should know you cannot compete with the white man as they are the owners and producers of the land. We can't be equal with the master until we have what the master has. We can become the equal and producers by securing land for our future as other nations. Land is needed not just for the Muslims and Elijah Muhammad, but for all of our people who have had nothing for their blood and labor during the more than 400 years they have been in America. We need a place of our own to put our foot on. Why should the leaders of our people be like puppies begging for a crumb? We can't expect to make a future for twenty million people by lying around the white man's employment office. The white man today, is having trouble creating and finding jobs for his OWN people! You will soon see, he offers YOU nothing but a promise.

Almighty God, Allah, has for you, a promise of truth. No black man who has been beaten and trampled underfoot of the slave- master should reject the truth when it is presented. It is time for intellectuals, preachers and professional leaders, to decide on something for the future of our people. the black man should demand something for himself. Unite with me and in the Name of Allah, we will get it! We have tried everything else, NOW the TRUTH!

SOME OF THIS EARTH

2-24-62

Listen brothers, regardless to your profession or trade, or you may be the poor in the mud, agree with me on common sense. We are a nation (20,000,000) in a nation. What do you see of good in the future for us, that is being subjected to the children of our fathers slave masters? The children of the slave masters have the same mind of their fathers - full of hatred and murder (death) for you and I.

You are over-deprived of equal justice and opportunity. You are at the mercy of a four hundred year old open enemy, who has deceived you ever since you have been in the Western Hemisphere. They have given us a picture of their bloody hatred of our black, brown, yellow and red races. They divide, rob, rule and hold out false promises to all they have swollen us up with these promises.

Where do you see any hope of a good future in our open enemies, for our sons and daughters? Are you depending on being a servant forever for them? Suppose the nations of earth push them out of their countries and cut off trade with this people. Will there be jobs enough for them and you, who number 20,000,000? Self- preservation is the first law of nature. Both nations (black and white) birth rates are ever-increasing. Your hope of survival is in the mercy of your enemies to provide employment for you and your children, or some soup and bread.

With educated people and scientists of our own, don't you think we are a universally foolish people? We have no unity, no love of self, and no desire to be self-independent, which is due to laziness. Some of our people think the Christian religion is sufficient - this the enemy has been successful in deceiving you. Actually, the Christians and their religion, as you know it will not see the hereafter.

We the Muslims, under the guidance of Allah, will rule forever. We are the righteous, the wisest and the powerful, in which whatever is in the heavens and earth obeys. Without some of this good earth, that we can call our own, it would be better that we all commit suicide. Come unite with me and my God, Allah, and you will get what you want (heaven in this life). My followers and I are an example of love and unity. We are the people of Allah (God) and are guided and protected by Him to Whom all praises are due forever.

A Muslim can live here or there. We will never be slaves anymore. Death is better than being a permanent servant to such enemies that you and I are subjected to. Come unite with me and my God, Allah and get some of this earth for ourselves and children, or die in the attempt.

THE GREAT DECEIVER

Arthur R. Gottschalk, State Senator, 8th District, Chicago, Park Forest, ILL, wrote our National Secretary, John Ali, asking him and my followers to disavow and repudiate publicly the truth Allah has revealed to me of the Caucasian race; the truth of them being REAL DEVILS and our (the black Nation's) open enemies.

A part of the letter was printed and published in the Chicago Tribune, June 15th, 1962. The Senator, Gottschalk, failed to include in his letter to Secretary Ali, proof or material that the truth Allah has given me of them being real devils, is false. This leaves my secretary and followers helpless to deny the truth.

Failed to Consult Messenger

I am surprised at the intelligent Senator writing a letter before first making an attempt to consult me of what Allah has revealed to me. The Senator's letter is a perfect insult to my followers. Without showing proof that what I am teaching IS NOT the truth, he is asking my followers not to believe it and tell the public that they do not believe.

What the Senator does not like is that my followers believe that the Caucasians (the white European race), are the real devils as Allah has said; also the true history and teachings of the Prophets and their scripture (Bible and Holy Qur'an) bear witness.

I think the Senator has attacked something that may surprise him and his race because of his intentions of

171

making my followers disbelieve in the truth of Allah as taught me.

One of the characteristics of the devil is to deceive. In last two paragraphs of his letter to our Secretary, John Ali, Gottschalk hoped to deceived him with the following words:

Words of Deception

"At this time when man and good will of all races are working hard to promote harmonious human relations and eliminate the social and economic conditions which has produced injustices, it is tragic that men like Elijah Muhammad are attempting to tear down their good work and accentuate racial tension and misunderstanding."

Mr. Gottschalk, we are not your slaves anymore; therefore, do not misunderstand us. We care very little about you or anyone or races who would think, after the knowledge of you, that a promise of promoting harmonious human relations, social equality with you will solve our problem. You are mistaken! We want nothing less than freedom to build our won economy and society, and on some of this earth that we can call our own!

We want to be independent as you and other nations are, to do what we think is best for our own selves. What kind of future can you prepare for us other than subject slaves to you and your kind? I am not attempting to tear down anything good, for I have not found anything of good that you or your kind have set up to tear down that was good for my people. Allah and I are the only one I know who are setting up any good work for our people, I think.

Let Us Enjoy Freedom

Since our government declares us to be free, why not leave us to go and enjoy this freedom to ourselves on some of this earth that we can call our own? The language used in your letter is that of a deceiver, who knows that he has laid hands upon a great value and hopes to deceive him to believe that, that which he has been given or found is of no value and what you have is the best.

The entire 20 or more million of my people here should learn a lesson from your letter, and be careful of you and your kind, erupted promises of social equality without some of this earth we can call our own.

Your dogs enjoy honor in your society; they are seen eating from the table and riding in the same seat in some of your best transportation. We do no desire any such place and level with all the evil you have done to us for the past 400 years and, you continue to mistreat us.

In For Great Surprise

Do you think we will be satisfied to settle with less than some of this earth we can call our own? I think you are in for a great surprise. The Senator is outright asking my followers to recant and make it publicly known that they disbelieve in the Truth Allah has revealed to me in the closing line of his letter to Secretary Ali in the following words:

"I call upon you, John Ali, as National Secretary of your organization to disavow and repudiate publicly all of the above statements that the Caucasian race is a race of devils says Allah to me by leader, Elijah Muhammad. "Failure to do so would be a clear admission that the statements of Elijah Muhammad accurately represents the policy of your organization which sponsors and operates the University of Islam."

For nearly 32 years the students of our school have been in the knowledge of you and good reason of being at peace in your midst. This comes from having the knowledge of you. If you fear this true knowledge of yourself will cause your mistreated, once slaves to hate you, then your argument is with Almighty Allah Who has revealed it. It is surely not with brother John Ali and my followers, for you will not be able to give up the truth of you, their God Allah, and their Leader and Teacher.

THE TRUTH

Truth is that which is opposed to falsehood and the father of falsehood (the devil). The devils (white race) are opposed to truth and the author of truth (the Divine Supreme Being). It is plain Truth only that is necessary to resurrect the mentally dead Black Nation.

God in the Person of Master Fard W.D. Muhammad, the long expected Messiah, the Muslims' Mahdi (Allah God in Person) has brought us this plain truth. The truth could not have come to us any sooner. It had to come from the mouth of Allah (God) in Person. He could not have brought it to us before this time.

He Had To Wait

He had to wait until the time given falsehood to rule had expired. Being afraid of the truth because it is not in favor of the enemy of truth is absolutely inviting death and the eternal anger of Allah, God Almighty, Whose purpose in coming is to rid the Black Nation once and for all of our chief enemy, the devil, the white race. This fear of the devils was put into our parents when they were babies, fear is even kept in us today by their beating and killing of our people without a cause.

FEAR is the real enemy that now stands between you and your salvation. The white man's strongest weapon which is FEAR, is keeping us divided. FEAR is the enemy that keeps us divided and from becoming an independent people. It is at the height of ignorance for any educated black man or Nation to seek the continued dependence upon the enemy for their future. Especially, when the enemy has no future for self! John 8:32 says: Ye shall know the truth...

Negroes Reared by Foes

This verse is directed to the so-called Negroes who were reared by their enemies, our enemies have never taught us the truth because the truth is in the Black Man's favor. The truth will free the so-called Negroes from the fear of the enemies (devils), and the truth will destroy the so-called Negroes love and worship of the devils as it has done for my followers and myself!

Allah is Truth. His religion Islam is Truth. White America is not losing time in trying to prevent the so-called Negroes from accepting it, Truth, Islam.

175

They are so afraid, the so-called Negroes are going over to Islam, that they are even disgracing themselves in their efforts to oppose the truth.

They are now even willing to have intermarriages between the so- called Negroes and white just to prevent the so-called Negroes from accepting the Truth (Islam). As some of the devils have said: "The best way to beat Muhammad is to make democracy work."

Tribe of Shabazz

Allah is the Greatest; it is incumbent upon Allah (God) to awaken and teach the truth to the mentally dead, lost and found members of the Black Nation from the tribe of Shabazz (so-called Negroes). Hell was not prepared for any black person. It was prepared for the devils (white race). This the white race knows. This is why they desire to take everyone of you to their doom with them. No pro white so-called Negro leadership will work for the good of black people regardless to what.

To speak for the truth, you need a fearless Muslim leader who knows people, their origin and destiny. The so-called Negroes need the unity of all darker people the same as white people seek and have the unity of one another especially against the non- whites.

The so-called Negroes have millions of members, the Indians and all darker Latin Americans of their own nations. But the so-called Negroes need certain qualification that is very much necessary for them to be respected by any member of their nation. They would even be respected by their enemies if they had self-respect, others are unable to respect you.

Truth Shall Make You Free

When Jesus prophesied: "The truth shall make you free," He did not tell what the truth was that would make us free. He refused to go into details even after being questioned by the devils who were claiming kinship to Abraham. Later admitted he could not guide them into all the truth. But Jesus prophesied that the Father (Allah) would send one in His Name who would teach and guide the people into all truth.

This one would only say that which he heard the father say (getting it directly from the mouth of God). This truth Jesus was referring to is the knowledge of God, the devil and the end of one and the rise of another. This truth Allah (God) has now revealed and it is being preached first to the so-called Negroes and then throughout the world of the Black Nation.

The real danger which now confronts and will destroy the future of the so-called Negroes is the great temptation which the white Christian race is now putting on just for the purpose of trapping the so-called Negroes.

That is their parading their bold, half-nude girls and women before the public along with some of the most filthy and indecent acts that is known to man. They were even more decent when they were savages. Then they did try to hide their nakedness with the skin of beasts! This is the truth! Believe it or leave it!

177

THOUSANDS TURNED BACK FAIL TO HEAR MUHAMMAD

Los Angeles, April 13 - Concluding a series of three of the most successful meetings held during the past seven months, Mr. Elijah Muhammad cut short his visit to Los Angeles and headed for Chicago to adjust pressing problems this morning. Each of the three meetings was a turn-away crowd. The meetings were held at People's Independent Church of Christ, 18th and Paloma, which has a capacity of 1000 seating, turned away more than 3,000 at each meeting.

Muhammad's powers to draw Negroes, even on Monday evenings, remains a mystery to those who are trying to analyze his popularity. Speaking to a standing audience, Mr. Muhammad, who refers to his speaking as teaching, taught on the history of the creation of the white man. He told his audience that if the Negro knew and understood who the white man really is, that he would not be clamoring for a seat beside him in restaurants. On the same token, he said, if Africans were killing white people in Africa, the white man in America would kill Negroes here in revenge. Thus, he said the sit-in-strikes in the South is one of the most disastrous activities Negroes have ever engaged in, in their four-hundred-year history in America. Thus, he continued, their activities are the sit-in-strike, marks the Negroes as the most stupid group on earth."

On the question of economics, he said the Negro has the power to acquire the same respect and status as other people by uniting and pooling their wealth. He said the Negro's money is put into white banks and savings and loan associations, loaned to white people to build businesses to discriminate against them. This activity marks the Negro as stupid. These same banks will not make a loan to Negroes. yet, the banks, many located in Negro communities, use the Negroes' money and openly fight them. The bankers, he said, reject Negro loan applications, thus driving the Negro businessman into the hands of shylocks. He urges Negroes to pool their wealth and build banks.

The wealth of the Negro American exceed 15 billion dollars and 85% of that money is tied up into monstrous churches. This money should be used to build factories. During this period unemployment, the majority of unemployed workers are Negroes. We cannot expect a white man to discharge white people and give employment to us. We have to make an effort to help ourselves. In this period of unemployment and starvation, the Negro masses throughout the country should make a demand upon the Ministers that they use this wealth to make employment for them. In demanding this, the members of the various churches will find that the deed and titles to these million dollar churches are in the names of the ministers and their wives and their families.

In comparing Islam with Christianity, Mr. Muhammad used both the Bible and the Holy Quran, comparing the scriptures as written by man to the word spoken by Allah. For instance, one passage of scripture stated: "And they said that Jesus went that way," but the Quran stated that "I am Allah Thy God." He pointed out that the Quran stated fully the word of God and not the saying of men as stated in the Christian Bible.

Muhammad also pointed out that Jesus was a member of the dark race proving this fact by stating that there were no cameras in that day to take the picture of Jesus and asking the question how then do we know that this is the true picture of Jesus as presented to us today? "Jesus," he continued, "was a Muslim and Christianity is a white man's religion created to enslave the black, brown and red people all over the world. The white man never had a God and never will."

Mr. Muhammad thanked his followers and those attending the meeting for the courtesy extended to him during his four-day stay in Los Angeles. He thanked those who made it possible for him to hold the meeting in this beautiful church. And said he hoped to return to Los Angeles again very soon.

Mr. John X., Minister of Muhammad's Temple of Islam in Los Angeles, said that he planned to purchase the People's Independent Church of Christ, and to turn it into a Temple. The church is for sale.

THE TRUTH PART V

If there ever lived on this Planet Earth a people who deserved a part of it that they could call their own, it is you and me, the lost-found members of the Asiatic nation from the tribe of Shabazz.

Today, Allah (God) offers you and me a chance to become the owners of some of His earth if we only submit to Him. I have submitted myself to Him and I am the first of the Lost-Found to submit to Him. Will you also submit to Him? We must have some of this earth for a home we can call our own as other nations.

20 Million In U.S.

Twenty million of us here in America at the present time depend only on the white man for a job to survive. We are increasing in population daily. Do you ever take time to think for a moment, that twenty million non-whites living and increasing in population among more than a hundred and twenty-five million whites, whose parents our parents were slaves to? We have become a Nation in a Nation and one of us MUST live (separate) from the other in order to survive!

The present condition of the white race engulfs them in a universal war that will force them to look out for themselves only.

Angry At Each Other

All the nations are angry with each other, and Allah is angry with them. What kind of future do we have in such a mad world who have carved it up among themselves, but to submit to Allah (God) for a home? He (Allah) has said to me that He will set us in heaven at once if we would only submit to Him.

Do you not hear and read how the white race is killing your own black people in Africa by the tens and hundreds of thousands?

They are killing them for no cause whatsoever, but to rule and rob them of their country's natural resources, and to enslave them with their false Christianity for cheap labor; just as they did our fathers here, and still have you in the status of a "free slave" with no hope but a job or the soup line. Yet, many of you glorify this same universal enemy enough to even integrate with them.

Paid For Our Home

We have paid well for a home on this soil with 400 years of shame. We have been disgraced, robbed of the knowledge of self and kind; we have sweated and bled for white America's riches, self independence, security of property and lives. Will you not wake up and stand up to God and the Nations of the earth like a man of YOUR place and home on a part of this earth that you can call your own?

Do you feel proud representing yourselves under the white slave maker's names, and claiming what is theirs to be yours or partly yours? We need and must have something of our own, a home! Get out and farm! Raise the foods and clothes that you and your people must have! Get the earth, and build your own civilization of freedom, justice and equality.

You are the real "Lazarus" charmed by the riches of the slave masters and are too lazy to go for self! Some of you (so-called leaders) are well educated in the "know how," but would rather give your educational values back to your white teachers in their factories, plants, laboratories and offices; even to the extent of teaching their children. You even refer to the wealth and to this country of America as being "our wealth, our country," or "we," while at the same time you are begging for Civil Rights (which they will never give you).

THE TRUTH

Often I am asked: (1) How can we live separately from the white people in the same country? (2) How can we be independent of them? (3) Would the white American agree to a separate territory for us in some suitable area where we could go for self and live alone in peace? (4) Would we get along in peace with each other?

The first question is very easy to answer: The black and white people, according to history, have always lived separately from each other. They were originally separated by God and the Law of God forbids their intermixing, or intermarrying. The earth was originally inhabited by the Black Man.

Families to Themselves

Later on as color (brown, yellow, red) began among them by the original scientists, (says the word of Allah to me) they became families to themselves, and from families to tribes; the term used today is "races" or "nations." Most of the black remained in the east along and below the equator of the earth.

The white race, after their creation 6,000 years ago, was given the part of earth today that is called Europe.

It is this race of people who actually started the sin of intermixing the two strange bloods, which is forbidden by God; just as they have disregarded all Divine Laws of Allah (God. They even seem to change the very natural laws of man in which he is made.

They first mixed with the original black Arabs, then, as they traveled over the earth, for the past near 500 years, they mixed with brown, yellow and red races. They captured the blacks and made slaves of them. For the past 400 years, they have used them (so-called Negroes) for experimental purposes and even uses them now as one uses his tool!

How Independence Is Born

The 2nd question: How can we be independent of the white race? Answer: When a people is smart enough to look and dig the earth and get what she produces, her secret treasures hidden under the surface, along with her water, air, and sunshine, that people can be self-supporting as other smart nations are, who are independent of each other.

Some may have in their part of the earth that which the other does not have; then comes the exchange of resource to others through peaceful means of trade and exchange of goods with each nation.

Only disagreement and war and fighting between each other would prevent such necessary union of Nations to get that from the other nations that she does not produce. A new nation should not isolate itself from national or international trade. However, this does not mean mixing blood with each other. The borders of a black and white separate state should be as strict as any nation's borders, protected by passports and visas for all people.

I think the so-called Negroes and white American should have such restrictions, and laws between them to maintain peace.

Intelligent Will Agree

The 3rd question: Would white America agree to a separate territory for us, the black, once slaves of the American? Answer: I do believe the intelligent minds of America would agree to the separation of us into some place other than trying to continue making us live with them with the same respect and justice that they enjoy not to mention the mixing of bloods and the complete care of us. If they see you and me in honest togetherness on some of this earth that we can call our own, even with some help as Egypt did for Israel on Israel's departure, they will respect us.

The 4th question: Would we get along in peace if we were put together to live together? Answer: I know we would if our national religion would be ISLAM; this I am proving to you daily.

It's God In Islam

See how peacefully my followers and I get along together? It is God in the religion of Islam who inspires love, unity and peace in the hearts and actions of every true believer. Once you accept Islam, you do not even like to dispute and quarrel with the brothers or sisters. Allah will soon put Islam in the hearts of all the lost found members of the Tribe of Shabazz.

Of course, there is the east continent of Asia and Africa who will welcome every Lost found Muslim in America to share with them, if others fall. It is a MUST that we be separated into some part of this earth that we can call our own.

Next do we have the qualified men and women among the black people of America to run a government for self?

THE TRUTH

The sower of the Truth is the Messenger or Apostle of Allah (God), but whose heart is fertile enough to germinate the Truth? In the same chapter 4:23, it says, *"If any man have ears to hear, let him hear."* This was the great trouble Noah had with his people. They would not lend their ears to hear the truth and were therefore drowned by a flood of water. Lot had the same trouble with his people. They just would not listen to the Truth. It is the same today, as it was in the past. The people just will not hear the Truth. *"Supremely exalted then is Allah, the King, the Truth" (Holy Quran 20:114).*

Author of the Truth

Allah is the Author of the Truth. The heavens and the earth bear witness that Allah is the Author of Truth. Regardless to how small or great, all life bears witness to the Truth.

Since the heavens and the earth bear witness to the truth of the existence of its Creator, falsehood cannot hope to gain a permanent place in the creation of truth. Darkness cannot find a permanent place because of forever being chase by light. So it is with the devils, the fathers of falsehood.

They now seek a hiding place somewhere in the Creator's Creation of Truth (the universe) which cannot now be done. Falsehood vanishes in the light of Truth as darkness vanishes before light.

The Light of Truth

Allah is the light of Truth in the Person of Master Fard Muhammad (the long expected Mahdi or Messiah). His appearance in the World of Falsehood is like that of the sunrise against the night of darkness.

We have lived in a night of falsehood for six thousand years under the rule of Satan (the white race). This evil false rule must be removed by Allah to allow the real Nation of Truth to rule as they did before the night of falsehood. This is the time the change is being made. Today, the Sun of Truth is casting her rays upon the dark western horizon.

Our Unity Demanded

We the darker people of the Western Hemisphere should unite and pull off our night garments and dress ourselves for today. Our unity is demanded. The original settlers (the Indians) of this Western Hemisphere and the Latin or Central American must unite and accept their own.

The earth was created by the black man, for the black man and this is universally known by all scholars and scientists of religion.

The earth has been divided between four families (black, brown, red and yellow) for many thousands of years. The fifth family (the white race) was grafted in to be tried at ruling us, the Black nation. However, they have proven to be unworthy of keeping the peace and justice among us., the aboriginals.

Instead of peace, love and brotherhood, they have been successful in bringing about hell, dissatisfaction, and have made enemies between brother and brother (divided us one against the other).

Whites Made Mischief

They have made mischief and caused bloodshed throughout the Nations of earth.

Now the nations that love peace and brotherhood are uniting behind our God of Peace and Justice to bring about the removal of this troublemaker, whom we have learned through experience, is disagreeable to live with in peace.

We should not hesitate to unite and take our place in our own. What future do the so-called Negroes have under their 400-year-old enemies? Of all people, should not they unite and do something for self and stop depending on their open enemies for existence?

THE TRUTH

"O Apostle, deliver what has been revealed to you from your Lord; and if you do it not, then you have not delivered His Message, and Allah will protect you from the people; surely Allah will not guide the unbelieving people" (Holy Qur'an 5:67).

When Allah (God) decided to reveal His Truth and bring an end to falsehood, that Truth must be delivered regardless of the cost! The Messenger of Truth should not fear to deliver it if that Truth is from Allah; He will be the Protector of it as well as the Protector of the Messenger who delivers it (Truth).

A true Messenger of Allah never fears to deliver the Message of Allah, nor does he ever fail to deliver it - even though most of them (Messengers) and their followers suffered severe persecutions and even death; yet, the message of Allah was delivered.

The awakening of the Arabs nearly fourteen hundred years ago to the ancient Truth (Islam) (not a new Truth) of Allah by Muhammad and his work, was typical of what will be done today. He was opposed by the Arabs for a while. Although the Arab Nation and their country are the birthplace of the great prophets and Scriptures, and from there, prophets are sent throughout the world from the time of Adam until today, the Arab history cannot be compared with the history of the so-called Negroes who have never had a Divine prophet nor a Scripture!

According to the past histories of the major prophets, one comes 2000 years until the end of the World of Sin. Moses came exactly two thousand years after Yakub (the

195

God and Maker of the evil Caucasian race). Jesus came two thousand years after Moses, and the last prophet came two thousand years after Jesus, fulfilling much of the histories of the Prophets before him; especially Moses, David, Jesus and Muhammad. The man Allah (God) raised up from among the American so-called Negroes in the West will unite his people to Islam with the guidance of Allah with a book of Scripture for his people prepared and written by the fingers of Allah (God).

His teachings will be called a "New Islam" and will be opposed by many who would not like a change from the old to a higher knowledge of the Divine. The present Holy Quran Sharrieff leads us right up to the door of that final book for our future though not admitting us in; yet we are able to get a glance of some things.

The devil (white race) watches the Believers, and when he finds one showing any sign of weakness, he helps him to become more weaker in the faith. Islam is the greatest unifying force on the Planet Earth. Islam is a religion that is backed by the power of its Author, Allah, to Whom be praised forever. Islam could save the world from its destructive fall, but the world has practiced evil for so long that she would rather go to her doom than to turn and do righteousness. Look at the silly things the world is doing, working "like mad" to destroy each other! For what?

Is not there enough earth for every one of us? Yes, there is enough if we would be satisfied with our share, and not seek to rob the other man of his share. Billions upon billions of dollars are being spent for the purpose of destroying humanity from the face of the earth; which is nothing but a waste of money that could be spent for the happiness of the Nations and not for their death. THE WICKED WILL BE THE LOSERS!

THE TRUTH SUBMIT TO ALLAH

(Holy Qur'an 2:12)

The power of all the religions of the world, other than Islam are losing their attraction and power on the people of earth. Why? Number One (1) because they are too proud to submit to God according to the word of Allah (God) to me. It was not possible for the world to submit, and believe in the religion of Islam before the end of the rule, and power of the devils (the white race).

The white race (devils) was permitted to rule (Genesis 1:26 us not according to Justice and Righteousness but by evil and falsehood. They were made wise enough by their father (Yakub) to deceive us in making falsehood to appear to be true, until the time and appearance of the Author of Truth (Allah), and Justice. They (the white race) make evil appear to be very attractive (Genesis 3:6) and in this way they capture many of the righteousness, for unlike attracts.

Murderers By Nature

By nature they are murderers and liars (Genesis 4:8; John 8:44), therefore, they could not believe (John 8:37-40) in a true religion like Islam which means man's entire Submission to the will of Allah (God).

Take a second look into the above said; if the devils were given the power to be the God of this world for a time (six thousand years), how could they by nature teach us to submit to Allah, and do the will of a God of Truth, freedom, justice and equality. Therefore, the people under a wicked ruler (the devil) of the world went astray from the True God and True Religion. They made for themselves all kinds of false gods and religions and bowed down and worshipped them.

The Time

Now is the time of the God of Truth and Justice to rule. The Black Nations are awakening to the knowledge of the time of our God (Allah) and are now seeking Him and His True religion called "Islam," to be united and live in peace together as they were before the creation of the white race (devil).

Negro Progress Slow

Islam was offered to this world by the Prophets of Almighty Allah (God), (see and read both the Bible and Holy Qur'an) but was unable to make their people believe in it (entire) submission to the will of Allah (God). Moses, Jesus and Muhammad failed in their efforts to get this world to submit to the will of Allah (God), not to mention the many other lesser Prophets who spent their lifetime and efforts trying to convert the world to submit to the will of Allah (God).

Even today, due to the poison effect of the teachings of falsehood, the progress of truth and Justice among the so-called Negroes is very slow, to what it would be if there were no opposition by the enemies (devils).

There are some white people better than others, but they are not to be mistaken for the righteous, because they are not as wicked as others of their kind. One reason why the so-called Negroes reject Islam, because they don't know what it actually means, which is only entire submission to the will of Allah (God). As today, the people have submitted to do the will of the devils, not the will of the God of Truth and Justice (Allah).

THE TRUTH

"Islam"

The religion of Islam is now for the first time being offered to us, the so-called Negroes, the lost-found, and the lost members of the chosen nation by Allah (God) in person.

Moslem Shriners

Before the coming of Allah, Islam was sold to the so-called Negroes in a secret order or society called the <u>Masons</u>. This order is made up of thirty-three (33) degrees and it is sold by degrees. If a member is eligible and able to pay for all the degrees he may do so, but only those who take the thirty-third (33rd) are called <u>Moslem Shriners</u>.

Though real Islam is not practiced in this secret order, it is made a <u>farce.</u> The first three (3) degrees are the base of the whole, they are full of significance pertaining to the <u>robbery</u> and <u>murder</u> of a <u>valuable</u> member of a significant Temple, and a friend of the wisest <u>King</u> that ever lives.

Islam Free

You do not have to buy Islam, it is free. Islam is the salvation of the Black Nation, and the only way out for the so-called American Negroes. Islam means submission to the will of Allah (God). What greater religion than a religion that demands us to submit to the will of Almighty God (Allah)?

The number one (1) principle of belief in Islam is the belief in One God. Is not this the teachings of the Prophets of old. <u>Abraham, Moses, Jesus</u> and <u>Muhammad</u>?

UNITY

Sincere unity comes from the love of one another and agreement is assured. The lack of unity is the real cause of the existing dissension among the so-called Negroes. There is no love for one another and this lack of love makes it impossible to unite and agree with each other.

Allah, in the Person of Master W.F. Muhammad (God in Person) brought the key to our unity by giving us the knowledge of self and others. This knowledge of self has made us to love self and our kind - not the evil. It is against the law of nature for us to love strange flesh as we love self and kind. Unlike is repelled by alike, through unlike may well attract. But the law of nature will rebel though unlike may well attract against it because of the lack of alikeness. Perfect unity is obtained then from alikeness and not from unlike. Every kind of life we see in this world is different; everyone unlike, but yet unity is at work among only the alike. We see that the world of mankind is intelligent enough to recognize their own likeness and repel unlikeness. Therefore. they like on a part of this earth alone to themselves - Black, Brown, Yellow, Red and White. But my poor people who like unlike and hate alike because they have no knowledge of self or kind; not to mention other than self. They are therefore called blind, deaf and dumb, and this is true even if it is offensive and disgraceful to be called such names.

Love and unity cannot be enjoyed without the knowledge of self and kind. The so-called Negroes should attend the meetings of the Muslims to learn about self and kind as revealed to us by Allah (to Whom be praised forever), Who came in the Person of Master W.F. Muhammad, the hoped for and long awaited for the last 2,000 years. The Great Mahdi, the Finder, of us, the Lost and the Last members of the Divine Nation of righteousness, the Great Restorer of the Kingdom of Islam). Everyone of us who accepts (entire submission to the will of Allah), Allah as our God and His religion, Islam, enjoys peace of mind, contentment and have no fear nor shall they grieve. This religion, Islam, is actually powered by Allah (God) and this power and the great wisdom - the secret of God, and the universe that we live in - automatically invites us.

One of the main purposes of His coming is to unite the Lost and Found members of the Great Asiatic Nation of Islam. His supreme wisdom given to the Lost-found Nation of Islam as He called us, will put us on top of civilization as Yakub's supreme wisdom and knowledge on how to trick the righteous into doing evil - just the opposite of right - put his people, the White Race. The Great Mahdi will make a nation from the product of righteousness and teach them a Supreme knowledge of the God of righteousness that has never been taught since the creation of the universe. He will make His people rule forever as that wisdom is the utmost of divine knowledge and as I have saith it is so powerful that it automatically unites us.

A UNITED BLACK NATION

WHY NOT A UNITED TWENTY MILLION BLACK PEOPLE OF AMERICA?

There is a United Nations, headed by America and England, which includes nearly all races and colors. There is also a United Arab Republic.

Twenty million black people of America are called after the names of their slave-masters. This means that they are still the property of white America; thus making impossible for them to become a free and independent people of white America. If they (the so-called Negroes) would united and throw off the white man's names - which have no divine meanings, for they (the devils) are not the people of the God of righteousness (Isa. 63:19; 64:3.5) - and the slavery teachings of the white man's religion (Christianity), they, in the Name of Allah and the religion Islam, could become one of the greatest and mightiest nations on the earth. (Let the disbelievers ask me to prove it).

We must unite and qualify for self-independence, for Allah's earth is vast. America kill off the original owners (the Indians) and took this country for their home. We must have some of this earth that we can call OUR OWN. Allah is with us. We must learn trades and professions of all kinds and build our own nation, which consists of twenty million so-called Negroes.

207

There is no hope of a future for us in the white race, because they have no future for themselves. THIS YOU MUST KNOW! Unity is the result of love and respect of one's own and others. We cannot expect love, unity and respect from others until we have these for ourselves. We should be ashamed of ourselves to ever want to integrate or mix bloods with the very enemies and murderers of our people. They are born haters and despisers of the black nation, they are also the robbers and spoilers of our nation.

Why not a united American black people (the so-called Negroes)? We have a world of people of our kind who would not hesitate to show us that they are our sincere brothers and sisters if we only would throw off the chains and yoke of the white man's slavery. You should drop their names and get out of their religion. Stop worshipping them (white man) and worship Allah (God) and His true religion, Islam. Islam means entire submission to the will of Allah and the entrance into His peace; there you will not fear nor shall you grieve.

Seek for yourself and kind, that which the white race seeks for themselves which is independence, freedom, justice, equality and a free country for their own kind. A dependent and begging people cannot hope for anything but the worse. This world is on her way out and another one is coming in, the new world of Islam (Peace and Righteousness) under the rulership of Allah and the Muslims. Let us buy farm land where we can grow our food and sell it at a price that our poor people are able to pay. We should produce our own needs, unite as one man, and sacrifice everything to accomplish this unity.

WE MUST BE OURSELVES

We are faced with the choice of accepting self or other than self. The absence of love for self, makes us to love other than self; hatred of self keeps us fighting and opposing self. We must do something for self and stop working against each other for the joy of our enemies. We must prepare for tomorrow. We cannot depend on the white race to continue to farm and grow food, cotton and wool to clothe us. We have to get rid of thinking like a child. We have to learn to think and do like men of all other nations and look after our own needs. We must unite and work together in order to make it easy for all. We must go to school and try to get a college and university education. We must learn engineering of all kinds, teachership, chemistry, medicine, astronomy and other sciences such as professions, trades, navigation, etc.

Learn to do for self and nation, what other civilized nations are doing for themselves. To long we have been lazy. Think in the way of being self-independent. Unite and build a better black nation, worthy of its name "the first." Speak good for self and kind; never join in making fun of your people with non-members of your people. Never seek to take advantage of your own black brother or sister. Be true to self and other than your own kind, defend each other against danger to lives and property of your own. Be clean internal as well as external. Stop using tobacco in any form. Stop eating the filthy swine (PIG). Stop being loud in the public and in secret. Stop using filthy language in public and in secret. Stop using drugs and whiskey.

Stop trying to mix with other than your own kind. Stop going to church and go to the Mosque of Islam where you will be loved and respected, and protected by the God of Islam and your Nation. Be yourself and fear Allah alone. Do not think the white man is being blessed in not asking you to take part in the third world war or final war of the western world's civilization. Join onto your own kind and be yourself!

WE MUST HAVE SOME EARTH

What good is it to serve a Master or God if that Master or God will not give you a home on His earth that you can call your own? There are 57,255,000 square miles of land out of water. Of a total of 196,940,000 square miles that make up our planet, and 29,000,000 square miles of producing land, how many square miles of this good earth do we, the so-called American Negroes, own here in America? Yet, we seek to be recognized as the equal of our slave-masters' children with nothing but a job that the masters allow us to do for them when we are wanted. Is not this a shame for us whom the slave masters claimed that they freed nearly one hundred years ago to go for ourselves?

We have never tried going for self. The white man drives us and forces us to do something for himself and his kind, and yet, we have made ourselves appear to the world of Mankind to be the laziest cowards, self-divided, shameful, disgraceful beggars of white people on the earth! Do not we ever get tired of being looked upon as fools without a home? Everyone has some of this earth that they call their own (if not, they are doing everything within their power to own some of it). For the past one hundred years of freedom (so-called), we have given the same slave masters our labor and our lives to help build them a home and keep it secure for them; though the white slave masters are responsible for our blindness - (but not after the light comes to us).

We need re-education!   The white man's education is helpful, but there is not enough light shown in it for the so-called Negroes to find the way to self. They beat and kill you, starve you, drive and kick you out of their presence and homes; yet, you love and admire them, and hate and dislike yourselves, and will not unite to find a home for self and children. You are a satisfied people with nothing!

We must have some of this earth that we can call our own! We have lost 400 years making our slave master's children rich, powerful and independent and are charmed by their riches (as the symbolic parable of "Lazarus" and the rich man) in that you will not go after something for self! No. (1) we are where we do not belong and by the Divine prophet's prophecy concerning us, there is not permanent home for us in this part of our planet; but promised us, a permanent home among our own people. Would not you like to live in peace and be recognized and treated as brother citizens by your own people in your own country than to be unrecognized and treated like a "dog" by other than your own kind and country?

Allah (God) wants to give you, the so-called Negroes, the best and most permanent home the earth has to offer. The white man came into possession of this part of our planet by blood and built up blood and established himself by evil (Hab. 2:12), and now must pay the price set by Allah (God) through the mouth of his prophets. We must have some of this earth that we can call our own for a permanent home. Come, follow me and you will get it. For this cause is the base of Allah (God's) coming. Do not let this world of our enemies deceive you.

WHAT THE SO-CALLED NEGRO MUST DO

All over the earth today, we see men coming into unity, oneness, or solidarity. The European Nations are in a bond or pact referred to as <u>WATO</u> or the Warsaw Pact. They are attempting to establish a European Common Market. In Africa, there is the Organization of Arab States and much work is going on toward uniting all the people of Africa. In the United Nations, those nations which have something in common or identical people, traits, culture or borders are in groups or blocks. Men everywhere are seeking unity among themselves. Every race of people want unity their own kind first, except my people, the so- called Negro in America. Our condition and lack of love for ourselves must be attributed to the slave-master. He has been our teacher until the coming of Almighty God Allah. The slave- master has robbed my people of their God, religion, name, language and culture. They are now deaf, dumb and blind to the knowledge of self.

The worst kind of crime has been committed against us for we were robbed of our desire to even want to think and do for self. We are often pictured by the slave-master as a lazy and trifling people who are without thoughts of advancement. I say, this is a condition which the slave-master very cleverly wanted and created within and among the so-called Negro.

Robert H. Kinzer and Edward Sagarin, in their book, "The Negro in American Business," Page 81, state that the history of America would be different today if the slaves, freed from bondage had been given, in addition to the three amendments to the constitution, the famous "forty acres and a mule." The slaves instead started not only without land and the money to purchase it, but with few avenues open to earn and save such money. Ownership of producing land is a prime and necessary part of freedom. A people cannot exist freely without land, and the so-called Negro in land ownership or limiting the areas in which such purchases or even rentals could be made. Are you not left restricted to the poorer sections the slave-master is abandoning throughout America?

Again, Mr. Kinzer and Mr. Sagarin give a hint in their book of the great psychological strategy of the slave-master on his slave - that is the original brainwash. On page 84, the authors state that the land sold to the slave was of poor quality and in an inferior location. They state, the so-called Negro faced pressure against his becoming a farm owner and pressure from the white community that he remain a tenant. We encountered credit difficulties, hardships of repayment of loans, and hardship with white executives from whom the loans must be asked. All of this is part of the clever plan to discourage my people from wanting to own producing land for themselves and to cause a great dislike, within them for having anything to do with tilling, cultivating, extracting and producing for themselves as other free and independent people. It is a shame! This shows you and me what White America is to us, and just why we have not been able to do anything worthwhile for self. They want us to be helpless so they can mistreat us as always. We must come together and unite. IT IS TIME.

I think it is a disgrace for us to be satisfied with only a servant's part. We should and must, as other people, want for ourselves what other civilized nations have! Let us do for ourselves that which we are begging the slave-master to do for us. Do not be fooled by the false promises of civil rights and the softening of their language. It is offered to you now to keep you from becoming free of their evil plans of depriving you of the offer made to us by Allah. If we would submit to Him, He will set us in heaven at once. It is only justice that we be given land and provisions for a start so, we may do for ourselves. This is what other new, emerging nations are given. We want good productive land; not earth that is scorched, but land that would produce crops and hold foundations for structures.

Let us make this clear, I am not begging, for if it pleases Allah, he will give us a home and I am with Him. Today, according to Allah's (God's) word, we are living in a time of THE GREAT SEPARATION of the black and the whites. The prophesied 400 years of slavery, which the so-called Negroes would serve white people, ended in 1955. The so-called Negroes must return to their own. Nothing else will solve their problem. The Divine power is working and will continue to work in favor of the so-called Negroes' return to their own. The separation would be a blessing for both sides. It was the only solution according to the Bible for Israel and the Egyptians; it will prove to be the only solution for America and her slaves.

WHAT IS UN-AMERICAN?

According to the dictionary's definition of un-American, it means: "one that is not American; not characteristic of or proper to America, foreign or opposed to the American character, usages, standards, etc."

As you know, any or all Negroes that seek freedom, justice and equality, is or are charged or accused of being un-American. They are accused with seeking to over-throw the government of America by force. (We Muslims, prohibit the carrying of arms, but yet we are accused of planning to over-throw the government by force). No Negro leader has been successful in helping his people to freedom, justice and equality, that was not opposed by both his own people and the merciless, wicked white Americans. Also, by those poison intellectual so-called Negroes who love and worship the devils and hate self and kind. Today, the Americans hope to unite all educated so-called Negroes, along with their already poisoned Negro Christian Preachers, against we the Muslims that preach freedom, justice and equality for the Black Nation. They are united against my followers and I. Thanks be to Allah, you are a little late to win. Allah (God) knew the tricks that you would use to try deceiving the Black Man before you were created.

UN-AMERICAN: I wish to prove, according to the English language in this article, that every so-called Negro, Indian, and all non- white Europeans, are un-American according to the dictionary's definition of an American. An American, according to the dictionary, "is a citizen of the United States or of the earlier British Colonies; one not belonging to one of the aboriginal races. (We belong to the aboriginal nation of the earth, the white or European race is not aboriginal). (2) Native or inhabitant of the Western Hemisphere. The above explanation makes it clear that we are not members of the white Europeans, nor descendants of that race. We are the aboriginal un- Americans. The above explanation also makes it clear that we (so-called Negroes) are not, and cannot be American citizens, since we are not American by nature, nor by race. A true American is one other than the aboriginal race or races that inhabited the Western Hemisphere, or the whole Planet Earth, before the coming of the white man from Europe. We, the so- called Negroes (members of the aboriginal -Earth, and of the tribe of Shabazz), were kidnapped from our native land and people by the white Englishmen and Americans. We were brought here not to be made Americans, nor American citizens; but rather, to be slaves or servants for the true American citizens - whites - who originally came from Europe. We, descendants of the Asiatic Nation from the continent of Africa, after 100 years of so-called freedom, cannot claim by the law of justice, to be Americans or American citizens. We are un-American; and by nature, we are different. Know from this day on, that if you are a so-called Negro, red, black, or an Indian, or any member of the aboriginal Black Nation, you are an un-American. Even though you may have been born in the United States of America you cannot be an American.

USED FOR CRIMINAL PURPOSES: What, or why are we called un- American? It is to classify us as criminals, or with crimes that we are not guilty of. They make the truth God has given to us un-truth, they use it to conceal our true intentions. But at the same time, they claim freedom of speech, freedom of the press and religious freedom lawful under the Constitution. Again, it is abundantly clear to you that have eyes, that the Americans never intended freedom for their so-called Negroes. She stands in the way and opposes true freedom, justice and equality from coming to the poor black man and woman in the Western Hemisphere. She is pleased with the foolish and ignorant worship of the so-called Negroes. She doesn't ever want the Negroes to accept the true religion, which is Islam. WHY? Here (In Islam) the Negroes have a true God and true friends on his side, and that means help to the poor Negroes against his open enemies, the white race. So YOU CAN SEE, or you will see why they do not want a so-called Negro Muslim people in America. It means independence, friendship, Divine guidance and help against the devils. As it is written in the Holy Qur'an, "know that Allah is with the Muslims."

TRICK THE NEGROES TO STAY IN DEVIL'S NAMES: For the first time, the so-called Negroes are awakening to just why white Americans still like to call their much hated and despised, once Negro slaves, after their names; or make the Negroes think names do not mean anything that they should remain in them. The devils have knowledge of the time. They know you will not be accepted by God, nor your own nation if represented under their names, which are not names of God - and will not see the Hereafter. The intellectual so-called Negroes think it is a disgrace to them to not be called by the slave-master's name; and if I wanted to be called "Muhammad," I should go to court and have my name changed legally. I laughed and said, I'm sorry, I have my legal name; there is no law to make me pay to be called by my legal name. I have been called by an illegal name. Now, I have gotten rid of that illegal slave name for a legal and Holy Name of God. Again, we must remember, the white race never intended anything like good for you. They are not seeking good for you today; death is really their aim for you. Why do they oppose our struggle for justice and freedom if they want to see all people free and enjoying justice and equality? They are not referring to you; you are not people in their eyes, it is their people they are referring to. Why do they oppose separation of us into a state or territory of our own, since we cannot live in peace with them? When we read of the evils done to us and to our fathers by this race of devils, we cannot foresee anything in them but evil hatred and murder for us and to our unborn children.

Read some of their books on what went on against our slave parents by the fathers of these modern murderers of ours. For instance, the book entitled, "Brown Americans," by Edwin R. Embree, printed 1946, page 54, tells the story of laws against education for the so-called Negroes. He quotes a devil, Henry Berry, as saying while speaking in the Virginia House of Delegates, in 1832, describing the situation as existed at that time in many parts of the south; "We have, as far as possible closed every avenue by which light may enter the slaves' minds... (The avenue of the light of Allah you are unable to shut out from coming to us). ...If we could extinguish the capacity to see the light, our work would be complete; they would then be on a level with the beasts of the field and we should be safe. I am certain that we would not do it, if we could find out the process and that on the plea of necessity." The above words, desires, and works against you, are still in the hearts of their evil, blood- thirsty children against you. Today, they go around in large cities like Chicago, at night, in cars, loaded with baseball bats, guns, iron pipes and knives to pounce upon and kill poor, harmless, so-called Negroes. We are living under the very shadow of death in such a place as America.

Unity under the guidance and protection of Allah will bring an end to this horrible situation. What do you see as a future in them for you and your children? - Nothing but hell. Remember, if you are black or a member of the Black Nation, you are un-American. If you want equal justice and a decent way of life to live, or have love for the black people, you are un-American. The American is the only one that can sing, "The land of the Free" - it is for the white Americans.

Elijah Muhammad

The Foundation Years
(1959 - 1962)

VOLUME II

By
Elijah Muhammad
(Messenger of Allah)

Published by
Secretarius MEMPS Publications
c/o 12685 Dorsett Rd. #187 n Maryland Heights, Missouri
[63043]
Catalog & General Info. (770) 907-2212
www.memps.com

223

ACCEPT ALLAH AND THE TRUE RELIGION OF ISLAM
Or Suffer the Chastisement of Almighty God Allah

I have warned you in this article of the consequences of rejecting Allah and the true religion of God and His Prophets: Noah, Abraham, Moses and Jesus.

Believe it or not, America is falling. She is under Divine Chastisement just as Egypt was in the days of Pharaoh and Moses (the servant of Allah). The same thing is being repeated here in America! Woe to the disbelievers in Allah! Egypt was made unfit for the Hebrews by Divine plagues. Likewise, America will soon be unfit for you! The Bible does not give us any knowledge of the previous condition of the slaves under Pharaoh until the birth of Moses. Only a prophecy of Abraham is given that they would sojourn in a land that was not theirs for four hundred years.

It seems as if their treatment under slavery by the Egyptians was kept a secret from the outside world. Just as the so-called Negroes' enslavement in America for three hundred years, and the true knowledge of our condition was known only to Allah (God) until about seventy years ago. Now, all of Asia knows where the lost-found members of their Nation are. For three hundred years, no outside teachers of our kind were allowed to contact us. Even now their movements among us are limited, because the Negroes were born blind, deaf, and dumb to the knowledge of SELF, not to mention other than themselves. Therefore, the so-called Negroes (who

225

are actually members of the Tribe of Shabazz) were reared and schooled by their enemies (their slave masters). They do not have the true knowledge of self, and kind, or the true knowledge of God nor His true religion of Islam.

The reason why it is so hard to get the so-called Negroes to believe in Allah and Islam, as mentioned in the Bible (Rev. 12:9; 20:10),is because the white race has spread their religion called Christianity all over the Black Man's World. He has deceived millions of Black People other than the so-called Negroes - the lost-found members of the Tribe of Shabazz. It is now only a matter of time before the so-called Negroes' eyes will be opened, and will believe and confess the truth of Allah and His religion, Islam.

…The REAL DIVINE TRUTH is un-American, if it is on the side of the poor Negroes, and it is! Do not fear what you will be called by accepting ISLAM (TRUTH) but rather FEAR ALLAH (and the loosing of your lives) for not accepting the TRUTH. AMERICA IS FALLING. She is a real habitation of devils, and every evil and unclean, and hateful person. There is no future for her. One destruction after the other shall come upon her until she has been laid low, even to the ground. The only thing that can check her fall is that she accepts Islam, and that, she will not do.

America has many of her own teachers warning her, but she will not believe. FLY TO ALLAH, MY PEOPLE, AND SAVE YOURSELVES AND YOUR CHILDREN FROM HER DESTRUCTION!

ALLAH REVEALED THE TRUTH

2-2-61

ALLAH reveals the real devil in human form that Man of Sin, the Caucasian Race. (Thess. 2:3). Why shouldn't the so-called Negroes and the whole of the Black nations know the Truth of the devil who has ruled us for six thousand years? The end of that race of devils has arrived. How are we to reject them and accept Allah (God) if we have not a true knowledge of the devils? Allah (God), the Best Knower, never destroyed a people without first revealing His truth and purpose through a Messenger whom He chooses of that people, according to the Bible and Holy Qur'an Sharrieff.

The wise tricks being used by the devils (White Race), on the American so-called Negroes to deceive them into sharing hell fire with them, could trap ninety-nine per cent of the Negroes into going with the devils to their destruction. The so-called Negroes must be given the true knowledge of this universal-arch deceiving race of devils, who have been the Negroes guides and teachers since slavery.

Shall I, for the sake of your fear and ignorance of the devils withhold from telling you the truth which Allah (God) has revealed to me THAT WILL FREE you of that fear and ignorance that is now hindering you from being set in heaven and power? NO! I will not withhold the truth from you to be called a friend of the devils, who have been the Negroes' guides and teachers since slavery.

Jesus prophesied that: "You shall know, that which shall make you free," (John 8:32).

Today it has come to you and me from the Lord of the Worlds; it is a true knowledge of the Person of God and the Devil. I am not responsible for your rejection. I am only responsible for the deliverance of it. According to the Bible (John 8:42), Jesus said to this race, "If God (The God of righteous) were your father, you would love me." In the 44th verse of the same Chapter, Jesus says: "You are of your father the devil." This proves beyond a shadow of a doubt that this race (Caucasian) cannot believe the Truth and especially Allah, His Prophets, and Islam. Being not of Allah, they cannot by nature love and obey Allah, His Prophets, nor the black Nations. Try teaching them of Allah and His religion, Islam; some of them will claim they never heard of Islam, to see how much you know of it, though their Father (Yakub), sometimes referred to as Adam, was once in Islam.

The American white race doesn't want the so-called Negroes to believe in the religion of Islam, but the poor lost-found members of the Tribe of Shabazz are now learning very fast that Islam is the TRUTH, but what they (Caucasians) hate the most is the teaching of the true knowledge of themselves. The Bible (John 8:44), (Thess. 2:3,4,8,9), teachers that they are nothing else but devils, and II Thessalonians, Chapter 2, makes it very clear to us, that the Man of Sin's (The Devil's) time is limited, and that he must do a work of deceiving, lying, murdering and opposing the true God and His Prophets. The Truth of them will put a stop to their deceiving the people of Allah (the Black Nation), which will only come after the time of the Man of Sin (the devil); this is True. He has come and I am sent directly from Him, to make this Truth known to my people, that they shouldn't love and follow the devils, for Allah (God) will destroy His enemy and the enemy's work. This country is now being plagued by Allah: Storms, Hail, Snow, and earthquakes. My people, ISLAM IS YOUR SALVATION. The devil desires to frighten you away from accepting Islam. Don't let him do that, for Allah is well able to protect you and me from the evil planning.

Hurry and join onto your Own Kind. The Time of this World is at Hand.

AMERICANS PERSECUTE THE MUSLIMS, WHAT WILL BE THE END OF HER? PART I

11-16-61

According to history, the breaking up or change of the OLD for the NEW, has always brought about the persecution of the representatives of the new. Again, according to history, the old was the loser.

Allah has taught me of the great persecution in the days of the grafting of the Caucasian race (white race), out of the original Black Nation. And the only solution was total separation. Gen. 3:23; Deut. 32:8; Matt. 25:32; Holy Qur'an 2:36, 38; 7:34. The proud Negro leadership is blind and cannot see that these are the days of separation. Therefore, they help persecute the Muslims (the righteous) and think they are beloved of God for doing so. They are self-made, self-sent, authorized by the devils on a script of paper. For such hypocrites, read: Matt. 23:13, 29, 34.

...And when the dragon saw that he was cast into the earth, he persecuted the woman (the Messenger of God) which brought forth the man ...Rev. 12:13. Persecution is the bitter pill for the new converts of a new change from the old. The old never wants to give way to the new. We are now in a change of worlds or civilizations. The previous changes of governments, and the persecutions of the Apostles and their followers at the hand of the old civilization, are put into the scriptures for our learning and warnings of that final change of worlds. Pharaoh and his dealings with Israel was a sign of what you and I are

231

facing today. Mentioned under the Bible's last book called the Revelations of John, under a very appropriate name, according to the character's nature and work, the "beast." They (white race) also once lived a life of part beast and part human. The symbolical "beast" of Revelation.

The so-called Negroes who refuse to believe in the false religion of the "beast" (Christianity), his name, his mark, or to worship him, suffers persecution. This persecution serves as a trial to both the believing (Muslims) so-called Negroes and the disbelieving so-called Negroes. The persecution of the so-called Negro Muslims in America is being carried on more for the purpose of frightening the others from accepting Allah, Islam, the true religion of God, than to change those who already believe in Allah and Islam. As we see and Hear, the poor, devil-made black Preachers are more enemy to the Muslims than the devils themselves. For the devils are wise as we are to what will be the end of their persecution of the Muslims. They know the black Preachers and black educated so-called Negroes are blind, deaf and dumb to the time and the end of these things. The black preachers and so-called educated Negroes are looking towards the white man as defenders for them against Allah and the Muslims. This class among the so-called Negroes is now being made manifest to those of the poor unlearned Negroes as their worse enemies.

For thirty years, we the Muslims, have been persecuted by the so- called Negro Preachers and so-called Negro Politicians. They care not for the love of Allah (God) and the Truth (Islam). Their love and worship is for the devils. (Though they are told in Rev. 9:20, that they should not worship devils.) The doom of one party and the disgrace of the other will not be delayed it is very near.

America's rotten government of injustice to the so-called Negro Muslims have not caused us to weaken in faith, but has strengthened us, and has given us more converts. For Allah desires to show Himself as God to these devils and our disbelieving people; that there is no God but He and I am His Messenger. The American white man ignores his own law of justice when it comes to the so-called Negroes. They are especially unjust to the Muslims whom they are afraid will win the so-called Negroes to Allah, that He (Allah) may bless and deliver them from their merciless hands.

This week in Monroe, Louisiana, the devils were again made manifest, that there is no law or justice under the flag of America for the black men and women that they will respect. After the Defense Lawyer, Sharpe, had proved by the laws of the U.S. Court the innocence of the Muslims, the court and its bloodthirsty, human-like beast, ignored it and sent the Muslims to prison.

The Defending Lawyer (Sharpe) was so surprised at such open action of the court, ignoring its own law of justice that he stood on the floor of the court before the inhuman devil Jury and wept. For he never thought his white devil teachers and instructors of their law could ignore it - without even the thought that they were disgracing themselves and casting aside their own laws.

We put up $19,000 in Monroe, Louisiana, as bond money for the Muslims; besides several thousand dollars to the lawyers and traveling expenses. We did this also for my son, Wallace Muhammad. For four years, the Muslims paid out more than $16,000 to obtain justice and freedom for my son, who was never a citizen of America and cannot ever be one according to what really constitutes an American citizen.

Will the U.S.A. have my son, Akbar Muhammad, arrested and returned to the U.S.A., claiming that he is a citizen of America and must take part in her defense in case of war; whom I have enrolled in the University of Al-Azar, Cairo, Egypt?

It is very clear that the Government of America does not mean to free us, indeed, without causing a lot trouble. I am asking for our freedom to return to our own people or give us (the entire 20 million) a few states here, where we can go for self with a little help for the next 20 or 25 years. Give us something to fight for other than just a job that you make for us. We will make our own jobs if given the proper chance and place. We don't want to be free slaves for you any longer! Let us go free for ourselves!

AMERICANS PERSECUTE THE MUSLIMS, WHAT WILL BE HER END? PART II

11-23-61

We, the Muslims, are persecuted from city to city, and from state to state at the hands of the universal enemies of the Black Nation, of Islam and the Black Man's period (the white race). For thirty long years, the government of America has been sending us in groups and by the hundreds to state and Federal penitentiaries throughout the U.S.A. under false charges and false excuses.

The Christian so-called Negro Preachers, Negro Educators, Negro Politicians, the Police Department are all united with the Federal Bureau of Investigation (knows as the F.B.I.) whose agents are so bold and frantic in their efforts to keep the blind, deaf and mentally dead so-called Negroes from accepting their salvation, (Allah, the true God; Islam, the true religion of God and His prophets) that they even approach some of my ministers, along with other devils, with offers of better jobs and more money if they would only stop following me and the religion of Islam. They approach both men and women of my followers.

By the help of Allah (God) and the true Muslims, I am well aware and well informed of most all the moves of the devils (white race). In the past, I have said little or nothing about these things, because I know they must come to past that the scriptures might be fulfilled; that the righteous will be persecuted and mocked by the devils and by the disbelievers of our own people. But out of all our haters, mockers and persecutors, the Negro Preachers are the worst enemies that we have. They are the hardest to get to see and understand the truth. We can convert a devil before we can convert tone of these spiritually dumb preachers. We cannot even talk to them. They never seek to learn from us just what it is all about. No wonder it is written: Matt. 21:31,

> *"Verily I say unto you, that the publicans and the harlots go into the Kingdom of God before you (preachers)."*

The Holy Qur'an also says, in words, that they (Preachers) will be the last to believe, and that their love and desires of this world is like rust on their hearts; that they will be forced to believe and will be ashamed and brought to disgrace because they had rejected, denied and persecuted the Muslims to no avail.

Allah (God) is making manifest their love and worship of devils. The so-called Negro old leadership does not want anything here but the love of the slave-master's children (but not Allah's love). Nor do they want their own people's love. They do not want independence - just servants forever for the white Americans. I am glad the Mayorship and the Commissionership of Police in Phoenix, Arizona, was not in the hands of these dumb professional class of preachers, when I came here to reside for health sake. If it had been in their power, I would not have had the chance of a rabbit before 52 hound dogs.

By the help of Allah, I will get all their followers to believe the truth of Islam and leave them with their slavery teachings to try surviving. Surely Allah and His servant will be the winner. Allah is blessing me with converts in all the devil's prison houses.

Allah (God) will soon free them and overtake and persecute our enemies. These are lots of Christians in Asia and Africa and they own much wealth over there. Plenty rain, hail, snow and earthquakes can also be used against the enemies of Allah and His servants. Separation and some of this good earth that we can call our own is the only solution to protect us from the inhuman treatment of the white Americans.

AMERICA PERSECUTES THE MUSLIMS, WHAT WILL BE HER END PART III

12-14-61

"And they (they that had accept Allah, and His true religion) cried with a loud voice, saying: How long O' Lord Holy True (Allah is the Author of truth and justice) dost thou not judge and avenge our blood on them (the white devils of America) that dwell on the earth?" - (Rev. 6:10).

We have lived under the unjust (white American) who has enslaved, beat, and killed us, their slaves, for 400 years without mercy. Today, Allah (God) has chosen us His people and will overtake them with persecution and death. As it is and will overtake them with persecution and death. As it is written:

"And ye shall leave your name for a curse unto my chosen; for the Lord God shall slay thee, and call His servants by another name." (Isaiah 65:15).

The so-called Negroes who refuse to turn to righteousness (accept the true religion of Islam) make themselves a prey in the hands of the wicked, as it is written:

"He that departeth from evil maketh himself a prey; and the Lord (Allah) saw it and it displeased Him that there was no judgment (no justice for the righteous). (Isa. 59:15).

There is no justice for us, the lost-found Nation of Islam, whom our enemies call Negroes. We can even BUY `justice' in the land of our enemies and it has been proven it is still being proven in the courts of the devils in Monroe, Louisiana.

I have preached many years, telling you that there is no law in this devil's law books that they will respect when it comes to black man, so-called Negro.

Their Supreme Court of Justice was not set up to give you and me justice. It is for white Americans, and some of them are even denied it. Why? Because justice cannot be executed by the very enemies of justice.

We are daily, with the Truth of Allah, making manifest in your ears and eyes that your BELOVED blue-eyed slave-master is your open enemy. The NAACP is suffering beatings and jail sentences to show white America the love they have for them. My poor people will learn that they have no friend but Allah (God) and His servant, Elijah Muhammad, though, we too are persecuted by the same enemies.

They will pay a dear price for persecuting the Muslims, but remember as it is written: "But thus sayeth the Lord, even the captives of the mighty shall be taken away, and the prey of the terrible shall be delivered."

There will never be an end to our persecution by white Americans because they do not have the nature of the righteous. The white race was created to break the peace of the righteous and shed the blood of the innocent.

They persecuted us before Islam, when we were their servants; now we are no longer their servants, for we are the servants of Allah.

AMERICA PERSECUTES THE MUSLIMS, WHAT WILL BE HER END?

12-21-61

The Americans racists have had power over us to do as they pleased. They have beaten and killed us throughout our history in this country until this day. It is nothing to see and hear the poor so-called Negroes show and tell you of some mark or a broken limb put upon them by the whites. Even our black girls and women carry some sign of evil on their person caused by them.

That same human, beast-like devil (white man), deceives the black man and woman even to making love and marrying them. He is a deadly rattler-like human being... killing and burning black people, depriving them of their own homes and families and the good earth Allah created for us alone to live in love and peace forever.

Despoiled, Enslaved Us

This heartless inhuman beast has robbed, despoiled and enslaved us and our beautiful saint-like women. They have and are still making filthy prostitutes of our women, right before our face; this has been going on for 400 years.

Now, the "frog' (Negroes) love the "snake" (white man) that has swollen them up with beatings. They even imprison those Negroes that seek justice in their courts, and if anyone speaks or even sympathizes with the poor mistreated so-called Negroes, he is hated, beaten and sometimes killed at the hands of our 400 -year- old slave master's children.

We Should Wake Up

The black people in America should open their eyes to see that these evil blue-eyed devils are only trying to deprive them of their salvation through tricks of integration. Integration is a foreign-like love, played upon the black people through filthy sweet hearting and marrying among the poor and unwanted classes. With the help of Allah, we intend to save our poor people, even at the price of death! They must be delivered from their enemies, the devils.

We who have accepted Allah to be our God and Islam, as our religion, which means entire submission and peace, are no longer servants of white America. Their persecution upon us will not bring them any good for it is like one eating fire without water.

Revenge With Allah

Their future depends on how they treat us, the Muslims. Revenge is with Allah and He, in His own good time, will repay this wicked, blue-eyed deceiver. Their persecution upon us, the Muslims, means that they are persecuting servants of a Master whose power extends over the Universe.

America robbed and killed our people, the Indians, and took their homes; he then kid-napped us from our native land and people to destroy under slavery. The time of justice for us has arrived, but due to our people's fear of these blue-eyed devils, we cannot get to all of them at once. Nevertheless, when they see what Allah will do with this devil, they too will bow in submission to Allah and will be saved.

AMERICA WILL DESTROY SELF PART I

2-15-62

A messenger or a Prophet of God is always sent to a people to warn them of the time. He is a Warner of some great and dreadful event to take place upon the earth's inhabitants for their wrong- doings and idol worshipping.

The Messenger's job was always to separate the people he was sent to from the evil doers, lest they all be destroyed. In the previous histories according to the Bible and Holy Qur'an, Allah sent Noah to his people to warn them and teach them of Allah's wrath soon to be brought down on them for their inequities and idol worshipping; if they did not submit to His teachings and separate from the ones who were leading the people from Allah, they were overtaken by destruction.

The Independent One

Allah desires His people to be obedient to Him. He does not need us as He is the Independent One and is able to stand alone. We are dependent upon Him.

Abraham was also raised to deliver his people and warn them of Allah's anger and His promise of death if they did not submit to Allah and separate from the one who rejected Him.

Moses was another Warner to his people to bring them into the knowledge of Allah and a death penalty if they did not submit to Him.

These histories serve as a sign to you today. It serves to make you see that if you do not submit to Allah, His wrath will most surely be brought down on you.

Signs and Warnings

These histories are signs and warnings to white America of what comes to nations that stand in the way, oppose Allah's message and mislead the very people to whom the message is sent.

Were not the people who rejected Noah and made mock of the believers destroyed? Abraham had to separate his people from the idol worshippers and all who refuse to separate were destroyed.

Were not the people destroyed who rejected Lot's warnings? What do you think Allah will do to the people today who reject his last message and will not separate from their enemy?

Allah's Last Messenger

Allah has sent me as His last Messenger. I am a Warner to my people, the so-called Negroes, to separate themselves from the slave master. Compare these different histories, prophets and their messages to that I am teaching my people, the so-called Negroes today.

I am also teaching you of Allah's anger directed to the slave master for his great sins and misleading the so-called Negro who is sacred in the eyes of Allah.

All those who did not separate themselves from the evil doers in Noah's time were destroyed. I am teaching you the same thing today.

My people separate yourselves from the enemy or burn in their prepared hell fire. Their fair-play shown to you today is only to deceive you. They desire to take as many of you to hell with them as possible. Mr. Preacher, I do not want to take your congregation from you, I only want to teach them the truth (Islam) and the consequences they must pay if they will not listen.

By nature we the Aboriginals are superior. We are not of the grafted race of white devils. We are the first and the last. They (the enemy) are those whom Jesus made mention of as being devils and by nature haters and murderers of the black nation. There can be no change in them unless you regraft them and time is too precious to waste time regrafting an evil people to good.

Their time is up on our planet. Today they are seeking ways to remain on the earth. They are by nature haters of Allah, the God of truth and justice, and have opposed Him and the righteous ever since being on our planet.

I am Allah's last Messenger and have been missioned to you (so- called Negroes). Come to Islam and escape the hell fire that has been prepared for the enemy of God and all those who follow after him. I am not of myself for

247

Allah has sent me to deliver you. Do not let them trick you to their death.

AMERICA WILL DESTROY HERSELF PART II

2-1-62

Separation of the two, (Negro and white) is the only solution to the every growing problem of "What must be done with the Negroes?" Both the so-called Negroes and the whites do not seem to want to let go of one another. While the separation of the two races would be an act of wisdom and justice, on the other hand, to force integration, which means socializing, inter-marrying of the two races (black and white) and the eventual swallowing up of the so- called Negroes' race by their white slave-masters, or mongrelizing the two races, this will destroy the respect of the society of both, nationally and internationally. Integration is against the wishes of the intelligent thinking group of both races - these want to preserve their race and the respect of their society.

The government is trying to enforce this wicked and contrary law to the Divine Law and place of God, which will end in revolution and war, and total destruction of the wealth of America. This integration is not the wise and proper way of solving the so- called Negroes' problem in America, but is an outright deceitful and wicked plan to Allah for the future of the so-called Negroes. Both are sure to run into trouble with Allah's chastisement - both Negroes and white, as it is plainly hinted and written in the Bible and Holy Qur'an. (I will gladly point it out to the disputer).

The wise white scientists know it as well as I, and hope to prevent it, but they are outnumbered by their wicked wise.

God created two kinds of everything, so it is with man. He didn't intend for them (Negro and white) to mix, and has set a day of reckoning for those who willfully, and knowingly break His natural law in which He hast created man. It is their purpose to try and make Allah (God a liar, so as to deceive the blind, deaf, and dumb so-called Negroes, as the devil deceived Adam and Eve in the garden of Paradise. While knowing full well that they would lose their place with Allah and a peaceful home if they accepted his advice, so it will be with the so-called American Negroes, who after being offered heaven at once by Allah, accepts the wicked advice and the office of a temporary enjoyment with racial intermarrying and having sexual intercourse with a people with whom Allah is angry.

He will punish both parties as he did Israel and the people whom Jehovah forbid Israel to intercourse with. Israel was punished, and finally lost the goal which Jehovah had set before her and the deceiving enemies of Israel were destroyed. I warn you to let Israel's history, from the days of Moses to this day, be a lesson to you. REMEMBER, both Israel and the Christians are on the brink of a pit of fire. The best and only solution of this problem of the so-called Negroes is SEPARATION and give them a start in a territory to themselves, regardless to the ignorant love of the slave for his master.

Take a look at the foolish plan of Martin Luther King for the poor so-called Negroes and how he and his plan were criticized by Mr. James B. Kilpatrick, recently, on the Television program, "Nation's Future." There we saw the man, Rev. King, a college man, a Christian Minister and

Pastor, with a plan to take our poor people and himself and throw them at the mercy of an angry Negro-hating mob, to be beaten and killed for nothing; only to be accepted as whites accept white, in white private-owned places, and finally allow his people to become white, and to mongrelize both races.

What does he think the intelligent white and black people think of his silly plan? What kind of foolish so-called Negro parents will let such foolish preachers use their babies as a test of the mob's fire? What will those children's think of such parents when they grow up and see the light of truth? Mr. Kilpatrick asked Rev. King, "Why do you want to integrate and make your race a coffee color, with complete integration, losing your race identity?" He was telling Martin Luther King, in so many words, that you and your race will not cause the white race to lose their identity, but the Negro will lose his. Such slander and mockery coming to the decent and intelligent so-called Negro by the ignorant love of a so-called religious leader of his people is a disgrace.

Such short-sightedness by Rev. King and the NAACP for the so- called Negro of America, is making the nations of the earth, both black and white, laugh us to scorn, to see us, a race of lazy beggars, great lovers of our enemies. Why doesn't Mr. King and his NAACP organization join with me on a decent plan; a plan that make sense and one that will make a future for our people. Ask for separation and some of this good earth that we can call our own, where we can live in peace together, away from those who do not want us. This is the plan of God and it will bring an end to the ever growing trouble between the two races. If the white man (some of them) wanted to colonize us in Central America back in 1867, why not a free territory today, for we will not accept colonization. It is the time of our FREEDOM, and we will not accept anything less!

The NAACP and Mr. King want the freedom of voting, and in this way they think they will be able to gain equal power in a white man's government and country. A Negro will never be the president under the Stars and Stripes of America. If he did, what could he do but to bow to the wishes of the owners of the Stars and Stripes? Let us seek some stars for our own nation and stop begging the white man for that which he has. We are not in such condition as being at the mercy of the white race, as long as we are members of the Asiatic Nation.

Everyone that reads this article, cut it out and show it to your friends; buy, or make your subscription to this paper now!

ANSWER TO THURGOOD MARSHALL, CHIEF COUNCIL, NAACP

Regardless to how plain the truth may be given, especially when it comes to the so-called Negroes, there is always those who would not like to see the truth triumph over falsehood due to their own selfish desires. Those who have love, honor, and respect for their enemies more than they have for God and their own people are not fit to lead or counsel their people.

The Negro Leadership is in love with the Negroes' enemies, and would like being one of the enemies. I have often said, the present leadership of the so-called Negroes, both political and spiritual, are blind, deaf, and dumb to the knowledge of self, and kind, and are more harmful to the love, unity, freedom, justice and equality of their own people than the enemies of our people. For, if the blind, deaf, and dumb cannot see, hear, and speak for himself, how can he see, hear, and speak for others who are blind, deaf, and dumb?

Take for example, the speech made by the NAACP Chief Counsel, Thurgood Marshall to Princeton University Students on October 21, 1959, which was published in the November 5, 1959 issue of the Jet Magazine, the U.S. News and World Report, and other news items. One would think that Mr. Marshall would be in sympathy with the freedom, justice, and equality for the so- called Negroes for equal education, equal justice (the same equal rights), good homes and good friendship in all walks of life, as a seeker of general advancement for the so-called

253

Negroes. But, the weight of his speech, slanderous remarks, and false charges made indirectly against me and my followers proved otherwise.

Mr. Marshall calls us "a bunch of thugs organized from prisons and jails, and financed by some Arab group, and that our Movement presents a real threat to law enforcement agencies." These charges are completely false, and I am ready to prove that they are false, and will prove that Mr. Thurgood Marshall is the most unfit, and worse enemy of all to the real cause of freedom, justice, and equality for the so-called Negro thugs. I have no knowledge of what other groups of Moslems are doing in America, and I am only speaking for my group (followers). We are not, and have not received not so much as a penny from the Arab Nation, nor any other than ourselves.

We have not been opposed to the NAACP's cause for the National Advancement of the so-called Negroes. Only we feel that the NAACP should have as its head a Black Man, and not a white man, and that the organization should not at this late date seek integration of the Negroes and whites, but rather, separation from this people which is the only solution to the 400 year old problem. [Securing a] closer relationship between the so-called Negroes and their master only will prove the total destruction of the Negroes by the wise old slave masters' children. Seeking love and equal recognition among this people is the most foolish and ignorant thing that a Negro leader could do in this late date, and it would eventually prove the total destruction of us, as a people.

Thurgood Marshall cares not for the recognition of his kind (the Black Nation). He is in love with the white race. He hates the preaching of the uplifting of the Black Nation, unless it is approved by the white race, and is totally against his brother Negro ever thinking or being the supreme. Mr. Marshall, we, the Black Nation of Islam, will be the supreme rulers in the Hereafter. That, I can prove with truth. You do not have to be numbered with us. The Negroes being without justice under the slave masters for 400 years should be seeking love and friendship among their own kind, and they would be recognized as a people who have some sense. I am by no means interested in what the white race is doing, for their people. It is my people that I am interested in. I think the white man is wise in trying to preserve his civilization, and all Nations should do the same. I want the same for my people. I want some earth for them, and by the help of Allah, I will get it as Moses got some for Israel.

THE BIBLE AND THE HOLY QUR'AN

The Bible is my poor people's graveyard. The Holy Qur'an would resurrect them if they would study its teachings, with someone to teach its meanings. It is fatal to read either Book without understanding. It would have been better that you played with rattlesnakes and been bitten than to have read the Bible without understanding. It is a "fixed Book" in which the truth has been added in and taken out of by the devils, the slave masters of my people. It is revised every few years and some of the filthy readings in it cannot be read in public by any decent person without feeling ashamed.

The Book was prepared for you and me (The Black Man) not for the white man. Is there any truth in the Bible? Yes, there is plenty of it if you understand it, and where to place it. The Bible is dedicated to King James and not to God! The Book is made up of many Books of histories, prophecies and poems. The first five Books are called the Books of Moses. In the First Book, called Genesis, there is an attempt made to tell us how God made the Universe, but not any of the knowledge of the Maker was given to us, which should have been the first of the Bible's teachings.

If the Bible is the world of God, He should be the One speaking and addressing Himself to us, and not His Prophet. Moses does not tell us where he received his knowledge of the history of the Creation here in Genesis. The histories of Adam and his sons, Noah and his sons, Abraham and his sons. Genesis does not begin with:

257

"Thus saith the Lord." nor does it read: "Moses said unto the people that God taught him these histories mentioned in the First Book called Genesis. I wonder how did you get your knowledge that it is the word of God? [Was it actually] the voice of God. Why did not the Angel speak, or was the Angel God?

According to the 2nd Verse, the bush was real and the fire unreal; and that the voice was real, but the Angel was unreal. If this was Moses' first experience with God, how about the Angel? Could Moses have known the Angel to be of the Lord, since he had not seen or met either one before? Allah (God) addressed Himself to Muhammad in the Holy Qur'an (2:1). The Holy Qur'an is the word of Allah (God), and not the Prophet. The voice of the Book is Allah (God) talking and not the Prophet Muhammad.

BROTHERHOOD OF BLACK MANKIND

5-4-59

WE MUST unite as brothers to all black mankind if we are to survive as human beings on this earth. We, the darker people of America, are the most disunited of all of our kind due to the evil and fear of the slave masters of America. Most of my people desire unity with all the nations, but do not know how to unite. Why should you fear to unite with your own people when you are trying daily to unite with other than your own? It is the will of Allah (God) that we be united.

Islam is a unifying religion, a religion of brotherhood, and the only true religion of Allah (God). Islam will be the only religion that will survive the great universal war which is now ready to burst upon the world of mankind. It is needless for you to put your trust in Christianity.

God has said to me that He will destroy if from the face of the earth. It stands true that Christianity has not helped us to unite, nor has it defended us against our enemies. It seems to have always been in the favor of our enemies. It even does not help the black preachers when the enemy attacks them, though they may be praying in the name of Jesus. You will come to know to the kind of Christianity that you are believing in is none other than the white race's tool used to trap the black people into a state of helplessness to the white race. God nor Jesus seems to care for it.

259

WHEN WHITE Christians go after the so-called Negroes, the Alabama black preachers should never preach the white man's slavery Christianity any more. According to this paper, the April 18 edition, one Rev. Charles Billups was beaten with a chain by a mob of devils and left on the highway. The poor black people are gravely deceived in their faith and belief in Christianity. There is no such thing as hell or heaven after death. Death is the end of everything, righteous or wicked. When we die that is the last of anyone.

All Muslims believe in the resurrection - a mental resurrection. Some call it a spiritual resurrection. This resurrection is now going on among you from the preaching of this religion (Islam). We cannot hope for a better religion than Islam to unite us with Allah (God) and the brotherhood of the righteous. we must remember that we cannot unite in the brotherhood of the white race. It is pure nonsense to seek them for brotherhood. They are our enemies and take them for enemies, not friends. While living under their law and order, obey it and those in authority. All the righteous will do it. Unjust and evil people do not make the righteous be unjust and evil. A Muslim is the righteous. The very name means one who has submitted himself or herself to the will of Allah (God).

TRUTH AND righteousness will be victors over this world; for the world of sin and doings of evil are now drawing to an end. It is the purpose of Allah's (God's) coming to you and me to unite us onto our own kind, the nation of righteousness.

THE COMING OF THE SON OF MAN

"AND THEN SHALL APPEAR the sign of the Son of Man in heaven: and then shall all the tribes of the earth mourn and they shall see the Son of Man coming in the clouds of heaven with power and great glory." Matt. 24:30. Here in the plainest words is the son of man on the Judgment Day. We are not told by either Moses nor Jesus to look for God on Judgment Day to be anything other than man. Spirits and spooks cannot be the judge of man's affairs.

Man is material of the earth. How long will you be ignorant of the reality of God? You are poisoned by the devils touch. Why are you looking for a god that is not flesh and blood as you are? Spirits can only be found in another being like yourself. What pleasure would you have in an invisible world? And on the other hand, what pleasure would spirits have in this material universe of ours? Your very nature is against your being anything other than a human being.

THESE ARE THE DAYS of the resurrection of the mentally dead so- called Negroes. The Son of Man is here. His coming has been fulfilled. He seeks that which was lost (the so-called Negroes). Many are now receiving His name and that name alone will save you. The wicked nations of the earth are sorry and angry to see the Son of Man set up a government of justice and peace over this, their wicked world. They see His signs of great power to execute judgment on the world of the wicked in the heavens (sky) and they mourn.

WE MUST HAVE A NEW RULER and a new government, where the people can enjoy freedom, justice, and equality. Let the so-called Negroes rejoice, for Allah has prepared for them what the eye has not seen, the ear has not heard, and the heart has not been able to conceive. The enemy knows this to be true and is now doing everything to prevent the so-called Negroes from seeing the hereafter.

THE COMING OF GOD IS HE A MAN OR A SPIRIT?

ACCORDING TO the Dictionary of the Bible: Teman, a Son of Esau by Adah, (Gen. 36:11,15,42) and in the (I Chronicles 1:36), now if Habakkuk saw God come or coming from the Sons of Esau (Eliphaz), then God must be a man and not a spook.

If Habakkuk's (3:3) prophecy refers to some country, town, or city, if there be any truth at all in this prophecy, then we can say that this prophet saw God as a material being belonging to the Human Family of the earth - and not to a spirit (ghost). In the same Chapter and verse, Habakkuk saw the Holy One from Mount Paran. This is also earthly, somewhere in Arabia. Here the Bible makes a difference between God and another person who is called the Holy One. Which one should we take for our God? For One is called God while another One is called Holy One. The Holy One: His glory covered the heavens and the earth, and the earth was full of His praise.

It has been a long time since the earth was full of praise for a Holy One. Even to this hour, the people do not care for Holy People, and will persecute and kill the Holy One, if God does not intervene. In the fourth verse of the above Chapter, it says: "He had horns coming out of his hand; and there was the hiding of His power." Such science to represent the God's power could confuse the ignorant masses of the World. Two Gods are here represented at the same time. (It is good that God makes Himself manifest to the ignorant World today).

263

"The Burning coals went forth at His feet, has a meaning: but what is the meaning? The ignorant do not know. "The burning coals" could refer to the anger and war among the people where His foot tread within the borders of the wicked (Here God has feet - Spirits do not have feet and hands). This Holy One does not refer to anyone of the past - not. Moses, Jesus, nor Mohammed of the past 1300. "For this Holy One measured the earth, drove asunder the Nations; scattered the mountains, the perpetual hills did bow, Cushan in affiliation; the curtains of the land of Midian did tremble." (What is meant by the curtains trembling?) (Who is Cushan?) "The mountains saw thee, they trembled." (Who does this mean?) "The sun and moon stood still in their habitation." (What does this mean)? The answers to the above questions are easy when we understand who this God called the Holy One coming from Mount Paran is.

The 13th verse should clear the way for such undertaking; for it tells us why all these great things took place on the coming of the Holy One from Mount Paran. It says; "Thou wentest forth for the salvation of thy people (Not for all people) for the salvation with thine anointed (His Apostle). He wounded the Head out of the house of the wicked, by discovering the foundation unto the neck (by excusing the truth and ruling power of the wicked race of devils).

"Cushan" represents the Black Nation who is afflicted by the white race. "The curtains of the land of Midian" could mean the falsehood spread over the people by the white race, and their leaders trembling from being

264

exposed by the truth. "The mountains" represent the great, rich, and powerful political men of the wicked; they also are trembling and being divided and scattered over the earth. "The Holy One" is God in person, and not a spirit!

THE COMING OF GOD

9- 29-60

For the past two thousand years, the world has been looking and expecting to see THAT GOD OF TRUTH AND JUSTICE appear; that God would destroy the Old World of the wicked, and set up a World of Righteousness. HE HAS COME. The world did not know the exact day of His arrival, but the Prophets have given us many signs that would appear as a warning to us that He is near.

Jesus gave us many good signs to watch for, and when we see these signs coming to pass, then we know when His arrival is near -

"When you see all these things, know that it is near." (Matthew 24:33)

In Matthew 24:27, a hint is given to the direction in which He would come: from the EAST)

"As the lighting cometh out of the east, and shineth even unto the west, so shall also the coming of the Son of Man be."

Jesus did not leave us to look for a spirit - unnatural, not human - but to look to face a Man Who is the son of a Man, and that this great Man is not to be expected to come from another planet. According to the signs of His coming, He is of the earth.

The 24th Chapter of Matthew make sense, that would appear to warn us of His Coming and Presence, that is, if we are able to understand them, and not be so foolish as the Parable of the Five Foolish Virgins who were mentioned in the next chapter (25:2). In the 28th verse of the 24th chapter of Matthew is a very beautiful parable, but not understood by many readers and scholars. There Jesus, after giving to us the direction of the coming of God, and comparing His coming with the lighting, the next verse (28th) he gives us the parable where the carcass is, there the eagles are gathered together. Let us see just what are we to learn from this parable: the carcass and the eagles must refer to people, one is dead and the other is alive - eagles are birds of prey. Jesus also mentioned that God would send His Angeles with a Great Sound of a trumpet, to gather His Elect from the four winds (or directions).

...These signs, most of them, are now fulfilled. The dead is the American so-called Negroes that must be brought to life (to the knowledge of Truth), before there can be a Just Judgment of the murderers (those who robbed and killed). The eagles come to remove the carcass that is offensive to the smell of the people. Since the mental death of the so-called Negroes, they have become hated and despised by their murderers.

We witnessed something, last week that never has happened before in America, the meeting of nearly all the important rulers of the Nation. This will probably never happen again in the life of this world - THE DEAD MUST RISE.

THE COMING OF GOD AND THE GATHERING OF HIS PEOPLE

2-9-61

The prophets have warned us of a time that would come when God would judge the wicked and punish, or rather destroy and wicked and give the earth over to the rule of a righteous people. So many of us have misunderstood just what we should expect. What will God look like? If we expect the destruction of the devil, what will the devil look like? How will I distinguish him? If the devil should be destroyed, in order not to follow him to his destruction, what does that devil look like so that I can recognize him so that he won't be able to deceive me?

What world's end will come and what is that world that is going to end? Does that include everything that makes up the solar system? - The planet earth? If so, what shall we expect? What kind of solar system will we have after the destruction of the present one? Think over these things. We must get down to the facts so that we can recognize them when they are presented to us. But you never questioned the first teacher. Shouldn't we be fair about this thing? Let us go after the thing right!

If we want to give each teacher justice, we should start with the first one. When Moses began to preach to the Hebrews, to make themselves ready to go out to another country that God had promised their fathers on the condition that they believe and obey, here was the reply: "Who made you a judge over us?" Let us question this as they questioned Moses. Why didn't you question Pharaoh, "who made you a judge over us?" Question me with facts. If they did not question Pharaoh, why should they Question Moses since Pharaoh didn't say that a God sent him? They should have made Pharaoh answer, "Who made you god over us?" They were born under Pharaoh's teaching, therefore, from their early existence, they believed in Pharaoh, right or wrong. They worshipped Pharaoh's God and when Moses made himself present, they wanted Moses to give them a good knowledge of who had sent him and made him such a man.

If today, a Moses was in your midst and he said, "The God of your fathers, has sent me" and "the Government of America has deceived you to the knowledge of God and has you indirectly worshipping themselves," wouldn't your reply be the same as the one given to Moses? That is right. You are asking me that. A man questioned me the other day when he said, "you mean to say that you talked to God face to face?

Where was Moses and what time was that? What did the God have in mind? If no one has gone to heaven or seen the face of God, then all of these prophets are liars. You must think these things over. You have a lot to learn if you understand it, otherwise, you are still in the dark to the Truth. We are here to know whether God has visited America or whether He is yet to come. The hour can come at any day, because it is prophesied that it will come in an hour that you think not. Naturally, I had expected it to come at a certain day but the book said you won't know the day nor the hour. If all of these signs of His coming are exhausted and I don't see any end of the world, that is to show me that it could take place at any time. If there is such a thing as a Judgment of the World, as you and I believe, if there are signs that will be produced before that particular destruction of the old world, how many signs do you know of today that have not been fulfilled that must now be fulfilled? If you know one sign that the Bible refers to that has not as yet taken place, point it out to me.

COMMON SENSE APPEAL TO UNITE

4-25-59

WHY SHOULD not we unite into one brotherhood? Are not white people united when it comes to black man-kind? Are not all other than the white race united; e.g., the brown and yellow races? Are not they our brothers, belonging to the same nation (black mankind)? Are not we all brothers under the same burden of white slave-masters' injustices? If you agree with me that we all are slaves and subject to the same injustice, why should we not unite as one nation of brotherhood?

In the eyes of our white slave masters, we are all Negroes - a people that no decent civilized nation will accept as equals. In the eyes of our black, brown, yellow and red brothers, we are the most ignorant blind, deaf and dumb people on earth. In the eyes of Allah (God), we are mentally dead and yet His choice.

Allah (God) is giving to us (the so-called Negroes) life to make us His special people - a people to be the head and not the tail...as it is written. When will you be convinced that our unity is all that is necessary to become a strong and most powerful and mightiest nation that ever lived? We know our slave masters have and are still doing all that they can to keep us divided, one against the other - then why not you and I unite?

IF A SMALL, well-twisted cord is hard to break, then how much harder is it to break 100 such twisted cords well twisted into ONE? We are well educated in the knowledge of what the slave masters dislike of us. If they are afraid of our unity as ONE nation of brotherhood, then why should not we unite? You know that they have deceived us in regards to the TRUTH of God, His religion, and our own selves. We have served them more obediently than we have the God of heaven and earth. In all our humblest submission to them, we received the most outright cruel injustice ever meted out to any human beings.

They make prostitutes of our American black women. They are free for them at all times, and you look on helplessly - not being able to put a stop to it because of our disunity. Why not unite? You see and hear of my work and the teaching of God's truth and power in your midst - how it is uniting those that believe and are following me, yet you are afraid to join in unity with us, regardless of the plain truth that you hear. Allah (God) has revealed and taught this truth to me to teach and warn you.

I am sure that you have learned that the Christianity taught to you by the slave master has not and cannot unite nor defend us against the injustice and brutality of the white race. You see and hear your leaders and preachers pleading to the white Christians to accept them as brethren and, at the same time, the white Christians and their government in many places do not even like to look on your black faces. In Islam, you will have love, power and help of Allah... the entire nation of black mankind with you. This earth is ours and the GOD of it. Why not unite with us? You see and hear the talk of white mankind...is there anything good in it for you and me? NO!

ONE OF THEIR preachers by the name of Herbert Armstrong (of Pasadena, Calif.) is on the radio at 1:30 P.M. weekdays, preaching both the destruction of white government and the salvation of his people after their destruction for their evil doings. He takes the Bible's prophecies of the salvation of us, the lost-found members of the Tribe of Shabazz (so-called Negroes) to be a promised blessing for his people whom God will destroy and give the kingdom to us, the slaves (so-called Negroes.) No one but Allah (God) and myself are preaching love and salvation for the so-called Negroes. No one can and is proving it from the same scriptures that Mr. Armstrong claims to be the salvation for his people (the enemies of Allah (God) and all black mankind), but Allah (God) and myself.

Why not unite with us? Regardless of the white man's opposition, we will be the winners, for God, Himself, is with me and those who follow me. I am your brother and a sufferer along with you. Let us unite.

THE DEVILS INCITE THE HYPOCRITES AND DISBELIEVERS

5-23-59

A HYPOCRITE is one who speaks that from his or her mouth what the heart does not agree with, or what is not in the heart. As the Holy Qur'an (2:8,10) says: "There are some people who say: We believe in Allah and the Last Day; and they are not at all believers. They desire to deceive Allah and those who believe, and they deceive only themselves, and realize it not." A hypocrite is far more dangerous than your open enemy (the devil), for the hypocrite seeks to learn that about you which will hurt you with your enemies. They always hope evil for you. They claim brotherhood and friendship with you only to hurt you. The true Muslims, my followers, are at the present time honeycombed with such rotten characters, of whom the believers must be aware of.

They are now joined with the devils receiving bribes to destroy me and my followers and the truth which Allah has revealed. Do you think that you will be successful in putting over this small- time evil murderous plan on Allah and His Apostle, and the true Muslims? Such plans, and the planner were not successful in the days of Prophet Muhammad (may the peace and blessings of Allah be upon him), and they will not be successful in putting it over my Allah today. He it is whom I put my trust in, though I am willing to give my life for the freedom of my people from this merciless devil, their real open enemy.

MY LIFE, and the lives of my true followers are in the hands of Allah. It belongs to Him, for He has brought it with a price of suffering. On Him we rely. We will not raise our hands to do you harm; we are brothers and sisters by nature (same flesh and blood), so think before raising yours against us for the joy of the devils who are your enemies as well as ours. I quote another few verses of the same chapter when it is said to them: "Believe as the others (Muslims) they say: Shall we believe as the fools believe? Nay, of a surety they are the fools, but they do not know. But when they are alone with the evil ones (the devils) they say: We are really with you, we are only mocking: Allah shall pay them back their mockery. He leaves them alone in their mockery, blindly wandering on."

FOR THEIR hypocrisy, the light of truth and guidance from Allah is taken from them and they think that they are being guided right when they are actually stumbling in the darkness of evil and ignorance. In another place the disbelievers are warned of their evil and proud attitude toward the Messenger of Allah in these words: "He said, (the proud disbelievers in the mission of the Messenger of Allah) - Tell me, is this he whom Thou has honored above me? If Thou wilt but respite me to the Day of Judgment, I will surely bring his descendants under my sway all but a few, and beguile whomsoever of them you can with your seductive voice, make assaults on them with cavalry and infantry; and mutually share with them wealth and children, and make promises to them. But Satan promises them nothing but to deceive" (Holy Qur'an 17:62,64).

The devils are playing this tricknowledge on my people here today. You shall soon comes to know that Allah is your best friend, and that the devils are your open enemies. They are sharing with you wealth and children only to make you sharers in hell fire with them and their doom.

THE DEVIL IN DISGUISE

4-26-62

Disguise: That which is under disguise; a false or misleading appearance, used to hide who one really is, make a person look like someone else, deception, concealment, unfriendly opponent. The first work of God on His coming was to make manifest to the world His and the Righteous One's enemies. The chief enemy of the Black, Brown, Yellow and Red man is the devil, the man of sin; created or rather grafted from the black man into a distinct, independent being. He was made an unlike, thus, enabling him to attract the alike. So said Allah (God) to me - unlike attracts and alike repels.

The devils, being endowed with the knowledge of both good and evil could, therefore, with such knowledge and power of attraction, appear as he is or like a righteous person, as a friend or a sincere adviser. (Holy Qur'an 7:21)

Misled Original People

The devils (white race have misled the whole of the original people of the earth. (The devils are not original, they are a new race made six thousand years ago as Allah has taught me). Read the Bible; Rev. 12:9: "And the great dragon was cast out, that old serpent called the Devil and Satan which deceiveth the whole world."

And Allah said to me that we allowed them to be created to try them at ruling the righteous until the righteous produced one Supreme in wisdom and power who by His

281

word or will is capable of bringing about that which He pleases.

(This is He who teaches me all that I know). He is the great Champion of our faith - Islam - Whose rule will be truth, justice and righteousness.

Evil Injustice In Rule

The devils have ruled the nations under evil and injustice; this Mighty One's rule will be righteous. We must come into the knowledge of our next ruler! But how can we appreciate or recognize a Ruler or God of righteousness until we first have a thorough knowledge of the present ruler of evil and unrighteousness?

You must know the truth of this pale face, blue-eyed race of devils who have deceived you and our fathers. The entire history of them is written in evil and bloodshed. They have shed your blood like water, but yet you love them; your love for them will surely get you hell! The Bible and Holy Qur'an warns you and me against taking them for friends.

Fear Governs Acts

Of course, your fear of them makes you act say and do things you would not if the fear had not been present. Accept Allah (The True God) and His religion, Islam and He will remove the fear of them from you. They were created and made to be our enemies and also they were made to be destroyed by fire. You cannot reform them (devils) unless you graft them back into who they came from (the Black Nation). (As Allah taught me to Whom be praised forever).

They lead or invite you to nothing but evil and filth - sport and play. And they make you to believe that they are God's chosen people to lead and guide you on the right way. The head of the church (Pope) the Christians call the "father" and vice regent of God.

Here in the church of the devil's religion is where he disguises himself as a Divine Guide. The Catholics are the chiefs of the Christian religion and are out to deceive the so-called Negroes in America to keep them from going over to the true religion of ISLAM.

The devils in Christianity are stripping their followers of their clothes. The women wearing their dresses above the knees - one of the most indecent things a woman could do, walk or ride in the public dressed half-nude. (to be continued) A RACE OF EVILNESS AND INDECENCY.

DO SOMETHING FOR SELF

The white man (the devil) poured into our hearts a belief in a God that does not even exist, and prayers to a dead prophet (Jesus) who cannot help us against the slave masters' children, who are constantly robbing, beating, killing, raping, and disgracing us and our women. All of this we suffer daily. Should not we have a home of our own on this earth that our fathers created for you and me to live happily on?

We are a race of bums, walking and hitchhiking from Los Angeles to Chicago, seeking a job, love, and friendship of the murderers and disgracers of our Nation. Put your brains to thinking for Self, your feet to walking in the direction of Self, your hands in working for Self and your children, and fight like hell with those who fight against you and the world of mankind will respect us as equals. Stop begging for that which others have and help yourself to some of this good earth where in you can produce something for Self like other Nations.

Actually, there are no jobs that the white man has for you that he and his people and machines cannot do. This is why you and I should start trying to create jobs for ourselves. If our leaders do not want to go along with us, then leave them and see which one will suffer the most - you or the leaders. We have been a good servant for the white slave master for 400 years. We have among us men and women who can do almost anything that we want; but at present, they are doing it for our slave masters. WHY should we not utilize our brains for Ourselves? This can be done overnight if we stop putting frightened leaders into office to lead a race of people who were born with the fear of the slave masters.

We have not been given anything but hell in return for 400 years of hard labor, sweat and blood, without Justice. We are not wanted in their society and are hunted like rabbits. They seek to kill our leaders if they attempt to teach and lead us into our Own. They have poisoned the so-called Negro preachers' minds, under Christianity, to help them against any Negro leader they do not like. The poor Black Preachers that fear the white slave master have become the most worthless and cheapest class of leaders for our people on earth. All so- called Negroes should refuse to follow and support such false and cowardly leadership which obey and follows the enemies of God and His prophets. They (the preachers) are satisfied if they can get just a few followers and a church to keep them from working.

We need a home that we can call our own. We have no more time to waste on our problem. We know our problem, and we know the solution to our problem. Now, let us solve it. We have wasted too much time arguing with each other.

On the 9th of this month the Chicago Tribune and a few other newspapers and magazines carried a false charge against me, that I was arrested in Detroit in 1934, for contributing to the delinquency of a minor. This is false, my record in Detroit can be found, and it proves that I was not arrested on no such charge. I shall do my best to make the guilty pay for such a false charge.

EVERYTHING HAS FAILED

Islam comes after everything fails. Its significance is the making of Peace. The Muslims' greeting to each other is. "Peace." What better religion could we desire after being divided, and made enemies of each other? Don't tell us that you have "Unity and Peace" in the White Race's Religion called Christianity. The White Race does not like Islam, because it is truth, entire submission to the will of Allah, and this is against their nature. They can't live the life of Freedom, Justice and Equality - not even among themselves.

Many of you sing that old song, "Give Me That Old Time Religion;" Islam is that "Old Time Religion." It is as old as God Himself; and God is the Author of Islam. Islam was not invented as in the case of Christianity and other religions. Islam came with Allah (God) and the Universe. The Holy Qur'an says: "This day I have perfected for you, your religion and completed my favor on you; and have chosen for you, Islam as a religion." (5:3)

Here, Islam claims to be a perfect religion; and its Author, the Perfect One (God). What can be imperfect about Islam when it means, "Entire Submission to the Will of God?" What can be wrong or imperfect about this religion Islam, which was the religion of Noah, Abraham, Moses, Jesus, and all the Prophets of God; to Muhammad, the last of the Prophets? Islam proves that its Author is God, inasmuch as Allah (God) is on the side of every True Muslim. This is easy to see today. Every one of you, who is accepting Islam in America, can bear me witness that-

287

for the first time in your life, you feel the Power and Help of Almighty Allah (God) on your side. Your whole life becomes a change, for the better. Your fear is removed; your grief is gone; your desire to continue to do evil things is leaving you for good. Love for your brother (your people) for the first time is now becoming a reality. It is the Aim of Allah (God), in giving to you and I, Islam to unite us and to remove fear, sorrow, and sickness; and bring us into that heavenly life, peace of mind, and contentment.

Do you mean to say that you don't need such religion? Or, do you say that the White Race made Christianity is giving you peace and contentment - whose world recognized Father is the Pope of Rome, not Jesus, nor Allah (God) is the Father of the Christian Religion, as practiced by the White Race, and those who believe in it.

Islam is universally recognized as being the True Religion of the Divine Supreme Being. The proof that it is the True Religion of God, and that it will get power and friendship for you, with Allah (God) and the Righteous: Why is the Federal Government and its thousands of agents doing everything in their power, except outright shooting you to keep you from believing in Allah and His True Religion, Islam? They are trying, and tricking you in many ways; under the false disguise as now being a friend of yours and wanting to forget the past. But, your agreement with them will not stand when you see the showdown.

Islam is the natural religion of the Black Nation. The nature in which they are made, and we are called to return to Islam in these words from the Holy Qur'an: "Set your face upright for religion in the right state. The nature made by Allah in which he has made men: There is no altering of Allah's Creation: That is the right religion, but most people do not know."

The Devils know the true Religion of Allah, and have always known it. But, they will not teach it, because it is against their nature to believe and teach the True Religion of God, which would upset his chances of ruling the people under Falsehood. WHY NOT ISLAM?

FOR WHERE SO EVER THE CARCASS IS…There The Eagles Will Be Gathered Together

(Matt. 24:28)

The poor so-called Negroes are the mentally dead carcass of the Nation. The robbers of them, even their own kind, come from every direction to eat (rob) them. Their enemies, (the white slave-masters) bleached them as a dried bone for 400 years. Yet, their own kind seek to grind the bones which are left. They are blind, deaf, and dumb, and every civilized person who finds them soon discovers that they are a prey, and go after them like eagle birds to finish them off. It is a shame and a sin on the robbers of my people. I find robbers of them from black, brown, yellow, red, and white races. They come from all walks of life, from the gamblers and dope peddlers to the religious leaders of all faiths and their members; even to the weak Muslims of America and Asia, not to mention the Christian leaders who have eaten the flesh and left the bones for the foreigners.

THE PRESENCE of Allah (God), Who wants to put flesh again on their bleached bones and life in the body through His word of Truth preached by me and those who follow me, has caused many eagles to come flying. Seeking to get a hold on what is left of them. They would like to charge me with grinding the bones of my people, but they cannot. Even after honey-combing my followers with dirty paid stool pigeons, many of them we now recognize and only await the hour to rid ourselves of them. The

291

eagles of prey envy the Shepherd of God among them because the Shepherd will light for the safety of his sheep, and he has Allah (God) on his side.

He is appointed by Allah (God) and Allah has given him the sheep to feed with the bread of truth, and will not give them to anyone else. Some of the eagles (robbers) even seek the help of religious scholars here and there to say that they are the ones who shall or should lead this people to us and God. But this is not so. You cannot send or authorize anyone to take over this job of giving life to my people, regardless to whom you are, or where you come from. Allah is the Sender of His Messengers.

Many a of the eagles (robbers) have nothing to offer but arguments against the Shepherd, telling the sheep that he (the Shepherd) is not the Messenger of Allah and that he is not an Apostle. They say, "He is not teaching Islam, he is teaching hate. He cannot speak or read the Arabic Language." They so foolishly do not know that the Holy Qur'an and the Bible have all their evil sayings and doings recorded in them. "And those who disbelieve say: You are not the Messenger. Say: Allah is sufficient as a witness between You and me and whoever has knowledge of the Book." (Holy Qur'an 13:43).
MUHAMMAD could not read or write, but was granted the revelations which made up the Book called the Holy Qur'an.

He was given the knowledge of it by Allah, Who gave it to him. Take a look at Allah's Servant in the Bible. It says: "Who was more blind, deaf and dumb as my Messenger that I sent? Who is blind as he that is perfect, and blind as the Lord's servant? Seeing many things, but thou observest not; opening the ears, but he heareth not. The Lord is well pleased for his righteousness sake; he will magnify the law, and make it honorable.

No prophet of the past brought forth judgment unto Truth. Judgment, for truth's sake, comes at the end of this world. Jesus and Muhammad both failed to convert the Jews and Christians, but the last Messenger will not make an attempt to convert them. His preaching is to close the door against the enemies of Allah (God) and His prophets. Judgment follows his message, for only God is left to act after him. He is the end of prophets because there is nothing left for a prophet to do after God has manifested Himself to the world along with the last Messenger.

DIVINE CHASTISEMENT FOR ANY MAN WHO WORSHIPS THE BEAST, THE HUMAN SERPENT' (REV. 14:9-10) PART I

4-4-59

WE ARE warned in the plainest words against the love and worship of the symbolic beast (the Caucasian race) and not even to receive his mark in our heads or hands. To do so will bring upon us the wrath of God without mercy, according to the 10th verse of the above Chapter 1. There are no darker people on earth who worship this race of people as the American so-called Negroes do. Due to the lack of knowledge of this race and their fear of them, they ignorantly love and admire them, their open enemies, who are the enemies of God and His prophets. While you faithfully pray to God that you may not be a follower of the devils, you even now love and worship them. Come out of them and save yourselves from the wrath of Almighty Allah (God).

INTEGRATION will not solve our problem in this late day and time of the judgment of the white race. Your problem can only be solved by your separation from the white race. This will be brought about by the work of God. Your names are of the beasts' (white race's) names. Your religion and God, language and everything, are of the white race. To escape their doom and the wrath of God, you are warned to come out of them.

"The mark in the forehead or in his hand," refers to your face or hands. It is the face which includes the eyes, mouth, nose and forefront. It is in the face where one looks for a sign of what the person really is. If the sign is not in his or her general expression, it is in the eyes or what comes out of the mouth in words. The hand is marked by the work they do in favor of the beast, which comes from the head of our bodies. Therefore, whatever is in us, the mark or sign is in our forehead or the work of our hands. Those who love the devils (the beast) are known by their works, looks, talk, actions, and guilt.

THE WORKS of the beast are evil and filth, sport and play, games of chance, love songs and temptation, drunkenness, murder and robbery. Under the above, they captivate you (the so-called Negroes). You need plenty of teaching along these lines of how to keep yourselves from being marked by the devils as unbelievers in your God. Remember, you were reared by the devils, and your flesh and blood are already marked by them. Today, they (the devils) are like roaring lions among you after your girls and women, and many of his women and girls are after you for the sole purpose of marking you as unfit to see the hereafter. God allows the devils to tempt you that you may receive the infidel mark of unbelief in God, but He will surely punish you who receive such mark.

The poor Negro preachers who understand not the scripture, nor God and the devil, preach that you should love everybody, which includes the devils, while God forbids us to love His or our own enemies, not to mention the arch-enemy devil. I warn you to receive not the mark of the beast in your head or hand.

DIVINE CHASTISEMENT FOR ANY MAN WHO WORSHIPS THE BEAST, THE HUMAN SERPENT' (REV. 14:9-10) PART II

4-11-59

FOR BEHOLD, I will send serpents, cockatrices among you, which will not be charmed and they shall bite you, saith the Lord." (Jer. 8:17)

The above said scripture is a warning to you and me against the love and worship of the devils, the human serpents. Here God promises the willful worshipers of his enemies that He will even send those whom you take for friends above Him against you, and make them bite you (do you evil). For believing and obeying the serpent (the devil) after knowledge of God and His religion, Adam and his wife were punished by the serpent (the devil): "And I will put enmity between thy seed and her seed. It shall bruise thy head and thou shalt bruise his heel" (Gen. 5:15). God is not to be mocked. He warns us against loving and taking the devils for friends. Allah, alone, is our friend and most certainly is able to make us know it.

The black man has ever suffered from his mistake in taking the white race for his friends. From that incident in Eden, six thousand years ago to this day, there is enmity and hatred between the two people (black and white). This cannot be removed except by the removal of one or the other race. The two could never come to and live up to a just agreement to do justice between each other. It is the impossible, unless their nature is changed. Adam and his wife accepted the advice of the devil against their

297

Lord, and the serpent (the devil) has misled and put to death the prophets and the righteous servants of God ever since the fall of Adam.

"THE SERPENT BITE" - To cause trouble, disappointment, imprisonment, the loss of a good friend, the loss of paradise (the hereafter), to cause sickness and death. They did bite the disobedient followers of Moses (Numbers 21:6). Regardless of your good intentions for the serpent, he will bite you just the same. Who is any more submissive and lovable to the white man than the Originals (so-called Negroes)? Yet they receive the worst treatment from the whites than all the others of his kind. A couple of weeks ago I was told a few devils in Texas lynched a black man right on the streets for just disputing the devil's word. I know of plenty of places in the South where you will be killed if you dispute a devil's word or even ask for justice. I was born in such a place, and his Northern brothers are not Angels to you and me; so do not feel safe anywhere unless you are a believer in Allah.

AS IT IS WRITTEN of us: "They lived their lifelong under the very shadow of death." The Originals (so-called Negroes) are now offered the sure friendship of Allah (God) but they prefer the friendship of the devils (the serpent) rather than God. They are being beaten and murdered daily by them and denied justice everywhere. There just is no justice for us under this kind of people. Allah (God) desired that we come to the knowledge of Him and His salvation which he holds for us; therefore, the Holy Quire- an teaches us that he will send the devils against the disbelievers. Since it is the devils whom you believe in, then by the devils you should learn from their actions and treatment that they are the devils.

ALLAH IS WELL able to prove His word true. The serpent cannot bite true Muslims - they are forbidden to him. The cockatrice mentioned in the chapter is just another name of the devils, which means: a monster, reptile, evil eye, a deceiver. So fly to Allah and keep away from the bite of the serpent.

ISLAM THE TRUE RELIGION

"Set yourself upright to the right religion before there comes from Allah the Day which cannot be averted; on that day, they shall become separated." (Holy Qur'an 30:43).

We are now living in the above mentioned time by the Holy Qur'an. When we as a people should begin setting our faces upright to the religion in the right state and stop believing in the slave master's slavery religious teachings, which are not in the right state, then we will be successful and the world will respect us.

Which one of these emblems represents a good religion, the cross or the Star and Crescent? To attract one to do good you must have something good. Our religion (Islam) has the best sign (the Crescent). There is no doubt about it. We have taken the best of everything for our own (the Sun, Moon, and Stars), ever since it was created by our father, we know the best. What can be more essential to our well-being than the Sun, Moon and Stars? The spiritual meaning of our emblem (the Crescent) is Freedom, Justice and Equality. Not that we "say" and do otherwise; a Muslim tries to carry into practice what he preaches. Not so with the Christians. They "say" and do not. But after all, their religious emblem (the cross) and its meaning compare with the nature of the so-call Christians. By nature they are murderers; by nature they love making slaves of others; by nature they are haters of the black Nation who loves Freedom, Justice, and Equality. It looks strange to see people accepting the

301

cross as a sign of a good religion. The Ten commandments which Moses gave to them (the white race) have never been practiced by them, nor those whom they teach. They (the white race) were condemned by Jesus as not obeying. Why should we be looking and begging them for that which is good (Freedom, and Justice, and Equality). The right religion (which by nature they cannot give us) - Islam - is that right religion.

According to the Holy Qur'an 31:30, one of the greatest teachings of brotherhood is laid down to us by Prophet Muhammad (may the peace and blessings of Allah be upon him) in these words: "A Muslim is not a Muslim until he loves for his brother what he loves for himself." The old Christians' religion has been the white man's whip to lash the Black Man, ever since it was organized. My people here in America are fast awaking to the slavery teachings of Christianity to the dislike of their enemies.

A few years ago the so-called Negroes could easily be frightened and worked up into emotion by the preacher, yelling and spitting out foam all over the pulpit, preaching hell fire and death, and the dying of Jesus on the cross. He would paint an imaginary picture in the minds of the listeners, of meeting some dead relative up in the heavens (sky) after death, or mourning them into grief and sorrow. They are leaving out such nonsense as they advance more and more educationally. After they have heard the Truth of it all, that Allah has and is teaching me, they will not go near that slavery teaching. Their eyes must be opened to the Truth at any price.

ISLAM VERSUS CHRISTIANITY

The truth has arrived for we, the lost-found members of the darker people of earth here in America, to stop playing the "fool" among ourselves and the World of Mankind. To make up our minds whether we are going to hold on to that religion which the white race teaches us, or believe in the religion of the God of our people, which is taught by our people.

We make fools of ourselves to please our enemies (the white race). The average so-called Negro in America is not concerned about Love and Unity among their own kind, but are really interested in trying to get Love and Unity among other than their own kind.

Love of Enemy

Of all the histories of people upon our planet earth, past and present, we can find no people who have loved their enemies and hated themselves but the American so-called Negroes. They love and admire their enemies and all that goes for their enemies. They are ready in an instant to dispute, oppose and kill you if you are not likewise.

I am a lover of my own people and a hater like God, of all our enemies, and fear only God, Who has risen me up from among my people to bring them out of the darkness of falsehood into His light of truth so that they may enjoy heaven while they live. There are but a very few so-called Negroes who have spent any time examining the truth of the Bible and the white man's Christianity. Therefore, they are without real truth of the Bible and Christianity. I know the consequence of trying to bring truth to our people, who are in love with those who have taken them and their fathers out of truth into falsehood. But, my life and my death are for this cause (to bring truth to the American so-called Negroes).

Examine the Truth

If we are to accept a religion that is said to be from God, we should diligently examine the truth and the author of that religion, its people, and the contents of its book or books, before we [believe] that it is the [true religion of] God and the right religion. Let the so-called Negro preachers take a second look at the Bible, which the white Christians want all Black people to believe that every word of it is from God.

There is no mention of a religion by the name of Christianity for God or the Prophets. Again, we must remember that God does not represent Himself to us in the opening nor the closing of the Bible. He is represented by someone other than Himself. There His creation is pointed out to us as a proof that there is a Supreme Being over all this Universe, and that it was made in six days. (Genesis 1:1-31) God does not address Himself to us throughout the first Chapter, nor His religion, nor even the name of the representative of god is mentioned there.

The reader is without authentic proof of just who the author of this book called Genesis is. You must remember that according to the preface of the Bible, under the authorized version of King James, it has been 346 years, and you have only been permitted to read the Bible for the past 90 years. The white man, our slave masters and

304

enemies, had the Bible over one hundred fifty years before we were allowed to read the book. Now, you seem to know more about the purity of the Bible than those who translated it into their own language. Not only do you try defending the Bible as being the word of God, but you equally try to defend the enemies and their wicked world.

ISLAM FOR THE SO-CALLED NEGRO

"Say: I seek refuge in the Lord of the dawn; 2. From the evil of that which He (Yakub has created; 3. And from the evil of the intense darkness when it comes; 4. And from the evil of those who cast (evil suggestions) in firm resolutions; 5. And from the evil of the envier when he envies." (Holy Qur'an 113:)

The dawn of a new day has arrived to Seek our place in that which is new, we must have a guide. Allah (God) has always provided guides for those who seek to walk in His path.

We should hasten (ourselves) to the light of truth, as we hasten to get (ourselves) into the light of the day (the Sun). The light of Allah (God) is even greater than the light of our day (the Sun). We must learn to be intelligent enough to distinguish between truth and falsehood, and to seek refuge in the God of truth.

If we shall know the truth (John 8:32), and the TRUTH shall make us free, can we truthfully say that we already have (long since) known that truth that Jesus was referring to is that we "Shall know"?

That TRUTH that Jesus referred to was yet to come, not in his days (John 16:8, 13). If that Truth had been revealed two thousand years ago there would not be any falsehood today in the world. However, Jesus, being a Prophet, foresaw the future, and the end of the devil's rule.

"Seek refuse from the evil of that which He (Yakub) has created." The father (Yakub) of this World created a World of evil, discord, and hate. If you do not agree with their evil doings, your goodness is then called hate or infidel, and peace-breaker.

This world of Christianity has gone mad, and they think that every cry is against them. They are like robbers who have robbed, and are afraid that they will be recognized by their victim. Thieves know that light makes them Manifest.

Since Christianity has falsely accused Jesus as being its founder, it is being plague with spiritual darkness and confusion. Under such darkness, the Prophet and his followers (the Muslims) are warned to seek refuge in the light of Allah (God), for under such spiritual darkness the wicked seek to persecute and kill the Prophet of Islam and his followers.

They are mad and cannot see, nor hear the Truth, so they call the Truth false, and the false they call Truth. The Truth Islam, has angered it (Christianity), the Revelator, saying,

> *"And the Nations (Christianity) were angry, Thy wrath is come, the time of the dead, that they should be judged, and that thou shouldest give reward unto thy servants the prophets, and to the saints, and them which destroy the earth." (Bible, Rev. 11:18).*

The white Christians and Jews are the guilty race, they have persecuted and killed the Prophets of Islam and their followers (the Muslims or black people in general). Now, should not they be destroyed or get what they put out?

Christianity is so afraid of the True religion (Islam), awakening the Mental dead so-called Negroes to the knowledge of Truth, that in nearly every Negro Church

308

you will see a white Christian sitting in on the meeting, to watch and see that the dead do not rise. They try to prevent it (the awakening of the so-called Negro), for they know the so-called Negroes think that it is an honor to have them present. If the so-called Negroes only understood their Bible (II Thessalonians 2:4-8), they are trying to make the so-called Negroes believe they too are the beloved of God, then why not believe in Allah?

(Seek refuge in Allah from the envier when he envies). The success of the Messenger and His followers of Islam is envied by the disbelievers and they are not leaving a stone unturned (trying to stop it with falsehood).

JUSTICE FOR THE AMERICAN SO-CALLED NEGROES

8-22-59

MONEY, good homes, friendship in all walks of life await us (on condition that we believe in Allah and stop practicing filth). Our leaders, teachers, scholars and scientists must give and practice his or her wisdom among our people to help elevate them. There are many well-trained professional people among us, such as construction engineers, building engineers, civil, electrical and mechanical engineers, school college and university professors, artists, draftsmen, biologists, chemists, and many others who are capable, if united and made to devote their time, of uplifting of their own people, could become independent over night.

The average Negro professors love giving their knowledge back to their teacher. It is really a sin that the poor so-called Negroes suffer because of the lack of knowledge of self. Their leaders, hungry for a place among the white race instead of their own race, have brought the Negroes to the present condition. Our very fine doctors and nurses in many fields, tradesman, salesmen, farmers, mechanics of all kind, just need only one dose of Islam to unite them to become the world wonder people.

THE CLERGY CLASS (Christian preachers) if they only could see the harm that they are doing to their people by teaching the white man's slavery religion called Christianity, and would accept Islam and preach it, would set their people and themselves in heaven at once. They see and know that the white man's Christianity will never get the so-called Negroes out of the power of their 400-year slave masters

This Negro clergy class is the white man's right hand over the so-called Negroes. It has proven to be true on Aug. 9, 1959, in Indianapolis. There, we had been promised in advance the use of the Gorham Methodist Church. The pastor, Rev. Hardin, who from natural fear of the devil more than Allah, changed his mind even before he had knowledge of us and the word of God which he had never before heard, and refused his, and his followers' own salvation. This was due to the lack of love, unity and true brotherhood among us (the so-called Negroes).

I WAS NOT present, but why did not they try getting acquainted with me and learn what I am teaching before accepting my enemies' version of the truth which I teach? But, fear made him disregard our friendship and brotherhood of the same nation. Would a white pastor of a church who had promised some leader of his race who was preaching love, unity, and white supremacy among his people shut him out because some Negroes are against white supremacists? I should say not!

If the Negroes only know what evil is now planned by certain whites against them, they would love me. Nothing would please me better than to have a meeting with all leaders of my people, both religious, civic, and political. Such a meeting would clear our misunderstanding of each other. Are you ready for such a meeting? God is with us, and Satan is angry, and wishes to keep you away from

God and the heaven which God desires to set you and me in.

The Indiana whites are guilty of lynching Negroes. They hate Negroes. Indiana used to be a Ku Klux Klan state. J.B. Stoner, Imperial Wizard, Ku Klux Klan leader, who claims to be the arch leader, is trying to stir up trouble for the Muslims, and especially me; but I think and can say with certainty, that if his people try doing such evil to my people who are at peace with Allah and the world, they will baptize themselves into trouble that is not peace. If the Imperial Wizard of the Ku Klux Klan attempts to be carried out on us. I will seek only Allah for our protection. Mr. Stoner knows that seven powers of Allah are ever ready to defend us in this resurrection, and he is not enough for one of the seven!

TIME FOR TRUTH KNOW THYSELF

3-2-59

You must know and remember that Almighty God Allah has sent me with a mission to unite you on to your own kind. I can do nothing without the help of Almighty God Allah. It is time for our uniting. Time is on our side!

On consulting history, you will find that you and I have been in this part of the world for some four hundred years. More than three hundred years were served in physical slavery. About one hundred years, we have been so-called free since our being made so-called citizens of America. Yet, why are we seeking civil rights if we are citizens of America? A citizen should not have to go to the government to give him civil rights. If the benefits of the 13th and 14th Amendments are written in the constitution and you and I, the so-called American Negro, are citizens, we should be enjoying them without asking for them.

Still, we are begging for justice. To whom were these particular amendments applying? You may say, "each individual." Perhaps we, the so-called Negroes are not considered individuals. We know today that we are having trouble trying to sit in the classroom with white people. If they hate us so much that they do not want their children educated in the same classroom with us, what should we do? Should we continue to beg for freedom, justice and equality from people who don't even desire to sit beside you in their educational institutions or to ride with you on the same vehicle?

We are twenty million or more in America. Yet during our four- hundred year stay in America, we have not enjoyed civil rights, protection or justice under the Constitution which states it is for every individual. What shall we do? We must remember that if we are to enjoy such rights, we first must create these rights in and among ourselves. We cannot ask other people to give us freedom, justice and equality, when we don't recognize it among ourselves. We have not been able to unite and respect each member of our nation as a brother. We have not been able to respect any of our kind from abroad as a brother. What is wrong with us? If we want freedom, justice and equality, shouldn't we first practice it among ourselves? We have not been able to do anything worthwhile since we left the cotton fields of the south under the lash of the southern white slave-master.

By worthwhile, I mean we, the so-called Negroes, have not done anything toward self independence. We have done a lot of great things. We have had rise from among us, great men who had good intentions and wanted to see you and me rise. They are gone. You and I are here. Some say, no one can do it, the other one may do it." The parable of David in the Bible states that David did not live to build a house. His son built the house. However, David did get the material necessary to build the house but death overtook him before he was able to build it. Nevertheless, David showed how the house would look and his son came behind him and built the house of David's desire. If I am not able to build the house, I will try to get you the material.

It is time we come into the knowledge of ourselves, God and God's religion. You will not find a civilized people today who are not aware of Islam. The Islamic believers number around a billion people on our Planet. The Islamic people do not refer to their religion among themselves, nor do the believers as an organization, group of people or a community. It is referred to as a world. The religion of Islam is a world as is the world of Christianity.

The world of Islam is the world of black mankind. Islam is a religion that black people love. Islam is a great world. The religion of Islam teaches you and me to believe in on God, Allah, believe in His prophets, believe in the scriptures that the prophets bring to you and me. The three fundamental principles or beliefs in Islam are the belief in the One God Who created the Heaven and Earth, belief in His prophets and finally, belief in His scriptures or book.

Islam is not recognized by the white people in America. Why? I have taught you that white people cannot accept Islam. Righteousness is the religion of Islam. Righteousness, the white man cannot accept because his nature is against righteousness. It is just as impossible for you to try to make yourself one of them! This is the secret of the white man that you have been deprived. This secret I am teaching and you misunderstand. I am teaching truth. It is wonderful for you to be able to live in the time we are living. All of us are blessed to be here today to witness the change from the old world to the new world. It is time for you and I to know these things. It is time that we unite. It is time for the separation of black and white... [I am so happy and thankful that Allah has given us the knowledge of the] time as now and to receive such revelations that He has revealed to me. They are revelations for your salvation.

WE MUST HAVE LAND AS OTHER NATIONS

YOU SAY, BUT, I don't want the white man to carry us. Just give us an equal chance," What kind of equal chance? What do twenty million people look like milling around in a factory of white people all the days of their lives and their children's lives, looking for a job? We need to look for some land. Who will recognize millions and millions of people who will not protest their condition? Yours and my condition here in America is the worst of any people on earth - it is unequalled, and we are without one tiny state in the union. We are till demanding equality. The white man will not accept you as his equal because he knows his slave is not his equal. He does not want you to marry his daughter. He does not want you as his son or his son- in-law even though you greedily desire to be. You are most eager for integration so you may have a chance of inter-mixing and inter-marrying with them than you are for justice for your people and getting some land - land for you and your children on this earth.

IF I AM YOUR equal as you are a citizen, then prove that I am a citizen of America by giving to me some earth like that which you own. The so-called American Negroes can never have a successful future in America as long as they do not own some earth. You are a nation within a nation. You have been carried by another nation all your life, here in America for more than four hundred years. Today you continue to beg them to carry you and recognize you as their equal without even asking them for something. You are not asking them for anything worth-while. why don't you unite as leaders an go down to Washington and tell the Washington leaders, "We don't want to sit in your schools beside you. What we really want from you, if you don't want to let us go, is a place for our people in this country. You have said that we are free. Let us go! If we are not going and you will not help us to go, then give us a chance to live to ourselves here. We don't want to force our presence on you and upon your children. If you will not let us go and seek earth somewhere else other than America, then set aside some of these states for us."

THE SO-CALLED AMERICAN Negroes say they don't want to be separated and that is because of their inferior knowledge of their own kind and the white race. If you had a thorough of yourself and a thorough knowledge of the white race, you would desire to be separated. What have the slave-masters done in the way of justice that we should want to live with them? What have they done in the way of justice that we should want to eat with them, drink with them, walk with them or marry them? What have they done for us that make the so-called Negroes desire them. It appears to be their greatest desire to make unity and love to the slave-masters children. You should first make unity and love among yourselves and your own kind. I think white people would be foolish to accept a so-called Negro as a friend or as a neighbor of theirs, when he is not a friend or neighbor to himself. we are divided. There is no unity among us. we have allowed the slave-master's religion to divide us one hundred percent. We do not have a knowledge of the Whiteman, or ourselves. I have told you the truth.

Some of you say and write that, "Elijah is teaching hate." What is there in the teachings of Elijah Muhammad that you can single out as "hate teaching?" What part or the whole of this teaching do you construe as hate? If I say that you should love yourself as a black man, is that hate? I say that black mankind are the people from whom you were taken. Is that hate? I say the white race came after the black and is a grafted race from the black man. Is that hate? I am not telling you to hate white people. I am only telling you who they are. We are very quick to single out one of our own as an enemy, when he speaks up for the good of black mankind. I am for the black man!

SOME OF YOU may not like me because I love my own kind. Any man that is brown, yellow, red or coal black is a member of the black nation. any man who has not accepted self or speak and love others more than his own kind, cannot be trusted. The time has arrived for the truth. You should know exactly where you stand. there are no people more blessed this day than the so-called American Negroes, who have been chosen by Allah Himself, The God of The Universe. You and I should be happy to know today that we have on our side a God who defends and guides us. You may believe in that which the slave-master gave to you for a religion. But you must prove to me that it was the religion of the prophets. You may say, "the Negro is not mentioned in the Bible or any Holy Book." If you don't see where you are mentioned by the name, "Negro," it is only right that you should discard the name. Then see if you can find yourself under some other name. Almighty God, Allah, has taught me the truth to teach to you. I must deliver it to you whether you accept it or not. It is not my fault if you reject it after I offer the truth to you. It is my fault if I don't offer to you the truth God gave to me.

WHAT DAY ARE we living in. We are living in the day of judgment of the Caucasian World. We are living in the day in which we should separate. You must know this even though your minds are filled with wealth, sport and play. It is the time of judgment of this world as you and I have known it. There are scholars who think this is the time of their judgment. Who is going to tell you, if one of your own kind does not? Are you looking again for a spirit God.

MR. MUHAMMAD SPEAKS

The Monroe, Louisiana, southern courts with their southern judges of hatred and attorneys of hatred and are Negro-blood thirsty take their own law of justice, twist it up and throw it back up on the shelf. And when they look and see a poor, innocent so- called Negro begging for justice as his grand-parents before their grandparents as far back as 400 years ago, they receive nothing but the spitting of anger and threats of murder from the Judge throughout the courts of America. Just to mention `justice' for a so-called Negro in the south is an insult to the judge who is supposed to be the judge of right and wrong between the state and opposing attorneys. He becomes more a vicious enemy against the poor so-called Negro than even the prosecuting attorney when he sees a so-called Negro before him.

The so-called Negroes have not justice under the law not only in the south, but nowhere in America. As I plainly stated this in Washington D.C., in 1959 in the Uline Arena before 10,000,000 people that everything has failed us as far as justice is concerned the Justice Department in Washington, the churches, the priests, and the preachers have all failed the so-called Negroes when it comes to justice. By the help of Allah, and by the blood of the original man whose father is the originator, I Elijah Muhammad, will fight for this cause to get our people justice in America. And by the help and power of Allah and the power of the universe, and the power that is in the Nation of Islam, and the power of every atom that is bound in the planet earth and that is bound in other planets. What angers America is just the idea of her 400-year old slaves now wanting to go over to the paradise of freedom, justice and equality under the crescent of the divine religion of Islam where they will have sincere brotherhood and friends throughout the civilized world.

America knows that under her flag we have received nothing but hell; beatings and killings without due process of law day and night - not in the past only, but the present. She wants to make some so-called Negroes believe that the religion of Islam can be thrown out the window by turning hypocrites themselves in trying to make democracy work. This is done just to deceive the so-called American Negroes.

But I say to everyone who reads this paper that Islam is here among these black people to stay as long as there is life in their bodies. The God of Islam (Allah) is with me and will back me and others up who are working hard to deliver our people from such an evil and merciless race of devils.

What glory and honor does a so-called Negro get under the stars and stripes? No honor, no glory - only hell. We have proof of this by their so-called courts and justice. There is no justice for us; and this America knows. She would like to hurt everyone of you and make you like it; it pleases America to do you evil. But not we Muslims; we will declare the truth and die for it! Thanks to Allah for removing fear from us, and I pray he puts it in them that they may fear and tremble every day until they be taken out of the way!

MR. MUHAMMAD SPEAKS ON NEGROES' SALVATION PART I

There is no justice for us under the white race. The past is the answer. The secret order of the Ku Klux Klan claims all loyal American citizens as their members . As for the principles of the KKK, who knows any better than we that all white people are Ku Klux Klansmen when it comes to us (the so-called Negroes). The whole of the United States of America's Police Department and State Attorneys are the Judges when it comes to the so-called Negroes. They are happy to get a chance to arrest you just for the privilege of beating and shooting you. On many occasions, the black woman gets the same kind of treatment as her black man. There is no justice in any of their Departments for you. This is the limit!

The KKK organization of cowardly devils who love going out doing evil to us, the God of Islam shall soon destroy. Therefore, why should you fear? America is like Sodom and Gomorrah was before their destruction. They were wealthy, full of filth and evil doings. The destruction of those cities was to serve as a warning and example for the wicked people of the present cities of the world - although there is a way of escape for all of the so-called Negroes.
The so-called Negroes fear of believing the truth, which they think will bring the anger of the devils (white race) against them, keeps them suffering at the hands of the devils who, by nature, enjoy mistreating the black people of the earth. Under such fear of their enemies, they will reject their own salvation and fight against their own God

325

and Apostle for the pleasure of the devils, who are their open enemies.

LET THE SO-CALLED NEGROES KNOW THE TRUTH that the time of our enemies has come to an end and that Allah will destroy them from the face of the earth. Such demons as J.B. Stoner, the Imperial Wizard of devils. Allah has made to expose himself and his whole race as devils. Now, without a doubt, so-called Negroes who believe that Heaven's doors to the hereafter are open to the white race as well as any member of the darker race and do not believe in the teachings that all of the white race are devils and cannot be accepted by Allah (God) to see and live in the hereafter in the World of Islam, can plainly see by Stoner's own admission that they are really the race of devils.

Mr. Stoner says in his letter to me. "If I can put you (Elijah Muhammad) out of business (teachings the truth) the Ku Klux Klan will once again become supreme throughout the North because the other niggers are easier to handle than you Muslims.

The Messenger

Though hell with all her power and fury should rise against me with the guidance of Mr. Stoner, it still will not be able to stop the spread of the Message of Truth that Allah has risen me to preach to my mentally dead people. But, what Stoner has said should open the eyes of all Negroes in these words: You know that the Niggers are too cowardly to support you. Their cowardice even causes them to fight you." In words to say that he did not doubt that I have the right way for my people, but that my people are too afraid of them (the white devils) to believe and follow me, and instead, my own cowardly people will fight against me and the truth to please the white devils because of fear.

The Negro preachers are great friends of the enemies of their people. Mr. Stoner calls the law that "you cannot hate anybody" unconstitutional. Those who write it were haters of Negroes and such a law cannot be enforced. It is even against the nature of God, for God, Himself, hates the wicked devils and has set a day for their destruction.

MR. MUHAMMAD SPEAKS ON NEGROES' SALVATION PART II

The so-called Negroes are the prey (Isa. 49:24) of the mighty U.S. as Israel was in the days of Pharaoh. They were a prey under the power of Pharaoh. According to the Bible, they had nothing like shares in the land of Egypt. A few cattle, the land or home given to Joseph's father's house, in the days of Joseph, all seemed to have disappeared in the time of Moses.

Jehovah appeared to Moses in the bush. Moses was made to see the bush in a flame of fire, though there was no actual fire. The fire represented the anger of Jehovah against Pharaoh and his people. It was the declaration of a Divine War against the Egyptians for the deliverance of Israel.

The TIME had arrived that Allah (God) should fulfill his promise made to Abraham. According to the Bible (Gen. 15:13, 14) we do not find wherein Israel had ever sought Jehovah through prayer or from any scripture, nor did they know of any prophet before Moses. The only knowledge we have is in the words of Jehovah's address to Moses - that they knew Him only by the Name of God Almighty (Ex.6:3.)

But, the real issue was not in the name as much as it was in the TIME. It was the TIME that Jehovah should fulfill His promise, though Israel was a disbelieving people in Moses and Jehovah, Jehovah could not lie to His prophet Abraham, though Israel was a rebellious people (disbelievers), and Pharaoh had to know the time of his end.

There was a limit to his rule over the people of God, though they knew not their God nor their father's. The time had arrived that they should be delivered from the power of Pharaoh, and that they should become an independent people in a land that they would be given that they could call their own.

MR. MUHAMMAD SPEAKS ON NEGROES' SALVATION PART III

If only the American so-called Negroes had knowledge of the TIME in which we now live, they would accept Islam at once, for it is just the acceptance of Islam which will bring the so-called Negroes the things they desire, good homes, money and friendship in all walks of life. This is the time that they should enjoy such heaven - the Time of God to be His people, and not the Jews and White Christianity. It is you, the American so-called Negroes, but it is only just you who are blind, deaf, and dumb to the knowledge of the TIME of your salvation and the judgment and death of your enemies.

Remember the story of Moses and his people. Jehovah said to Moses; "I have surely seen the affliction of my people which are in Egypt, and I have heard their cry by reason of their taskmasters; for I know their sorrows." (Ex. 3:7). Jehovah had seen and heard the cries and afflictions of His people while His people were yet dumb to the knowledge of Him, for they called not on Him. They worshipped the gods of Pharaoh and his people, and not Jehovah, Who was the God of their fathers. Jehovah had not represented Himself as being the God of Pharaoh and his people. It was to the slaves of Pharaoh and the slaves' fathers to whom Jehovah, their God, was to show mercy and deliverance.

Pharaoh was against Jehovah and his religion, and the people of Jehovah who were his slaves. So it is with white America. She is against Allah, His servant, and

Allah's true religion of Islam. But it is TIME that the mentally dead Negroes, who are afflicted day by day by the evil hand of white America, should be delivered and given freedom, justice and equality and from the devils when by nature there is none in them. All the daylong the Negroes are mistreated. If Allah and I, His servant, will not stand up for them, who shall stand up for them? You, by far are unable to do so for you know not God. The devils have you afraid and worshipping that which you know not. FEAR NOT and come follow me and God will love you and will set you in heaven at once while you live.

Jehovah told Moses to go first to the elders of Israel and say to them: :The Lord your God (not Pharaoh's) the God of your fathers, He has appeared unto me saying: I have surely visited you, and have seen that which is done unto you in Egypt (America.") EX 3:16. But the elders would not even meet with Moses, only by way of disputation.

MR. MUHAMMAD SPEAKS ON THE NEGROES' SALVATION PART IV

"The Lost is Found Must Be Restored"

White America is in great fear of the rise of her sleeping, mentally dead slaves, the lost found members of the Black Nation of Asia. The long south, the Bible's symbolic lost sheep (Matt. 12:11; 18:12) is now found after having been kidnapped by the evening wolf, and held a prey by the power of the Beast in the wilderness (Dan. 7:7, Rev. 18:4, Isaiah 49: 24: 25). The finding of the lost members of the great Asiatic Black Nation means the end of the world that you and I have known. These truths are of the utmost importance to the future of the so-called Negroes, although they have no knowledge of their importance.

The so-called Negroes must be separated from the White race and given a home on this earth that they can call their own. The prophetic 400 years of slave service for the slave-masters in a country that is not their own (Gen. 15:13; 14) and the history of the lost and found members (the so-called Negroes) of the Original Black Nation begins in the Bible's first book called Genesis, and ends in the last book called Revelations (read Rev. 14:19; and 20). But there are no parables in the Bible more fitting to our history here in America than the parable of the "Lost Sheep," and "The Prodigal Son" (St Luke 15:1; 8; 11). These parables show the great love and joy for the Finder (God in the person of Master Fard Muhammad) who in the year 1930 to 1933 made known that he had found us, and immediately began preparing for our return.

The return of the lost - found so-called Negroes to their own people and country, rises and completes all of [what righteous] teachers are said to be prophecy. It also closes the present Holy Qui-ran which was revealed after the Torah and Gospel, whose message is directed at giving the necessary qualifications for the return of the lost found which are absent in the Bible.

Without saying it, the Holy Qur'an, whose author and teacher is God Himself, is unlike the Bible, whose authors and teachers are said to be prophets, historians, theologians who were sent from God. The Holy Qui-ran was revealed at the right time and place. It is called "Al-Hudd" or "The Guidance" (2:2). "Al-Furqan" or "That which makes a distinction between truth and falsehood" (15:1). It is also called "An-Nur" or "The Light" (7:157). Divine light, right guidance, and the truth that will show up the false teachings under which the found Negroes have been reared, are the first and [the last in the] necessary steps toward a return to your own. This truth is now causing much annoying talk, false charges and threats of death for the bearer of truth to the so-called Negroes (my people). But they, the Negroes, must know the truth.

They must be separated and joined again to their own people. This will be done unless you are able to make God and His Prophets liars, and this you cannot do, even with the aid of all the devils. Symbolically, the Negroes are the absent sheep of the one hundred, and the tenth piece of silver that demanded the sweeping of the house (the Nations) in order to find it. They are also the Prodigal Son who was lost, dead and alive, requiring that the father go after him in order to find him.

MR. MUHAMMAD SPEAKS

"Say to those who believe that they forgive those who do not fear the Days of Allah, that He may reward a people for what they earn." (Holy Qur'an 45:14)

What is meant by "Days of Allah (God)" are the battles between right and wrong. They are often mentioned as follows: the Days of Judgment, the days of the Resurrection, the Days of the Son of Man, and the Days of Allah (God). These days must not be mistaken for the regular twenty-four hour day. NO, the Days of Allah, the Days of the Resurrection, the Days of Judgment, and the Days of the Son of Man mean years; not the common twenty-four hour day.

What will make us know when we are living in the Days of Allah (God)? It is by the fulfilling of the predictions made by the Prophets of Allah (God), long before they come to pass. I quote. Maulvi Muhammad Ali's foot note 2276 on this verse, in which he says: "The Days of Allah are the contests in which the righteous shall be made successful." That, no one can deny; for this is a sign for the disbelievers who have enjoyed great temporary prosperity; and who thought that they were too rich and powerful to be brought into a state of helplessness. Although they had the histories of those who were before them, there is no difference between the disbelievers - today or the past.

We are living in the Days of Allah (God); the earth and its people have been ruled by the evil race known as the white race. In these Days of Allah (God), the righteous (the Muslims) are now gaining power over the wicked, and will soon rule the earth again as they did before the creation of the white race.

Take notice of my followers (the so-called Negroes) who have given up the wicked ways of the white race and their self-styled Christianity, and have accepted the Truth (the religion of Islam). They are gradually becoming the most successful people in the world. Allah has chosen us, we have chosen Allah.

Who can successfully oppose Allah (God) in His Days and time of rule? It is easy to give up a weak and poverty stricken people, but it is not so easy when they are powerful and wealthy. They think there will be no end to their power and wealth which is made to deceive them.

MUHAMMAD SPEAKS

"None calleth for justice, nor any pleadeth for truth: they trust in vanity, and speak lies; they conceive mischief, and bring forth iniquity." (Isaiah 59:4).

Well has Isaiah and other prophets foretold the condition of these days, when we would be seeking for justice and justice would not be given? The black man has not enjoyed one day of justice since he was brought to America by the devil slave trader, John Hawkins, in 1555. The history of the enslaved black man of America is very sad to read. As J. Saunders Redding, the author of the book rightly entitled, "They Came in Chains," I bear witness that they are still in chains - the chains are not on their hands and feet, but rather on their brains. The unforgettable and unforgivable evils heaped upon these poor black slaves in America for 400 years have no equal in the histories of man since creations. The evil deceiving enemy devils have now doped the American black man into believing in a false show of friendship, while at the same time, the Congress in Washington is on a sit down strike to prevent the black man from enjoying equal justice (Civil Rights) but yet, he calls him a citizen of America.

The evil slave masters know that they can never sincerely accept their slaves as their equals, in fact this is against the very nature of the white race; they were not created to accept the black man as their equal. They were created to enslave and kill off the black man for six thousand years but their time was up in 1914. Due to the mental death of the American black man an extended time has been given to them.

There are non who are actually seeking justice for them (the so- called Negroes) but Allah and myself, His Servant. It makes me feel ashamed to read and hear over the radio, and to see my people on the TV in Washington praying and begging the same murderer for justice (Civil Rights), for they don't have that to do. If they would only accept their own God and religion (Islam) and follow me, they would enjoy Freedom, Justice, and Equality at once. As I said to you in Washington, May 31 1959, the devils have failed to give you justice; you are hated, despised, beaten, and killed all over America by the devil white man but yet, you think there is salvation for you in your enemies, that is like the frog charmed by the snake.

The poor proud Negro clergy class is afraid to unite with me to make a strong stand for justice for our people, due to the fact that they are missioned by the white man, and not by God to preach the white man's slave making Christianity. Therefore, their licenses can be provoked any time their preaching is not liked by the white man. The poor so-called Negro preacher was first missioned by this slave master to preach to the slave obedience to his master, in turn he was given a little more freedom and better food than his fellow slave and until today the Negro preachers are the white man's best slave makers. They are against any Negro leader that the white man in against, but they will become my good helpers in the near future.

You have nothing to fear if you believe in Allah and the true religion (Islam). You are not pleading for the truth, which God has sent by me, unless your white man approves it. This he cannot do, therefore, you believe in other than the Truth, and other than the Truth causeth mischief. The white man runs to do evil, and makes haste to shed innocent blood (kill the Negro) the way of peace they know not: wasting and destruction is in their path. We must forsake their way of life. Come and I will teach you a better way.

The Chicago South Side could, if united with me and my God, get salvation for every Negro in the country: not by violence, just by being united on the right path and doing the right thing for the black man. I beg you EDUCATORS, PROFESSORS, and SCIENTISTS to help me solve this problem.

MUHAMMAD SPEAKS

Let us take a look at the devil's creation from the teachings of the Holy Qur'an:

"And when your Lord said to the Angels, I am going to place in the earth one who shall rule, the Angels said: What will Thou place in it such as shall make mischief in it and shed blood, we celebrate Thy praise and extol Thy holiness." (Holy Qur'an Sharrieff 2:30).

This devil race has and still is doing just that - making mischief and shedding blood; and it was the Black Nation from whom they were grafted:

"When your Lord said to the Angels: Surely I am going to create a mortal of the essence of black mud fashioned in shape." (Holy Qur'an Sharrieff 15:28).

The essence of black mud (the Black Nation) mentioned is only symbolic, which actually means the sperm of the Black Nation; and they refuse to recognize the Black Nation as their equal, though they were made from them by a Black Scientist (name Yakub).

Their every cry is: "Beat, kill, kill the so-called Negroes!" The day has arrived that Allah will return to our murderers that which they have been so happy to do to the poor innocent so- called Negroes. They love to shed the poor innocent blood of their Negro slaves, and even seek and plan to kill anyone who is teaching the Truth. Allah will give you your own flesh and your blood to drink like water. (Isaiah 49:26.) Your arms and your Allies will not help you against Allah (Rev. 12:7-9.)

The heads and bodies of the so-called Negroes are used to test the power of your clubs and guns. Yet, the poor foolish so- called Negroes admire the murderers regardless to how much they are murdered. The day is near, even at your door, when you shall reap fully what you have sown. There is no justice in your courts for a so-called Negro. Most of the judges are more anxious than the prosecutor, to see that we do not get justice. He charges the jury in a way to get a verdict of guilty against us. Most of their police are like brute beasts or savage leopards, when they come to arrest us. They come rejoicing to beat and kill a Negro (their hated slave), bashing in your skulls and mouths, kicking and stamping you even after you are hand- cuffed and "hog-tied." Then the heartless brutes laugh and make mockery of you after disfiguring your face and body. They threaten to kill you for no excuse other than: you are a so- called Negro whom they always beat and kill at will because they know there is nothing to it but just another beaten or dead Negro.

Will Allah forever suffer such injustice to we, His people? NO! He will give repayment to them soon. Leave this brute beast and go to your own God and people, for there is no justice in them for you and me. We are in a strange land and are living among strange people who are not our friends - they are friends of each other. What we should do as members of the darker Nation: join onto our Own Kind, and there we will have a sure friend, it is our Salvation to believe in Allah, and His religion of Islam, and our Own Nation. Otherwise, we will remain a friendless Nation subject to destruction.

Mr. Muhammad Speaks

FOR THE PAST 2,000 YEARS the world has been looking and expecting to see THAT GOD OF TRUTH AND JUSTICE appear; that God who would destroy the Old World of the wicked, and set up a World of Righteousness. HE HAS COME. The world did not know the exact day of His arrival, but the Prophets have given us many signs that would appear as a warning to us that He is near.

Jesus gave us many signs to watch for, and when we see these signs coming to pass, then we know when His arrival is near - "When you see all these things, know that is near." (Matthew 24:33) In Matthew 24:27 a hint is given to the direction in which He would come; (from the EAST) "As the lighting cometh out of the east, and shineth even unto the west so shall also the coming of the Son of Man be." Jesus did not leave us to look for a spirit - unnatural, not human - but to look to see a Man Who is the Son of a Man, and that this great Man is not to be expected to come from another planet. According to the signs of His coming. He is of the earth.

THE 24TH CHAPTER of Matthew gives us many signs that make sense, that would appear to warn us of His Coming and Presence, that is , if we are able to understand them, and not be foolish as the Parable of the Five Foolish Virgins who were mentioned in the next chapter (25:2). In the 28th verse of the 24th chapter of Matthew is a very beautiful parable, but not understood by many readers and scholars. There Jesus, after giving to us the direction of

343

the coming of God, and comparing His coming with the lighting, the next verse (28th) he gives us the parable where the carcass is, there the eagles are gathered together. Let us see just what are we to learn from the parable: the carcass and the eagles must refer to people, one is dead and the other is alive - eagles are birds of prey. Jesus also mentioned that God would send His Angeles with a Great Sound of a trumpet, to gather His Elect from the four winds (or directions).

IN THE 31ST VERSE, same chapter these signs most of them, are now fulfilled. The dead is the American so-called Negroes that must be brought to life (to the knowledge of Truth), before there can be a JUST JUDGEMENT of the murderers (those who robbed and killed). The eagles come to remove the carcass that is offensive to the smell of the people. Since the mental death of the so- called Negroes, they have become hated and despised by their murderers.

WE WITNESSED something last week that never has happened before in America, the meeting of nearly all the important rulers of the Nations. This will probably never happen again in the life of this world - THE DEAD MUST RISE.

NEGROES SALVATION IN RECOGNIZING THE TRUTH 5-7-59

The main thing is getting the Christian to admit the truth.

> *"O followers of the book (Bible) come to an equitable proportion between us and you that we shall serve any but Allah and we shall* not associate aught with Him. O followers of the book, (Bible) why do you dispute *about Abraham, when the Torah and the gospel were not revealed till after him, do you not then understand?" (Holy Qur'an 3:63,64).*

The Jews and the Christians both take Abraham to be the father of their religion or faith, while Abraham was before both Moses and Jesus. Moses brought the Torah, Jesus brought the (Injil) gospel. Abraham was an Arab Muslim and not a Jew nor a Christian. Says the Holy Qur'an:
"Abraham was not a Jew nor a Christian but he was an upright man, a Muslim, and he was not one of the polytheists." (Chapter 3:66).

A Muslim is an upright person, a believer in one God (not three). The Jews and the Christians both agree that Abraham was a believer in one God. The Christians cannot take Abraham as a father of their faith because the Christian's faith or religion is a belief in three Gods: Father, Son and Holy Ghost. This kind of belief is called Polytheism, and this is the true name for all Christians.

Abraham submitted to Allah (God) to serve and obey Him. The Jews nor the Christians never have submitted entirely to Allah (God), Moses, nor Jesus to do righteousness. Do you say they have when the Jews and the Christians are charged with killing the Prophets of God? It is a manifest proof that the Prophets' religion was Islam: (submission to the Will of Allah (God). Surely the

345

Jews and the Christians would not have killed the Prophets if the Prophets were of their own religions:(Judaism and Christianity). Abraham is mentioned throughout the Holy Qur'an as being a Muslim, and you also bear witness that he was a Muslim when you say that he was a believer in one God even through you do not have a detailed knowledge of Abraham.

As the Holy Qur'an says:

> 'Behold you are they who disputed about that of which you had knowledge; why then do you dispute about that of which you have no knowledge?" (Chapter 3:65).

This stands true of the Christians. They like to dispute with you on that which they have knowledge and that which they do not have knowledge. The Qur'an further says:

> "And the Jews will not be pleased with you nor the Christians until you follow their religion. Say: Surely Allah's guidance that is the true guidance and if you follow their desires after the knowledge that has come to you, you shall have no guardian from Allah, nor any helper." (Chapter 2:120).

NEGROES SALVATION IN RECOGNIZING THE TRUTH PART II

Why Do the Heathen Rage and the People Imagine a Vain Thing! (Psalms 2:1).

The average Negro has been so thoroughly changed into the devil that the only way to distinguish the real devil from his imps is by color. Their great deceiver (the white race) has so thoroughly corrupted and divided our people until now they have no love for self and kind; only for their enemies, the white race. Almost all of the news of the Negro press is filled with Uncle Tom's language, discord, indecent language, filthy, indecent, bold, front-page pictures of half-nude, indecently posed girls and women of their own color. This is representing their people to the world as being the dumbest, the filthiest, the most divided, the most self-haters of Black Mankind, and the greatest lovers of their enemies, the anyone will find on the earth!

No one can help such people but Allah (God). I am for justice, peace, security and a home on the earth that we can call our own. I have been preaching and writing this doctrine for 27 years. The Negro press knows it all, but as soon as their white god wrote some false charges against me three weeks ago in their magazines and papers, the so-called Negro press carefully picked out all the false and evil things said, and wrote against me and my followers. They made headlines out of it for their papers to show the world their love for the enemy, and their hate for the leader among them.

The Time Magazine and the U.S. News Magazine were prompted by the leader of the Ku Klux Klan, whose doctrine is "to keep the Negroes down, even if you have to beat or shoot them down." They control the south and part of the rest of America when it comes to the Negroes. They have their members in key positions wherever the Negroes and whites are concerned. They also have knowledge of the glorious future for the Negro in Islam, and are now in hopes of crushing it to keep the Negroes at the mercy of the white man. They confess that they are the devils by using the Bible Scripture, John 8:44, following the arch-leader of the Christian Party to represent themselves to their brothers. They are the real murderers and liars from the beginning.

The Time Magazine Page 25, of the August 10, 1959, issue had to admit that: "We (Muslims) are law-abiding (peaceful), a fact that worries some cops more than minor outbreaks of violence." Think over these words. "We are peaceful, unarmed, non-aggressive, non-alcoholic, do not indulge in tobacco or dope, we bathe often, we pray toward Mecca five times a day, our women are modestly dressed, using no lipstick, and are never allowed alone in a room with men other than their husbands, and that I (Elijah Muhammad) am against all forms of dependency (begging) upon whites." (This is the type of leader that the Negroes need). But yet, the cops are worried over such clean and peaceful Negroes because they do not get an excuse to beat and kill them. The F.B.I., who has watched for a chance to do the worst against us with their paid Negro stool pigeons among us (even to making false charges of stealing the charity given for the expenses of the temples and laborers,' all will fail.

One U.S. Marshall told me when I was arrested by him in 1942 that he had also arrested one of my followers. When he was carrying him (my follower) to jail, he asked the brother: "Why did you not run?" The brother replied, "For what?" The marshal said, "So that I can get a chance to shoot you." Can we hope for justice from such people? They all are united to destroy Elijah Muhammad and his followers, but I ask my followers to fear not their evil plans against us, for all of their plan are against ALLAH, and ALLAH is with us. HE is sufficient as a HELPER; and ALLAH IS NOT A SPOOK! He can deliver us, and our enemies are heading in the direction to soon learn! They would like to make it appear to our blind, deaf, and dumb people that it is a crime for a black man to preach black supremacy, while the preaching of white supremacy is a common thing among them. They preach the end of their own world, then who will rule after them if it is not the Black Man. But they do not like for you to believe in your own nation.

The U.S.A might have to learn the hard way, as Pharaoh had to learn the hard way that Jehovah had visited Egypt and talked with Moses. He appeared to be in a flame of fire (the burning bush was the sign of war between Jehovah and Pharaoh). His anger burned against Pharaoh for Pharaoh's injustice, and Pharaoh's anger burned against Jehovah and Moses, His servant, and openly told His senators to leave him alone that he may kill Moses, and to let Moses call on his Allah. The time has arrived that we must have justice and liberation from a people bent upon our destruction day and night. And Pharaoh said: "Let me alone that I may slay Moses and let him call upon his lord. Surely I fear that he will change your religion." (Holy

Qur'an 40:26). The above verse is the answer to today's rage against me. They would not like to seek Islam in America.

I HAVE NEVER TAUGHT ANYONE TO HATE

Negroes' Salvation Recognizing the Truth

For the past few weeks, the newspapers, radio, magazines, some police departments, the big Negro church leaders, and a few ignorant Muslims, who know not Allah, nor the devil, nor do they understand the scriptures of the Bible and Holy Qur'an, have been working together to keep the poor blind, deaf and dumb of my people from accepting the truth, after it has come to them, by calling the truth of God which I teach - "hate teachings." Their intentions are to put fear into my poor people (who are born in fear of the white race (the devils) without even telling you what they classify as "hate teachings."

They also want you to think it is a crime for me to preach Black Supremacy, while the preaching of white supremacy has been their text and teachings and hate for us ever since they have been on the plane Earth. Now the truth of them (John 8:44 - Thessalonians 2:2) Allah is now revealing to us; and they (the devils) know how easy it is to frighten our people. They know that once the Negroes learn that they are the real devils, naturally, they would not have love for them. Therefore, they call TRUTH TEACHINGS, "hate teachings" against the white race. (The devil does not like TRUTH).

Hate means dislike. Can the Righteous like the devils, or can the devils like the Righteous? There is not one so-called Negro in America who does not know that white people hate Negroes. Let the coward Negro preachers who fear and worship the white race, as they should Allah (God) answer this: - "Was it love or hate for the Negroes why the white race made our fathers slaves and still have us as free slaves?" "Is it love or hate for us why they will not give us equal justice equal chance equal education, equal respect?" "Is it love or hate why they beat, rape, and lynch us?" "Is it love or hate why they do not give us (their 400 year old slaves) any part of America which we can call our own?" "Is it love or hate why they do not want you in their schools and societies?" - (Of course, we Muslims like being in our Own). TRUTH CANNOT BE CLASSIFIED AS "HATE TEACHINGS."

The white man of America has always feared the truth coming to the so-called Negroes; but it has arrived, and your fighting against it will only spread it more; for Allah, HIMSELF is actually the One Who is spreading. You may make mockery of me and the Message of Life which I am giving to my people, but you shall soon come to know. The devils are taking my words and twisting them with lies to make my people afraid to come near me, but if it pleases Allah, He will make my people understand the TRUTH and bring their lies against me to naught.

The devils and their followers would like for you to believe that I am a self-styled leader of a cult, self-named "Muhammad," and that my legal name is Elijah Poole." "Poole" is illegal, "Muhammad" is my legal name. They know that every Negro who is called by their (devils) name will never be recognized as a Righteous Muslim in heaven or hell. They know that the name "Muhammad" will live as long as God lives. They further know that their names are not attributes of Allah (God), for their names will be cut off. The names of Allah (God) will live.

They (the devils) also know that Islam is the true religion of Allah (God), and that God will make it overcome and vanish all other religion - and this is the time that is will take place. They try to make you think that it is a crime to preach that the Black man is the first and the last, and will rule the earth after them (which they know is the truth, and you also know it to be the truth).

They would like to make you think that the Old Islamic World is against me. What if it is? Was I missioned by them, or the Imam of Shah Jehan of Working, England, or any other than Allah (God)? No, my mission is from Allah, and He is sufficient enough for me. He will make a New World of Islam, and you will be made to bow to it. so, fight against me, ALLAH IS MY HELPER AGAINST YOU.

NEGROES SALVATION IN RECOGNIZING THE TRUTH PART III

The greatest thing that ever came to you and me is: - The Truth - especially when it is in our favor. Of all the knowledge a man may have, the best is the knowledge of self, God, and the Devil. Without the above knowledge, you are not considered a civilized person; for, if we know not ourselves, how can we know God and the Devil? How can we serve one and escape the other, without the knowledge of both? Real Truth brings about a change.

The Truth is never wanted by false believers. The people, who have not known the Truth, must be taught it before Judging them. If a liar has deceived the people, then Truth will make manifest the Liar. Yakub's race of devils were made unlike the original Black Nation, for the purpose of being able to attract the original Nation to follow them. It stands true - White attracts Black and Black attracts White; but, where the attraction differs is, the Black - and especially the so-called Negroes - love the unalike)the White Race), while the unalike, by nature, can't love the so-called Negroes.

As you have learned, they were made to hate and kill off the Black. They have killed on an average of 100.000.000 to every one thousand years that they have been on our planet; and, hope to carry 97% of the so-called Negroes here in America to their doom, and two-thirds of the entire Black population of the Earth. Maybe a thorough knowledge of their enemies will reduce this figure.

355

The secret of the White Race, just couldn't be exposed before their time of rule was out. If the Original Black Nation had known that this new, unalike, blue-eyed race would not be accepted by the God of Righteousness, at the end of six thousand years of their time, there would not have been one left on our Planet. The knowledge of them was kept as a secret, from the common people, as they are symbolically spoken of under the name of "Cain," who murdered his brother. God marked Cain so that the people would not recognize the murdered of their righteous brother, lest the people would kill him." (Genesis 4:15)

Though God pronounced a "Curse on Cain, coming from the Earth, which had opened her mouth to receive the righteous blood from the murderer's hand, he was to be driven from the face of the earth and from the face of God. The earth shall not yield her strength to Cain; and he shall be a fugitive and a vagabond." (Genesis 4:10, 12).

Moses reminded them of this curse in Deuteronomy (28:45-52). Of course, the so-called Negroes are warned in the same Chapter, to let the Divine Chastisement or Destruction of their enemies serve as a lesson to their future greatness, or they will meet with such fate.

NEGROES' SALVATION IN RECOGNIZING THE TRUTH PART IV

We cannot expect to see that which cannot be seen. A spirit cannot be seen, only felt. It is like electricity. Electricity is a power produced by friction from a substance that has such power (electric) in it, produced by the Sun and Moon upon the Earth. It is not seen, but we know what makes it. So it is with God.

We know that God exists and is All Wise, All Powerful, and that this quickening power called spirit if from Him. But, who is this God? A spirit cannot think, but thinking can produce spirit. So, according to God's own words, through His prophets, He must be a man. He is interested in man's affairs, according to the Bible (Genesis 1:27) "God made man in His own image and likeness, both male and female." If we believe that alone God created man in His own image and likeness, that is sufficient for us not expect God to be anything other than man.

A father has pleasure in his sons' affairs, because his son is a part of himself and his very image and likeness. There is no true scripture that teaches us that God is something other than a man. The Bible teaches us (Hosea 11:9): "For I god and not man; the Holy One in the midst of thee." Here the latter part of the verse makes it clear that God is a Holy ONE (Man) and the man He refers to that He was not is an unholy one (man). This only means that the Holy God is not the wicked man's God (The Caucasian Race.)

Ever since Adam (the Caucasian race) has been referred to as the man (the man made man or race and mankind); the world has taken it to include all men. *"No man hath seen God;" (I John 5:19).* This is another confused teaching to the ignorant masses, for if no man hath seen God, then there is no God for you and me to look forward to seeing on the Judgment Day. If such is true, how will we know Him since no one has ever seen Him? But we do know Him and what He looks like.

"We know that we are of God and the whole world lieth in wickedness." I John 5:19).

The whole world of the White Race is full of wickedness and this is the world referred to. We are not of this world (the White Race or Devils) nor is our God the God of this world. Our God is One, today, as we had only One God in the beginning.

"In that day (this is the day) shall there be One Lord and His name One." (Zechariah 14:9).

This refers to the time when the True God is made manifest. Before His manifestation, the people worship what they think or what they want to be their God. The devil's teaching is a division of Gods - three Gods into one God. The Hindus have many Gods. The Muslims worship One God (Allah). "Say: He Allah is One God." But yet 99% of the Muslims think that Allah is only a "Spirit" and is not a man. Then they too need to be taught the realty of Allah (God).

Certainly He is One God, but not a spirit; for a spirit cannot be said to be "One God," If God was only a spirit, then we do not wait on the coming of [that which is said to be around us day and night].

NEGROES SALVATION IN RECOGNIZING THE TRUTH PART V

Both Books are called Holy. The word of Allah (God) is Holy, and His word is true. Therefore, all truth is Holy; for Allah (God) is Holy and is the Author of Truth, without the shadow of a doubt. Allah is the representative of the Holy Qur'an (not a Prophet) in these words: "This Book, there is no doubt in it, is a guide to those who guard against evil." (2.2) translated by Maulvi Muhammad Ali. Abdullah Yusuf Ali's translation of the same verse reads near the same: "This is the Book: in it is guidance sure without doubt, to those who hear Allah (God)" (2:2).

The Bible does not claim God to be its author. Jehovah called Moses out of the burning bush to go to Pharaoh (Exodus). There is no mention of a Book or Bible that is found that Jehovah gave to Moses in the first five books of the Bible, which are claimed to be Moses' Books. Moses' rod is the only thing used against Pharaoh and the land of Egypt; and tables of stones in the Mountains of Sinai. The miraculous Rod of Moses, and not a Book brought Pharaoh and his people to their doom. The Ten Commandments served as a guide for the Jews in the Promised Land. Where do we find in the Bible that it was given to Moses by Jehovah under such name as Bible or the Book?

But, on the other hand, Allah (God) says that He gave the Book "the Holy Qur'an to Muhammad." "I am Allah, the Best Knower, the revelation of the Book, there is no doubt in it, is from the Lord of the Worlds." (Sur 32:1,2). Allah says to Muhammad in the same above Sura (32:23) - "We gave the Book to Moses, and be not in doubt in receiving it, we made it a guide for the children of Israel." (If Moses' rod and book were given as guide for Israel, and the Gospel God gave to Jesus as a guide and warning to the Christians, and the Holy Qur'an to Muhammad for the Arab World, will God give us (the so-called Negroes) a Book as a guide for us? Will He bring it or send it? - For, those Books were for other people, and not for us.

If we are in the change of the two Worlds (Christianity and Islam) then surely we need a "New Book" for our guidance; for those Books have served the people to whom they were given. But all or both Books are guidance for us all. Yet, we must have a "New Book" for the "New Change;" that which no eye has seen or ear has heard, nor has entered into our hearts what it is like. We know these Books, they have been seen and handled by both the good and no good. Certainly the Holy Qur'an is from the Lord of the Worlds; there can be no doubt in the Word of Allah (God). But if the Book or Books have the world of someone else other than Allah's words in it for them; there is doubt in our hearts concerning the receiving of such Book or Books!

NO JUSTICE FOR SO-CALLED NEGROES

Let us united and pull our people who are down trodden out of the mud of civilization. Let's put clean words in their mouth. Teach them to rid themselves of the evil and indecent habits. Put them on the road to justice. Carve out a way for our people. Put them to themselves so they may see and use the fruits of their own labor. Seek a country for them. You cannot make a future for your people with a people who are not willing to give you a chance to do for yourselves. America never has nor has she been willing to give the so-called Negro the right to go for self. America has always worked against the Negro acquiring and using the right to go for self. America wants the so-called Negro to remain subjects to her people. No mention is ever made for the so-called Negro to go for himself.

Now, as a means to keep the so-called Negro from awakening and coming into his own, intermingling and integration is offered to him. Integration is not a sincere affair. The slave master has never had sincere love for his former slave. Integration is only a trick to stop you from having the desire to be free and independent as other nations. The slave master knows it is time for the so-called Negro to go for self. They know Almighty God, Whose proper name is Allah, is offering you freedom.

The slave master never offers you a home of your own. They say, "Live here in my house. I won't let you own it, but you may use one of the rooms. Also, I will allow you to marry my son or daughter." The clergy, the educators

361

and other leaders of our people stand by and speak in behalf of integration to persuade their own people to a way of destruction. The Negroes should reject such leadership. why should we desire, want or agree to integration? What will our children fifty years from today think of us, permitting the very people who kidnapped us, destroyed us in slavery, for over four hundred years, and never gave us equal justice, deprive us of a chance to go for self, while a caller was in our midst, uniting us to freedom, justice and equality under the guidance of Allah? What will they think if we permit blind leadership to bind us again to the slave master? What man once free, then captured, wants to remain with his slave master? What nations captured want to remain in captivity? Why should the leaders of the so-called Negro seek to destroy their own people as they seek to please the slave master? Does the so- called Negro want history to show that his leadership carried him into integration, a path to destruction?

We must not, since being freed, bind ourselves over to the wishes of any people! We must have some of this earth for ourselves! We must build! We must make jobs for our own people! We must build factories! If we unite, we can build factories. Only now, the so-called Negro is too much in love with an independent nation to see his fallen and dependent nation. I have Allah (God) with me to unite my people! Come and unite with me. Throw away your shame which you have because of the temporary enjoyment you have now. There is eternal joy and happiness in the program God Almighty has given to me to give to you.

Let us all unite and reason together on a better future for the so-called Negro. If Africa desires a better future without the white man, who robbed them and the world respects Africa for doing so, then certainly, you and I who number more than twenty million should seek something for our own! We have given our life blood and every ounce of our labor to America. America won't give you equal justice because it is not in her blood. Why should we remain under the rule of such evil and unjust people? What future have we in such people? Would you accept sweet-hearting with the murderers of your people for the price of enslaving, lynching, and burning your people here for 400 years? Our murderers were never punished for the crimes they did to us and our fathers. We got nothing and have nothing. We are not being offered anything now, but a chance to mongrelize the two races. I say, there is no such thing as peace and agreement among a people who have had our nation subject to them for more than four hundred years. How is such a peace possible? The only way out and solution is for our people to be totally separated into a land, state or territory of their own. The fools who love the murderers and want to remain with them, are welcomed to do so. The separation will bring peace to you and your government.

THE ORIGIN OF GOD BEING A SPIRIT AND NOT MAN

"Take heed to yourselves, that your hearts be not deceived, and you turn aside, and service other gods, and worship them;" (Deuteronomy 11:16)

THE AMERICAN so-called Negroes are gravely deceived by their slave-masters' teaching of God and the true religion of God. They do not know that they are deceived, and earnestly believe that they are taught right, regardless of how evil the white race may be. Not knowing "self" or anyone else they are a prey in the hands of the white race, the world's arch deceivers (the real devils in person). You (the so-called Negroes) are made to believe that you worship the true God, but you do not! God is unknown to you in that which the white race teaches you (a Mystery God).

THE GREAT ARCH DECEIVERS (the white race) were taught by their fathers, Yakub, six thousand years ago, how to teach that God is a spirit (spook), and not a man. In the grafting of his people (the white race), Mr. Yakub taught them to contend with us over the reality of God by asking us of the whereabouts of that First (God). One Who created the heavens and the earth, and that, Yakub said, we cannot do. Well, we all know that there was a God in the beginning Who created all these things, and do know that he does not exist today, but we know again that from that God, the person of God continued until today in His people, and today a SUPREME ONE (God) has appeared among us with the same Infinite Wisdom to bring about a complete change.

THIS IS HE of Whom I preach and teach you to believe and obey. The devils call Him a Mystery God, but yet claim that He begot a son by Mary. They call on you and me to take this son of Mary for a God, who was a man before and after his death; yet they deny the coming of God to be a man. If Jesus was a son of God, what about Moses and the other prophets? Were they not His sons since they were His prophets?

THE BELIEF IN a God other than man (a spirit), Allah has taught me, goes back into the millions of years - long before Yakub (the father of the devils) - because the knowledge of God was kept as a secret from the public. This is the first time that it has ever been revealed, and we, the poor rejected and despised people, are blessed to be the first of all the people of earth to receive this secret knowledge of God. If this people (the white race) would teach you the truth which has been revealed to me, they would be hastening their own doom - for they were not created to teach us the truth, but rather to teach us falsehood (the contrary to truth).

It stands true that they are enemies of the truth by their ever warring against the truth. They know that Islam is the truth; they know that the history of them that God has revealed to me is the truth, but do not want you to know such truth of them. Therefore, they seek every means to oppose this teaching. They try everyone of you who says that he believes it and is my follower. They are watching you and me seeking a chance to harm us. They are so upset and afraid that they visit you at your homes to question you of your sincerity of Islam.

AS DAVID SAYS in his Psalm (37:32): "The wicked watcheth the righteous, and seeketh to slay him." Also, Psalms 37:30: "The mouth of the righteous speaketh wisdom, and his tongue talketh of judgment." And, in another place: Psalms 94:16: "Who will rise up for me against the evildoers? Who will stand up for me against the workers of iniquity?" I have answered Him and said, "Here I am, take me." For the evil done against my people (the so-called Negroes). I will not keep silent until He executes judgment and defends my cause. I fear not my life, for He is well able to defend it. KNOW THAT GOD IS A MAN and not a spook!"

OUR UNITY

Our unity is not sufficient alone. We must have Divine Power in back of us as Moses had four thousand years ago, and that power is in tack of us. That is why we should unite and get rid of all that hinders our unity. Sometimes our worst enemy is FEAR. Why should we let fear keep us from uniting when we know, and the whole world knows, that the unity of the American so-called Negroes is all that is needed for our salvation - that is, if this unity is protected by Allah (God).

We are in the same position that Israel was in four thousand years ago under the Pharaohs of Egypt. Israel knew nothing of the God and religion of her fathers. She worshipped the gods and religion of Pharaoh and his people, the slave masters of Israel. This they had practiced for 400 years. So has the American Negroes practiced the worship of the white slave masters and their religion for four hundred years. Israel was not united until they believed and accepted Moses as their leader, and Jehovah as their God. They doubted the power of Jehovah as being sufficient to protect them against the power of Pharaoh and his people. For not only was Jehovah a new and strange God to them, but His Name was equally as strange to them, and Moses - being one of them - how could he have met with a God that they too had not met with? So they doubted both Moses and Jehovah's power to deliver them from Pharaoh.

The American so-called Negroes having no knowledge of Allah and His Name, have a dead Jesus as their God, and

369

therefore they doubt Allah's power to protect them against the power of their American slave masters. Though they (Israel) saw the people of Jehovah working on the side of Moses, yet their inborn FEAR of Pharaoh and his people prevented them from uniting on the side of Moses and Jehovah. Who had sworn to Abraham, His friend, that He would deliver them from Pharaoh with a Mighty Power.

So it is with the American Negroes. You see the power of Allah working on my side to save and deliver you, but you yet doubt Him due to your being born with fear of the white slave masters. If the so-called Negroes would unite on the side of Allah and follow me, Allah would remove their fear, and destroy that which they now fear, as Jehovah did in the case of Israel's enemies. FEAR NOT, and come follow me.

PRAYER IN ISLAM

"O Allah, we beseech Thy help and ask Thy protection and believe in Thee, and trust in Thee, and we laud Thee in the best manner and we thank Thee, and we are not ungrateful to Thee, and we cast off and forsake him who disobeys Thee."

IN THE ABOVE PRAYER we learn that the whole of the Muslim Prayer, as Maulvi Muhammad Ali says, in the preface of the Holy Qur'an, "is only a declaration of Divine Majesty and glory, Divine holiness and perfection, and of the entire dependence of man on his Maker." If you would only adopt the saying of the Muslims' prayer, you would be helped. Of all the praying people on earth, the Muslims' worship to God in the best manner. The words used in their prayers are the best and humblest. They cast off and forsake those who disobey Allah (God).

THE CHRISTIANS teach love for the enemy because they are really the enemy and desire to mingle with you for the purpose of misleading you. It is nothing but right to sever friendly relations with those who do not care to serve and obey Allah (God).

THERE ARE MANY Muslims and black Christians who, for the sake of certain privileges, do not carry into practice the casting off of those who disobey Allah (God), and think it is a sin for the true righteous Muslims to do so. Today I am often asked, "Can white people attend your service?" When told that white people are not Muslims, some of the ignorant Muslims falsely charge me of not

371

teaching Islam. They also falsely charge that my teachings do not represent Islam, and that we're not recognized by the Muslim World. This is exactly what the enemies of Islam desire that the so-called Negroes believe. They sow such lies in the hearts of the weak Muslims and the so-called Negroes. YOU ARE GOING TO BE GREATLY SURPRISED. If I have Allah (God) on my side to bring my people out of the darkness and power of our enemies; is not He (God) sufficient? Most surely He is with me, and I with Him. If you are not on our side you will most certainly be the losers.

THE LORD'S PRAYER, as it is called, contains some words that should not be written there - such as: "lead us not into temptation" - GOD WILL NOT LEAD US INTO TEMPTATION. It is the devils that tempt us to sin. The above words show a lack of confidence in God to lead us aright; that He must be reminded just how to lead us. Another, "Give us this day our daily bread." Here again, the words, "this day," could lead one to believe that on that day the prayer was given, there was a shortage of bread, or that Christians' prayer seeks their physical bread first, and spiritual bread last; even though the Bible says (Luke 12:31), "you first seek the Kingdom of Heaven, and all these things shall be added unto you." In another place (Matt. 4:4)a, "Man shall not live by bread alone, but by every word that proceedeth out of the mouth God." These scriptures are contrary to the prayer, although it stands true of the Christians who seek bread, swine's flesh (the poison), whiskey, wine and beer first, and the prayer for spiritual food last.

THE BIBLE SHOWS (Exodus 16:2,3,8) that is was the want of bread and meat, first of all, that gave Moses and Aaron much trouble trying to lead the Israelites into the spiritual knowledge of Jehovah and self-independence. They even said, when they were hungry: "Would to God we had died by the hand of the Lord in the land of Egypt" (Exodus 16:3). Often they angered Moses and Aaron by their longing for the food of their slave masters even while on their way to freedom and self-independence.

THE MUSLIMS pray in their oft-repeated prayer to seek Allah's help in guiding them on the RIGHT PATH, the PATH of those whom GOD HAS FAVORED, and not on the path of those who hast caused His anger to descend upon (the Jews and Christians). This want of the slave masters' bread, meat, and luxuries is depriving the so-called Negroes of their independence.

THE DEVILS GOING RAMPANT

5-16-59

THE ADAM's (devil) children, the great trouble-makers, the demon, the fiend, Shaitan, the Adam's human beasts, the hell-raisers, the open arch-enemies of God, and all black mankind, who in the beginning disobeyed the law of God and introduced evil, filth and disrespect for God and His law of justice and righteousness among the nation of righteous (the black, brown, yellow and red people) are now on their traditional rampage against us, the so-called Negroes (their good old 400-year old slaves).

They have been murdering and raping us throughout the centuries and yet you are foolish enough to love and adore them (the devils) after all of their evils poured upon you and me. It just does not make sense.

Do not be surprised at anything like evil that you see them do; only be surprise when you see them do an act of good in your favor. Evil is the nature of Adam's children. They even have you believing that you are from Adam which is absolutely false. Never say that you are from Adam. Adam was the father (devil) of sin and disobedience, the devil of you and me.

THE RECENT Parker lynching and the Florida rape of one of our girls, who was gagged and tied by four devils taking turns one after the other on her last Saturday morning (May 2) outside of the capital city of Florida (Tallahassee), a savage beast could not do worse. They

375

swooped down upon two of our original girls like hungry wolves after lambs with drawn shot guns and knives to destroy the virginity of our daughters and kill their black boyfriends if they attempted to try to protect the girls.

Of Course, the boys would have been given more credit if they had received death in trying to defend their women against the filthy devils' attack. What good is our lives to us to allow our enemies to come into our families and rape our wives and daughters and lynch our men at will? Unite on the side of Allah and He will help us to put a stop to it, or die trying in the name of Allah.

APPEALING FOR justice from the lynchers and rapists brothers will avail us nothing. Parker's Mississippi mob of devils, the law's excuse is that the murderers cannot be found. The sheriff knew that Parker was charged with rape. Why did not he try to protect his prisoner by keeping the jail well guarded from an attempt by his lynchers? How did the lynchers know where the keys were? Why did the nurse wait until the outlaws (lynchers) had captured their prey and was out of the town before notifying the sheriff's office or his home of the cries that she heard coming from the mouth of the murdered prisoner in and out of the jail? If it had been Negroes trying to take a white man out to lynch him, it would have been known at once; even to the U.S. Army!

Florida will protect her four devil rapists. She is already preparing a defense for them now by claiming the four devils to have been drunk, which we all know will be false. There is no justice for you under the American flag from their Supreme Courts to the jailhouse kangaroo courts. You fear to accept Allah and His true religion, Islam (Peace), and you will continue to suffer disgrace, beatings and killings at the hands of these devils. Remember, we live in a lawless world.

THE AMERICAN SO-CALLED NEGROES' SALVATION IS IN ISLAM, THE ONLY TRUE RELIGION OF GOD

The poor people that are called Negroes, who are not Negroes but defendants of the Tribe of Shabazz, are the victims of every known cruelty and evil treatment known to Mankind. Through being ignorant to the knowledge of self and others, they bring a lot of it upon themselves. The One and powerful God is now seeking them to believe in Him alone - that He alone will defend and deliver them once and forever from the cruel hand of those that hate and kill them daily.

Their fear, and belief, is not in God, nor Jesus, it is the white race, their slave masters that they fear. Were we to put all of our faith and fear in the One God Allah, we would never suffer. The so-called Negroes are home - born slaves and they think that they should be recognized as equals in everything with their slave masters. They boast in calling themselves slave names of the slave masters, the citizens of America, and at the same time begging their masters for civil rights (justice) - and their so- called Spiritual leader disgracing themselves by preaching and offering up prayers to a dead Prophet (Jesus) and an unknown God, that they imagine is living somewhere in the skies. When one enemy mistreats them, they seek refuge in the enemies' brothers that they may punish their brother for the wrongs done to them. This shows how blind and ignorant the poor so-called Negroes' Spiritual leaders are.

379

They sell themselves to be the friends of the enemies of their own people to oppose their own salvation, and become agents of the slave masters to work against their own people. They are leading themselves and their poor blind, deaf and dumb people to destruction. May Allah help me to open their eyes before it is too late.

The Black Nation's religion, Islam, is a True and upright religion of a True and Upright God of Whom the So-called Negroes are members; who are blinded, robbed, and spoiled by the slave masters. They really feel and think that they are the same as their masters. They seek their masters' friendship above Allah (God) and feel secure in doing it. May Allah have mercy on my people in America.

Of all the histories on people being enslaved by others, never have you read where the slaves loved and worshipped their slave masters - but the so-called Negroes who live under death from the enemy, beaten and killed in the Public like wild animals and never are recognized in the slave masters' so-called Courts of Justice as an equal citizen of the land. The smart enemies keep their eyes and ears open on the so-called Negroes night and day seeking an excuse to kill them.

The lack of love, unity and self-respect among us is one of our greatest enemies. Love your Black, Brown, Yellow and Red brothers as thy self; do good by each other; never think of shedding the blood of your own kind; treat all human beings right as you are the righteous - then do righteous by all; but if we do good only to self and evil to others, we can't be called the righteous. The above said must not be taken to mean that we should love the devils, but do righteous and Justice according to the law of Justice. God doesn't love the devils, but His work of righteousness and Justice extends over all.

THE BATTLE IN THE SKY

THE FINAL WAR between Allah (God) and the devils is dangerously close. The very least amount of friction can bring it into action within minutes. There is no such thing as getting ready for this most terrible and dreadful war, they are ready. Preparation for the battle between man and man or nations has been made and carried out on land and water for the past six- thousand years. Man has now become very wise and has learned many of the secrets of nature which make the old battles with swords, and bows and arrows look like child's play.

Since 1914 which was the end of the time given to the devils (white race) to rule the Original people (Black Nation), man has been preparing for a final showdown in the skies. He has made a remarkable advancement in everything pertaining to a deadly destructive war in the sky, but Allah, the Best of Planners, having a perfect knowledge of His enemies, prepared for their destruction long ago, even before they were created. Thanks to Allah, to Whom eternal praise is due, Who came in the flesh and the blood: He has been for more than seventy years making Himself ready for the final war.

Allah, to Whom be praised, comes in the person of Master W.F. Muhammad, the Great Mahdi, expected by the Muslims, and the anti- Christ (the devils) under the names: Son of Man, Jesus Christ, Messiah, God, Lord, Jehovah, the Last (Jehovah) and the Christ. These meanings are good and befitting as titles, but the meaning of His name "Mahdi" as mentioned in the Holy Qur'an

Sharrieff 22:54 is better. All of these names refer to Him. His name, FARD MUHAMMAD, is beautiful in its meaning. He must bring an end to war, and the only way to end war between man and man is to destroy the war maker (the troublemaker).

According to the history of the White race (devils) they are guilty of making trouble; causing war among the people and themselves ever since they have been on our planet Earth. So the God of the righteous has found them disagreeable to live with in peace, and has decided to remove them from the face of the Earth. God does not have to tell us that they're disagreeable to live with in peace; we already know it, for we are the victims of these trouble-makers.

Allah will fight this war for the sake of His people (the Black people), and especially for the American so-called Negroes. As I have said time and again, we the so-called American Negroes, will be the lucky ones. We are Allah's choice to give life and we will be put on top of civilization.

THE DANGER OF TAKING ENEMIES FOR FRIENDS

6-6-59

"O, you who believe, do not take for intimate friends from among others than your own people; they do not fall short of inflicting loss upon you; they love what distresses you; vehement hatred has already appeared from out of their mouths, and what their hearts conceal is greater still. Indeed, we have made the communication clear to you if you will understand." (3:117).

WE, THE LOST and found members of the tribe of Shabazz (so-called Negroes), have for 400 years sought the friendship of our enemies - the white race, "the devils" - to the destruction of our own nation. The white race does not desire sincere friendship with black people. They may pretend to be your friends if you have something that they want, such as your women. Through her they corrupt your nation and bring it to disgrace before the nations of the earth, as they have done for the poor black people of America. Because of disunity among us and no control over our women, we stand by with folded arms, cowards to the core, and allow the human brute beast to take our women and little girls out of our arms, to beat, rape, and destroy the most priceless gift of a nation (its woman). We cannot produce a pure, chaste nation with a "free-for-all" woman. If we are too cowardly to protect her against the human beast's advances, we should kill ourselves and our women. This suicide of the race would get us more credit in the eyes of the civilized

385

nations of the earth than for us to continue to allow our girls and women to be corrupted by this human beast.

WE DO NOT love our girls and woman as we should. If we did, we would protect them as other nations do. We should compel all of our males under the oath of death, regardless of faith, to regain control and protect our black girls and women from being corrupted by both our enemies and non-enemies. The white race has made us to respect him and his women; now let us make them and all races respect us and our women. First, by self-respect. Second, with the help of Allah and our lives.

We are friends to everyone but self and kind. Our enemies love what distresses us; but we are like the next verse says that we are: "Lo, you are they who will love them while they do not love you." (3:118).

Allah, to Whom all praises are due, said that: "You love the devils because they give you nothing." That is so true. They lynch, burn, rape, beat and kill you; yet you love and want to be like them in every way. Their way of life will get you and me hell fire, for they were created for hell fire and know it. But, their greatest desires is to carry you with them.

MAN GOES TO hell or heaven in this life, and to the grave or earth after death. To love the devils is to be one of them and an enemy of God. There is a Bible teaching that: "God so loved the world (the Negroes) that He gave His only begotten Son that through Him (the Son) that they may have eternal life." This is misunderstood. Allah (God) has never and never will give a prophet's (a son's) life to save the world of devils. That scripture refers to the so-called Negroes, who were born and reared up in the devil's world, who must now be redeemed by the God of Righteous (the promised Mahdi) or one whom He will choose from among the so-called Negroes to be His apostle (Messenger). This man is the one the scripture refers to as the first begotten of the dead mentally dead so-called Negroes). He is also the first born of God because his first birth and teaching was of the devils, which is considered a dead race without eternal life, for the life of the devil race was limited to 6,000 years. So, the scripture makes a distinction between the races, or race and nation (black and white) by calling one (the devils) the dead or wicked, and the other (the original black nation), the people of eternal life; for the black nations have no limitation of life on the earth.

THE FINAL WAR AND THE CAUSE

Without a clear understanding of this FINAL WAR between right and wrong, my people the so-called Negroes) will all be lost, that the scripture might be fulfilled: "Destroyed for the lack of knowledge," (Hosea 4:6.) If Allah be with me, I do not want to see or hear that you were destroyed in the FINAL WAR because of the LACK OF KNOWLEDGE, for Almighty God, Allah, has given to me the truth, and I shall give the same to you. You will believe if you are made to understand the Scriptures. The devils are the cause of this most dreadful and frightful war, ever to be forced upon the Nations of earth, since it was created more than seventy trillion years ago.

I am so interested in the safety of my poor people here in America that I cannot hold peace. I have seen, I have heard it from His mouth, and He has made me to understand the words of His prophets of old - how it began and how it will end. There is no defense for anyone in this FINAL WAR between Allah (God) and the devils; only in Allah (God) alone will there be a place of refuge.

The earth itself will shake and tremble and seem as though she is frightened and desires to run away from the heat of the smelting elements that make up the atmosphere over North America. All life and water clouds above shall disappear and will not again appear for one thousand years. South America will not escape the effect of that awful and dreadful destruction of her Sister, North America. The white race is exceedingly wise, but not wise enough to behave themselves as they should and be satisfied with the great blessings of God, in a large country of untold wealth, that her peace may be secure. How can she cease from making mischief and causing bloodshed when her father was a liar and a murderer (John 8:44)?

My poor people must know that there is no love or mercy for them in this people. They should stop allowing themselves to be deceived by this arch deceiver of the world, who is the chief troublemaker of all people on Earth.

It is the purpose of this FINAL WAR to rid the people of Allah (God) of these troublemakers who delight themselves in making war. These troublemakers beat and slay the innocent so-called Negroes without justice. As it is written concerning them: "Ye have lived in pleasure on the earth, and been wanton; ye have nourished your hearts as in a day of slaughter. Ye have condemned and killed the just; and he doth not resist you. (James 5:5,6). The above prophecy is fulfilled here between the slave master and his slaves (the so-called Negroes).

Regardless to how the devils slaughter and kill the poor so- called Negroes, they, like sheep, do not resist their murderers for fear of being murdered. If they would come to Allah and submit and believe in Him and His true religion Islam, they would not fear anymore and would have a "Mighty One" on their side against this blood-thirsty enemy. A God Who will answer their prayers when they pray.

The devil has deceived us about the true God. There's nothing to what he has taught us to believe in as God. It naturally does not exist - a spook for a god, and a dead prophet of two thousand years ago, whom they want you to believe is somewhere in a heaven, alive. Nothing could be worse, and the people believe it without any proof. I would like to make you prove such a false doctrine or suffer the consequences. There is no such thing as a Heaven nor Hell for one to go to after death. This is one of the first lies Yakub taught his made devils to teach to the people (you and me. Even to this day, there are millions of people believing such a lie. These are two conditions in our life: Heaven and Hell - not beyond the grave. DEATH SETTLES IT ALL!

THE GUILTY

11-15-62

What can the guilty say when the truth of their guilt is made known? I have been teaching for over 31 years what Almighty Allah (God) has revealed to me of the truth of this subject. The origin of sin, the origin of murder, the origin of lying, a deception originated with the originators of evil and injustice - the White Race. I am sick, tried, and worn out with suffering from the persecutions cast against me and my people by the hands of the most wicked and deceiving race that have ever lived on our planet. I say as David in his Psalms: "Oh Lord persecute them and take them." None of them are righteous - no not one - they are ever seeking to do you and me harm every second of the day and night.

They (White Race are not hostile towards me because I am a Muslim and because I am teaching the true religion, Islam, to my people and the worship of the true and living God who is not a spook, but flesh and blood (Allah). They are hostile against me and my followers because we are of the Original Black Race who they were created to hate from the very beginning of their existence 6,000 years ago. They were not created to love or respect any member of the darker nations, for they are by nature, as Almighty Allah has taught me, incapable of loving themselves! They cannot love Allah and His religion, Islam, for it is against their nature to submit to Allah, the Lord of the worlds. All manner of evil and corruption have come from the White Race.

Though we as a people have become affected by over 400 years of contact with this race of devils, we have become like them in many ways; but we are not by nature evil or unrighteous. For we are not a grafted product from any other race, so we are not weak physically or mentally toward doing evil.

Almighty God, Allah, has appeared in the Western Hemisphere (North America) to tear off the voices of this wicked nation for their evils committed against our people, the so-called Negroes. We have been living under the God of darkness while in the absence of the God of light. In the same way that the light of day appears to put out the black of night, so it is that Almighty Allah has come with Truth to cast out and destroy falsehood. As long as the Devil is on our planet, we will continue to suffer injustice, unrest and no peace.

The guilty who have spread evilness and corruption throughout the land must face the sentence wrought by their own hands. I am offering you from Allah a Kingdom of Righteousness that will never decay; a New World that will be based upon the principles of Truth and Justice while we live.

THE GREAT DECEIVER

My greatest desire is to deliver the message of truth, that Allah has revealed, to my people (the lost and found members of the tribe of Shabazz), who are blind, deaf and dumb to the knowledge of self and others; owned and reared by the world's greatest deceivers that the original nation of earth has ever seen, and never will see the like after them the Caucasian race. Allah has revealed the real truth of this race, and also the so-called Negroes. Allah has said to me that the end of this race has come, and the time of the rise of the original nation (the Black Nation and the return of their lost-found members the so-called Negroes) in America, who were robbed and spoiled by our enemies (the slave masters and their children.

The time is now, not to come but has come. The arch-deceives know too that this is the time of the rise and return of the so- called Negroes to their own. They are not losing any time in trying to prevent this rise of their four-hundred-year-old property (the so-called Negroes) who originally did not belong to them, but after kidnapping them from their own people and native land, for the past four hundred years they have robbed the slaves of the knowledge of self, God, His religion, and other nations of earth. They also call them after their names, such as; Bird, Fish, Bear, Cat, Roundtree, Wood, Brier, Gnat Sawyer and Waters. Such silly names for human beings - these are what the lost-found members of God's people are being called. Allah (God) desires to give the so-called Negroes eternal names after his own, while the Caucasian race's names, which are not of God, shall perish from the face of the earth - so has Allah said to me. The devils, being aware and having a thorough knowledge or the time, are now tricking the American so-called Negroes into following them to their DOOM, which is now at their very door, even after my many hard years of teaching and warning them to believe in Allah, and His religion of Peace, Islam.

The fear and love of the devils by my people (the so-called Negroes) make it all the harder to teach them the truth and their salvation. As much hell, beating, murdering; the killing of both fathers, sons, mothers, and daughters, the denying of Justice the lynching and burning of both Negro men and women by the hands of this devil race of people, the blind, deaf, and dumb poor scared Negroes of America are today (the Days of Judgment of these enemies of Allah. Truth, Justice, and Righteousness) losing their lives for the love of their open enemies, and murderers. These Universal deceivers of the Black man, the robbers and spoiler of the so-called Negroes, are now even intermarrying with them. The wise Serpents (the devils) know fully their time and end is here; they are making a great false show of love for our foolish black women knowing that through her, they might be able to get the black man to follow them to their doom. This shows how dumb the poor Negroes are in America, though they are no more forsaken, and no longer lost from their people. The devils' universal show of temptation to deceive the Negroes and all black people is now being displayed in the eyes of the world. The filthy love songs, the filthy dancing, and the display of half-naked women and girls of their race in the public eye, without the slightest sign of shame - on the TV, public halls, and shows. The Negroes, following after them, up to their necks in a hell of filth, shame and disgrace before the face of the intelligent being of God, are now stinking in His Holy nostrils. We, the Muslims, are hated and despised by this evil and filthy world, and the devils hope to destroy us but Allah is the Greatest and I am His servant.

THE RICH MAN AND THE BEGGAR

We must remember that we just cannot depend on the white race ever to do that which we can and should do for self. The American so-called Negroes are like the Bible story of Lazarus and the rich man, the story that Jesus must have foreseen in mind at the time. This Bible beggar was charmed by the wealth of the rich man to whom he was a servant, and he could not make up his mind to go seek something for self.

This beggar was offered a home in Paradise but could not make up his mind to leave the gate of his master, the rich man, wishing for that which God had in store for destruction along with its owner. The beggar's eye could not turn from that perishable wealth. So it is with the American Negroes, they are charmed by the luxury of their slave master, and cannot make up their minds to seek for self something of this good earth, though hated and despised by the rich man and full of sores caused by the evil treatment of the rich man. On top of that he is chased by the rich man's dogs and still remained a beggar at the gate, though the gates of Paradise were ever open to him and the gates of hell were open to receive his rich master.

The American Negroes have the same gates of Paradise open to them, but are charmed by the wealth of America, and cannot see the great opportunity that lies before them. They are suffering untold injustices at the hand of the rich; he has and still is being lynched and burned, he and his woman and children are beaten all over the country by the rich slave masters and their children; the slave's houses and churches are bombed by the slave masters, his girls are used as prostitutes, and at times are raped in the public's eyes; yet, the Negroes are on their knees begging the rich man to treat them as the rich man treats himself and kind. The poor beggar kindly asks for the crumbs, a job or a house in the neighborhood of the rich man.

The Negro leaders are frightened to death, and are afraid to ask for anything other than a job. The good things of this earth could be his if he would only unite and acquire wealth as his master and other independent nations have; the Negroes could have all of this if they would get up and go to work for self. They are far too lazy as a Nation, 100 years up from slavery still looking to the master to care for them and give them a job, bread, and a house to live in on the master's land. You should be ashamed of yourself, surely the white race have been very good in the way of making jobs for their willing slaves, but this cannot go on forever; we are about at the end of it and must do something for Self or else.

The slave master have given to you enough education to go and do for self, but this education is not being used for self, it is even offered back to the slave masters to help them to keep you a dependent people looking to them for support. Let us unite every good that is in us for the up lifting of the American so-called Negroes to the equal of the world's independent nations. Ask for a start for self and the American white people, I believe, are willing to help give us a start if they see you and I are willing to do for self. It would remove from them not only the worry of trying to give jobs and schools to a lazy people, but also would get them honor and sincere friendship all over the

Asiatic world, and God, Himself, would prolong their time upon the earth.

THE SO-CALLED NEGROES IN AMERICA

IN A SMALL monthly paper printed in Morris Plains, NJ, in the language of true Moslem Shriners, the following appeared in the January 1959 issue:

It says: "The greatest shame upon the escutcheon of America, is its treatment of Negroes. These Americans are here because their forefathers were ruthlessly kidnapped in Africa, herded into suffocating ships, chained, beaten and sold into slavery.

"Much white blood is in the veins of American Negroes. Southern aristocrats had children by Negro women (and are still getting them by the Negro woman). Union occupation armies fathered many children by Negro women. Those fierce racists opposing the inevitable dawn of justice for Negroes ironically are fighting their own flesh and blood.

"These persecuted descendants of slaves go right on (like fools) defending the democracies of (white) Americans. Ralph Bunche, Negro Noble Prize winner, UN Under Secretary, refused an invitation to become U.S. Assistant Secretary of State because Washington, D.C., had Jim-crow laws.

"American Negroes dress American, talk American, live American, die American. Over a million Negro soldiers took up arms for America in World War II (some 400,000 fought for America in 1917).

"Dead Negro American are buried with white soldiers on every Revolutionary War battle field, only to be denied justice by the white soldiers of America (the Government). The first (fool) American patriot killed in the Boston Massacre was a Negro. The first (fool) woman to fight in the American Army was a Negro who disguised herself as a man to fight for America's independence.

"NEGROES paid the crimson cost of liberty at Antietam, Vicksburg, San Juan Hill, the Argonne, Chateau Theirry, Leyte Gulf, the Ardennes Bulge, Aizio Beachhead, Iwo Jima, Hungnam, the Yalu and Inchon Reservoir.

"Every other tie on the road-bed of the Union Pacific and the DL&W is the worked-out, sweated-out body of a Negro. The fiery tongues of molten iron pouring out of American Negro workers.

"And without recrimination. They sang `Swing Low Sweet Chariot' and `Come Down Sweet Jesus' as they lifted and existed on next to nothing, lived in unsanitary firetraps, ghettoed, Jim-crowed.

`Negro Americans can be the deciding factor in world power. Today two-thirds of the world are `people of color.' It further takes a snap at Masonry which the Negroes buy, seeking justice and respect as a man and as the brother of man in these words: "If Masonry is for light, then there can be no lamp-shade on its light. If the brotherhood of man is all-inclusive-not a cruel joke-then Masonry must be honest with itself or go down as history's great mockery."

THE SO-CALLED Negroes are tools in the hands of their enemies and were made blind, deaf and dumb by their enemies (the slave masters) when they were babies. Yet they think their devil enemies are their friends. They give their lives for their enemies to be free to keep them subjects, beaten, lynched, raped and killed. They help the white devils destroy their own women by giving her all the freedom she wants in their homes, stores, restaurants, hotels, offices, factories, farms and as baby- sitters. They strip her before the devils and ask the devils to accept her, and she foolishly accepts the devil to destroy her family's morals and to spot her children with the devil's blood, even after having knowledge that the same white man will not give her and her men-folk justice in any court.

Negro Masons, do not buy the white man's masonry. There is no brotherhood there for you. It is only a farce of justice. Come and accept the real Islam, the Muslim. I am the door. I will let you in. For our slavery, sweat, blood and life, one-half of America is not enough as pay.

THE ST. NICHOLAS ARENA NEW YORK CITY

ON Sunday, July 26, 1959- First- We thank Allah (God) for the safe trip there and return, and for the peace and protection we enjoyed. Second - We thank the people of New York, and especially the nearly ten thousand who greeted us with such warm welcome at the St. Nicholas Arena, 69 West 66th St., Downtown, New York. Thanks to the police department for their presence. Of course, there is very little work for the police officer among us. Wherever we go, there is peace. My people are good. This was my second public lecture in New York City. Last July, 1958, was my first. On that visit, we were received by an estimated seven thousand people who jammed the hall for the two days that we were in the city.

Harlem has the most, and best race - minded people in America. There you will find the Black man who wants something of his own for which he can be proud of. They welcome you if you have a sound program for the people. They are a wonderful people. Once Harlem is united into the Brotherhood of Islam, she could command the whole twenty million American dark people. She only needs to rid herself of worthless orators who have no constructive program for this half of a million dark people.

WE, THE NATION of Islam, have been given that constructive program, and by all means, we intend to give it to our people in Harlem, New York. The readiness in the eyes and actions of the people of Harlem tell you and me that these people are now ready for something which they can proudly call their own. If it be the Will of Allah,

407

I will visit my Harlem people again within two or three weeks, for it would be a shame on the part of the Brotherhood of Islam to leave this great half-million people to be exploited by hungry want-to-be leaders without a constructive program.

Last Sunday, I wanted to spend my time in making clear to Harlem our program, but having to defend false charges made against me by the enemies of teaching hate - (the white race is the father of hate) - I did not have time to tell my people all that God wanted me to tell them. The enemies of our people see and know that it is time for the rise of our people, and are seeking every evil and deceitful way to prevent it. The Shepherd must forever be on his guard to show up the wolf, whose only desire is to eat the sheep. Our enemies desire to make the truth, which will free our people from the power of their enemies, and which will sit them in heaven at once, look so dangerous that they will fear to accept it.

GOD HAS FOR our people here in America the greatest blessing that ever was bestowed on any people at any time in the past. He wants to make us the permanent rulers of the earth. He wants to give to us the Kingdom. The so-called Negroes must not follow an Uncle Tom for their leader. They just do not relieve you of the yoke, for their greatest desire is to please the slave master and leave you displeased. In this enlightened world of today, the slave master's Tom, Boot-lickers, and stool pigeons we cannot use, and must weed them out from among us as other nations have, and still are doing. They are the hold back of our progress among us. Remove them or isolate them and enjoy success. We have a few who are being paid to keep the enemies well informed of all we say. One day they will be out. The poor man in the mud is my friend. His friend is Allah and myself, and five hundred million Muslims all over the world.

THE TRUTH PART IV

3-15-62

The devils hope to deceive the lost-found people of the Asiatic Nation, the tribe of Shabazz (the American so-called Negroes). The truth should prevent the devils from deceiving the black man, and it will if the black man would only listen to the Truth.

On the 25th of this month (February 1962) between 10,000 and 12,000 people attended our annual Convention. Many different nationalities attended and all seemed to have been pleased with what they saw and heard.

Only one of our professional black Toms expressed his desire to be nothing but an American (white). Almost all the intellectuals in America are poisoned against their own.

They Love Intermixing

They love intermixing the imitating our enemies, the devils. They have enough education to build a self-independent nation, but they have been schooled and patted on the shoulder by their slave masters.

They are in love with their slave master and forsake the society of their own people. They seek membership into the society of white America who cannot intelligently accept them without losing her self-respect.

The slave and the master are not equal. It is time for the freedom, and freedom indeed, of the so-called American Negroes. They are divinely destined to become the universal ruler of tomorrow. Read Deut. 28:13, 44. Matt. 13:31; Luke 15:24; Matt. 18:12, 13.

Know Future of Slaves

White Americans are well aware of the future of their slaves. They hope to deceive and make the slave remain with them and receive the Divine Wrath of Allah (hell fire). They are working very fast since they have learned that Allah and the Truth (Islam) has come for us that Allah (God) is now naming us (calling us by His Holy Name).

My people should be well schooled into all the trucks these devils are playing or intend to play on them in these days of the Resurrection. If you were out to the International Amphitheater, 42nd and Halstead on the 25th, you saw and heard between 10,000 and 12,000 people voice their approval of Allah's (God's) program of salvation for the so-called Negroes.

A program of salvation for the lost-found sons and daughters of the members of the Tribe of Shabazz, whom their slave masters call after their names and the name NEGRO which means no future. The white man cannot be accepted in this day and time under any one of the attributes (Names) of Allah (God). N E G R O also means something that is dead or neutral, neuter gender. It means something that is not either this nor that and will have to be told what to do or carried to that which you want it to do (dead, or neutral).

Blasts Len O'Connor

As I sat and listen to radio and listened to radio and television broadcasts of our Convention, some tried to make the public believe that there were only about 3,000 out to this great meeting.

A certain television commentator, by the name of Len O'Connor, wishes to deceive the so-called Negroes by calling me after my grandfather's devil slave master's name which was Poole, instead of my right, God-given, Nation name of Muhammad.

The devils want you to remain in their names which means you are their property. What other reason would they have in trying to force you into being called after their names: Their names represent something other than human and are not Divinely given.

The devils swore to God (Holy Quran 7:16,17) that they would deceive us and make us become deserving of hell fire with them. Read in the Holy Quran and Bible of the tricks they are now pulling on you.

The things we must have is some of this good earth for a home. We must unite and do something for self. We must raise food for self and others, clothe our nakedness and shelter ourselves from out of doors.

413

THE TRUTH HAS COME

5-2-59

"Say: The truth has come and the falsehood shall vanish. It neither creates nor reproduces anything new, nor restores anything; it shall not come back." (Holy Qur'an 34:49.)

WHAT has falsehood created or produced in the heaven and earth? We are now living in the time of truth, and falsehood cannot survive in the light of truth any more than darkness can survive in the presence of light. Allah has revealed the truth to me, and I am teaching it to you, but you do not believe it because of your love an fear of the slave-masters. They too will be made to lick the dust, by the power of Allah. There never has been an enemy of His that He lacked power to rid Himself of. Neither does Allah lack power to rid Himself and the Nation of Islam of this enemy that you fear and love; though you are even disgraced, beaten and killed by them, from your ministers of their slavery religion (Christianity) down to the lowly, ignorant man in the mud.

YOU HAVE MADE yourselves the most foolish people on the earth by loving and following after the ways of slave masters, whom Allah has revealed to me to be none other than real devils, and that their so-called Christianity is not His religion, nor the religion of Jesus or any other Prophet of Allah (God). You are a hard-headed, stiff-necked, rebellious people who are proud of your enemies and their slavery religion.

Allah is now sending the devils against you, that you may learn that His word is true, that they are heartless.

Although they may do me and my followers evil, but by my Allah, they will not able to get away with it; for every harm done to or against us will be returned doubly and tripled. Allah (God) is with me in person to bless you and me with right guidance and protection if we believe and rely on Him; otherwise, He can do us evil.

ALLAH (God) has not come to bring about love and peace between us and the devils (our slave-masters), but rather to separate and make manifest to you and me our open enemies, the enemies of God and His prophets. We are now living in the judgment of this evil world of the devils, and the separation of the Bible's symbolic goats and sheep is now in effect. How blind you are, unable to see the truth, though it is like sunshine.

Do you not see and hear how your people of Africa from whom you were taken 400 years ago are separating themselves from the same enemy and establishing themselves into a united Africa for the African? Do you think the spirit of unity was created by themselves? No, it is the work of Allah to fulfill all that is written of Him by His prophets that He would do in these last days of the devils' world. (It is in your Bible.) If you are afraid of the truth, then how can truth help you when you disbelieve and are afraid of it? For such, the truth becomes your enemy.

ALLAH HAS revealed the truth of Jesus and His religion - that he was only a prophet (and was not the equal of Moses and Muhammad), and His religion was Islam, and not the Christianity of the Pope of Rome. Allah also revealed that Jesus was sent to the Jews and the Jews rejected him; therefore, he was unable to lead or convert them to Allah's religion, Islam, and that he died for his failure to accomplish that which he desired to do.

The truth of Jesus' death and burial God has revealed, and has condemned the fancy story of your Bible, of Jesus' rising from death and is somewhere alive sitting on the right hand of His father waiting for the judgment of this world to return to earth again. No one after death has ever gone any place but where they were carried. There is no heaven or hell other than on the earth for you and me, and Jesus was no exception. His body is still embalmed in Palestine and will remain there. Truth has come and false will vanish.

THE WHITE RACE'S FALSE CLAIM OF DIVINITY

THERE are several false teachers sponsored by the devil to deceive the black people by misinterpreting the truth in their favor, especially the Bible's teachings. Most of the white teachers of the Bible make the white race God's divine people. (Adam's race, Israel). These white teachers (beware of them) would love to have you and me (that is, if they could) believe that they are the beloved people of God. Their false claim is easily disproved. But, since they are the deceivers of the black nation, naturally, the so-called Negroes who were reared and taught all they know by white slave masters are made easy victims to such false teachings and claims.

The Bible itself, being tampered with and poisoned by them is made to read as though the salvation in it is for the white race. The so-called Negroes who are the real chosen people of God today are not mentioned under their name. The name "Israel" is used to blind the black people, especially the American so-called Negroes. For example: Mr. Herbert Armstrong of Pasadena, Calif., a radio and TV preachers, and Theodore Fitch of Council Bluff, Iowa., the author and writer of a small 56-page book titled: "Our Lord's Plan for the White Race," with a sub-title, "Who we are? Where we came from? Why he chose us? What our work is? Why our descendants must remain white?" These questions I will truthfully answer.

MR. FITCH is against the mixing of race (intermarriage) which he calls "an awful sin," of which I, or any sane

417

lover of his or her own people, will agree. Mr. Fitch does not seem to know himself and race. Of course, the true knowledge of the white race was first revealed in 1930-1933 by Almighty God, in the person of W.F. Muhammad, the God and Saviour of the American so-called Negroes. To him I submit and give praise all the days of my life.

Mr. Fitch and others will agree that Adam and Jacob (Yakub) was the father of the white race. Adam, according to the Bible (Gen. 3:6) Holy Qur'an (2:30), was the first sinner and divine law- breaker, liar, mischief-maker, murderer and world deceiver. As for Jacob (Yakub) whose name was changed to Israel (Bible-Gen. 33:28) because he wrestled with the Angel and did prevailed, according to the world and teaching of Allah (God) to me, the only Angel that Jacob (Yakub) wrestled with was the black man, to bring out of the black man the present white race - for the white race was and is in the germ of the black nation.

Mr. Yakub was the first to discover this germ in us and grafted this germ of the black man into an independent race of people. Mr. Yakub taught his people how to rule the black nation for 6,000 years. Their time expired in 1914, but they have been given an extension of time, until the black man could be awakened out of his 6,000 year sleep; so as to restore the American black people (the real lost-found members of their people) onto their own kind.

JACOB (YAKUB) the great deceiver who deceived his own father and brother (Gen. 27:19,35,36) robbed his father-in-law, Laban, of his cattle (Gen. 30:37-43, 31:12). This Mr. Fitch would like to deceive you in making you to believe that the white race is the chosen people of god and Jesus. This is not true, and I will disprove it.

Herbert Armstrong would like that we believe that the white race, even after they are punished for their sins, will yet be chosen by God to be the rulers. If it pleases Allah, I will defend my people with His truth, and make the devils' falsehoods manifest to the world.

The white race is not a divine chosen race. It is the black nation. The so-called Negroes of America are really God's choice to build the kingdom of peace on earth. The Negroes are the lost sheep of the Bible and not Israel. The white race has built a world of evil and bloodshed. We could not build our world in the time given to them to rule. We had to wait until their time was up.

THE WHITE MAN'S CLAIM TO DIVINE SUPERIORITY

7-4-59

THE TRUTH that the world has been waiting to know is just the answers to the questions Mr. Fitch asked in his book titled, "Our Lord's Plan for the White Race" (the God of righteousness never had a plan for you), with a sub-title, "Who We Are?" (the enemies of God and the righteous); "Where We Came From?" (from the black man); "Why He Chose Us?" (the God of righteousness did not choose you; if He had, He would not destroy you); "What Our Work Is?" (evil); "Why Our Descendants Must Remain White?" (certainly, you should remain white).

The average so-called Negroes would be misled by Mr. Fitch and his answers to such questions if it were not that Allah (God) had visited us and revealed the true knowledge of the white race. The best of it all, He is making the white race manifest to the world of the original black nation that they are our enemies, the devils, and that their father (Yakub) that created them is also classified as the father (Yakub) of the devil race because of his idea and making of the devils.

SINCE THE truth of the devils has been revealed, the devils are still trying to hide their true selves in order to fool the black man and woman, and especially the American so-called Negroes, whom the white man has fooled for 400 years-and mean to keep them fooled regardless to the truth. But, as it is written: "The truth would be made so plain that a fool should not err."

"What I teach you that Allah has taught me is just that plain. You that read what I write, and you that listen to what you hear me say of the truth, cannot have an excuse for a misunderstanding; for there is none. I leave nothing for you to be misled in. If you are blind to this, you will be blind in the hereafter.

"Who are the white race?" I have repeatedly answered that question in this article for nearly the past three years. "Why are they white-skinned?" Answer: Allah (God) said this is due to being grafted from the original black nation, as the black man has two germs (two people) in him. One is black and the other brown. The brown germ is weaker than the black germ. The brown germ can be grafted into its last stage, and the last stage is white. A scientist by the name of Yakub discovered this knowledge (that white could be grafted out of black) 6,645 years ago, and was successful in doing this job of grafting after 600 years of following a strict and rigid birth control law.

WHITE IS not a superior color by nature to black, but it is inferior. If you allow them to teach you the truth of themselves, you will never know the truth. Many white writers on the race and color issue today, which has become universal because of the whites' claim to divinity and superiority, claim that the color of the skin is due to certain climatic conditions, such as, hot Africa produces the black man; the cold. frigid zones above the equator produce the color white. This claim is as false as darkness is to light. Ask yourself these questions: If our colors are caused by certain climatic conditions of earth, why should not the white man become black in hot Africa, South and Central America? Also, why should not a black person turn white above the equator in the cold frigid zones of the north? If not, then beware of the devils' tricks on the truth of Allah (God). Does the climate of Japan and China make them brown and yellow? Did the climatic conditions of America make the Indians red? Then, why are we all not red?

THE WHITE RACE'S FALSE CLAIM TO DIVINITY

7-25-59

THE devil's struggle against us, their power, and authority, is now slipping since the appearance of Allah. Now they have begun to spread false teachings to trap the so-called Negroes. As soon as truth comes to them, they are prepared to try to crush it and keep their 400-year-old dumb slaves. It is actually a race between God and the devil to win the American so-called Negroes. Allah wants to sit the Negroes in heaven and the devil wants to keep them in hell. As it is written of them:

"And the serpent (the devil) cast out of his mouth (false) water as a flood after the woman, (the Messenger of Allah and his followers) that he might cause her to be carried away of the flood." (Rev. 12:15)

Here, you have that the devils will flood the people with false teachings to try to prevent the progress of the truth. But the falsehood is destined to come to naught, for God has revealed to me the truth - it is the salvation of my people. With it, I will fight the world of Satan and his followers until they submit and are destroyed. (The white race hates the truth that is now making them manifest for fear of losing the Negroes).

The Lord God of Islam is my defense. He will defend me against my enemies. He loves me and I love Him because I seek to do His will, and He knows that I love my people, whom He loves, and has come to deliver us from the power of the devils, that we may become His servant, and dwell in His presence in peace and security.

THE DEVILS SAY to you that they are better than you and I. Really, they are after the so-called Negroes whom they have crushed, made blind, deaf and dumb. They have robbed and experimented on us for 400 years, and all other darker people whom they have come in contact. Now they stand before you saying, "I am better than you." As he says in the Holy Qur'an: "I am better than he; thou hast created me of fire, while him thou didst create of dust." (7:12)

According to the world of Allah to me, the white race was created in haste. (See Chapter 21:37). Their father, Yakub, was in such a hurry to put his new people on earth as rulers, that he married them while very young (15 and 16 years of age). Knowing that they had only 6,000 years to go, he rushed them, so says the world of Allah to me. This makes them hasty by nature. They have a fiery temperament; while the original black man is meek and humble. They were made to attract the black people. With this attraction, and other actions of evil and filth, they intended to take you to hell with them. As they say: I will certainly lie in wait for them in Thy straight path; I will certainly come to them from before them and from behind them and from their right hand and from their left hand; and Thou shalt not find most of them thankful. And the devil swore to them both; most-surely, I am a sincere adviser to you." (7:12,16,17,21)

MR FITCH, in his book (page 28) states that they the white race, are much stronger physically, mentally, spiritually, and morally. I will agree that on an average they are larger in stature than we are; but, they cannot out-work us if we want to work. They claim 60 per cent more brain space than we. This is not true. They are not as wise as we are. Our father created and made the universe, and one of us made them. As we made the present universe, we will build a new universe. Can the white scientists do the same? We played sleep while they worked; now we are awaking and will build a new world which will make yours look like child's play. We have above you seven inhabited worlds - they are with us These seven worlds or heavens, the stars and the moon show the weight of our brains. What do you have that we did not give you? You shall soon come to know who is the wisest and the most powerful.

THE WHITE RACE'S FALSE CLAIM TO BE DIVINE CHOSEN PEOPLE

ACCORDING to the Bible (Gen. 3:20-24), Adam and his wife were the first parents of all people (white race only) and the first sinners. According to the Word of Allah, he was driven from the Garden of Paradise into the hills and caves of West Asia, as they now call it, "Europe," to live his evil life in the West and not in the Holy Land of the East. "Therefore, the Lord God sent him (Adam) forth from the Garden of Eden, to till the ground from whence he was taken. So he drove out the man; and He placed at the east of the Garden of Eden Cherubims (Muslim guards) and a flaming sword which turned every way to keep (the devils out) the way of the tree of life (the nation of Islam)." The sword of Islam prevented the Adamic race from crossing the border of Europe and Asia to make trouble among the Muslims for 2,000 years after they were driven out of the Holy Land and people, for their mischief-making, lying and disturbing the peace of the righteous nation of Islam.

The Holy Qur'an says:

> *"But the devil made them both fall from it, and caused them to depart from that (state) in which they were; and we said: Get forth, some of you being the enemies of others, and there is for you in the earth an abode and a provision for a time."*

(The time here refers to the limited time of the Adamic race. The time is 6,000 years). According to the above verse (2:36), they were driven out because they were the enemies of the people of the Garden, in these words: "Get

429

forth, some of you being the enemies of others." The "others" cannot refer to any others than the people of the Garden (the Muslims).

THE ADAMIC RACE is still the enemy of the Muslims (the black man). Nevertheless, Allah did not deprive the Adamic race of right guidance through His prophets, whom they persecuted and killed. The Adamic race's (the white race) history is a proof that they are the enemies of God and the righteous, for they never did sincerely accept a prophet of God. Can they now claim to be the chosen race of God? Where is their proof? Is it because they were allowed to rule us for 6,000 years? If they are the chosen race of God, why would God limit their time of rule? Why did God send His prophets to warn them that He was going to destroy them? Holy Qur'an (7:14):

"He said (the devil), respite me until the day when they are raised up."

Those that are referred to as being "raised up" refer to the resurrection of the black man into the knowledge of the white race as being the devils, the enemies of Allah (God) and the black nation.

"He said (the devil), as Thou hast caused me to remain disappointed, I will certainly lie in wait for them in Thy straight path." (Holy Qur'an 7:166).

What Allah disappointed the devils in was the limiting of their rule over the nations and making them manifest to the world of black men that they are the enemies and great deceivers of the righteous.

The white race is not, and never will be, the chosen people of Allah (God). They are the chosen people of their father (Yakub, the devil).

TRUTH IS CONFIRMED

"And the devil will say, when the matter is decided: Surely Allah promised a promise of TRUTH, and I promised you, then failed you, and I had no AUTHORITY over you, except that I called you and you obeyed: so blame me not but blame yourselves. I cannot come to your help, nor can you come to my help. I deny your associating me with Allah before. Surely for the unjust is a painful chastisement." - *Holy Qur'an 14:22).*

The time of the fulfilling of the above verse of the Qur'an is now going on among the so-called Negroes and their slave-master's children. It is the greatest desire of the devil: to deceive the people of God against the Truth and God's Messenger of Truth. The poor American so-called Negroes were born and reared by this great enemy (The Devil) of Allah and the Truth. They (the so- called Negroes) do not see nor know God, the devil, or even themselves. Therefore, spiritually, they are called blind, deaf, and dumb. They cannot see nor hear the Truth. The vicious enemy, the devil, has them scared to death. He put fear in the Negroes when they were babies, four hundred years ago - says Almighty God Allah.

The devil will not confess the Truth until he has no alternative - he has already deceived those who follow him. At the present time, nearly 90% of my people in America are following the devil and are actually unaware of it. It is almost hopeless, when it comes to trying to make them understand. They will even turn against you, their friend and sincere well-wisher, to the inducement of the devil's empty promises.

The devil in the above verse, is not a spirit, but a human being who is in the flesh and blood as you are: "the Caucasian race." The above verse, take and keep it before

433

your eyes as a warning, for it is TRUE. They will soon confess that Allah's is true, and that I , Elijah Muhammad, am His Messenger,, and that I have brought to you the true promises of Allah (God), but you are denying them for the false promises of the devil. You have taken the devil to be the equal of Allah (God), and when the showdown comes he (the devil) will deny misleading you. Note (the above words): "I called you and you obeyed me," though he had no authority over the believers of the Truth (Islam), but he did know that they were afraid of him from the cradle, and that if he called them they would be afraid to disobey his call.

It is a very dangerous time in which we are living in to ignore the Truth, when it means your life or death. The great tricknowledge (their false friendship and promises) which is being played on you by the Caucasian race, and especially your slave-master's children, you should not accept.

I have brought you the Truth and the True promise of Allah (God), believe it, and He will save you from fear and grief. See, and read Chapter 7:21 of the Holy Qur'an (a most true scripture) where the devil swears that he is a sincere adviser.

"And he swore to them surely I am a sincere adviser to you."

The white race rejects the religion of Islam, its God, and Holy Book (Quire- an), because it is a Universal Truth, and that both the Arab Prophet Muhammad and Jesus were dark men, and brothers of the darker Nation, though they (the white race) naturally object being a follower of a black prophet.

TRUTH AND JUSTICE FOR THE SO-CALLED NEGROES

Allah (God) has come to us to give to you and me truth and justice and to sit you in heaven at once. But our enemies have ever kept the truth and justice from us and have never, never given justice to the so-called Negroes. To prove their hatred and wicked, unjust rule over us, they are out to prevent that truth and justice from getting to you by using the old trick on us--"divide the Negroes- use one against the other."

The world knows that I am teaching you the truth and most of all, desire justice for my people in America, with whom I have suffered all of my life. Allah (God) has given to me the key to loosen them from the power and bondage of our ever-relentless, merciless, evil, indecent murderers, our open enemies, the devil slave masters; so that our people maybe free indeed and know their God, Allah (our only true friend) and their enemies (the devils), who have deceived them and the world of the black nation.

This truth and justice preached to the blind, deaf and dumb of my people in America is hated by the white race of America, and they would like to fool my people and make them hate me and the truth, which will free them by teaching hate. They know that the Negroes are already fools for loving them, and they would be worse fools to love them after having knowledge of them being the real devils.

THIS IS that TRUTH which the white race and their black lovers call hate teachings-THE TRUTH OF GOD AND THE DEVILS. We must know the truth and must have justice for our people. If not, it would be better to commit suicide than to continue to be slowly destroyed by our white slave masters' children. They make fools and Uncle Toms out of all of our educated professional class of people with a false show of social equality.

We, the so-called Negroes, must and will have what other nations have for themselves - some of this God-given earth that we can call our own, and protection for our wives and children from the murderous and raping hand of the American devils. We love our women and children as other nations love their women and children. We must have good homes to live in and protection for those homes, or die trying to get it. We will never enjoy peace, freedom, justice and equality under our enemies (the white race), for there is no justice and peace in that race.

IN THIS MODERN day and time, we should know that love and unity FIRST among our own kind is the key to power, justice and equality. But envy of those who can do, from those who cannot do, are the hindering causes of the black man. Talid Ahmad Dawud and his TV blues-singing Miss Dakota Staton (who the paper says is Mrs. Alijah Rabia Dawud in private life) and whom the world can hear her filthy blues and love songs and see her immodestly dressed, were successful last week in getting a chance to breathe their venomous poison against me and my followers in this paper and in a local Chicago paper, The Crusader. Mr. Dawud is from the West Indies (Antigua) and was born a British subject. He was known by the name Rannie (sounds like a devil's name). He is jealous of the progress with which Allah (to Whom praises are due) is blessing me and my followers, and this jealousy is about to run Mr. Dawud insane. (The Crusader erroneously called him an Imam.) Mr. Dawud and Miss Staton should have been ashamed to try to make fun of me and my followers while publicly serving the devil in the theatrical world. I do not allow my followers to visit such, nor do I allow my wife and the believing women who follow me to go before the public partly dressed. If they would, never would I claim them to be mine any more.

MR. DAWUD has been trying for some time to do me and my followers harm in the Islamic world through the Muslim Embassy in this country and abroad, but he is only hurting himself.

THE FOUNDATION YEARS OF ELIJAH MUHAMMAD VOLS. 1 & 2

UNIVERSAL BROTHERHOOD

5-20-59

IT IS the aim of Allah with His religion called Islam (Peace) to unite the world of darker people into one single nation of brotherhood. The lost-found members of the darker people (so- called American Negroes) must first be resurrected into the knowledge of Self, God, and the devil before they can recognize the importance of this plan of Allah (God) to unite the darker people of earth. This Universal Brotherhood cannot be a success unless we all believe in one God and one religion; and that one God is Allah, and that one religion is Islam (the only unifying religion of the human family of earth, and the only true religion of God).

We cannot successful unite under any other religion. Christianity and the Church, as we know it, after a hundred years of experience in it, is not a unifying religion for the darker people. Really, it has failed to unite the white race, for they are at war with each other. The power of the Divine Spirit of God in Islam makes such sincere love for the brother believer that war or fighting among them is made impossible. When the so- called Negroes in America learn more about this unifying brotherhood religion called Islam, they too, will come into it by the thousands and millions. We have here in America today all groups, including my followers, a little over one-half of a million. All over the world over a half of a billion Muslims.

THE POOR BLACK man of America cannot and should not hope to have a sincere brotherhood with the white race. The nature of the races is opposed to it. This is why Allah must resurrect the darker people of America and teach them a knowledge of Self and others. The truth of it all is now being made manifest. Do not be surprised on learning that you were deceived in that which you have been believing to be the truth. We want unity of love, respect and protection. That can only be assured and enjoyed in the Universal Brotherhood of Islam and no other.

You should know today that you are a free people according to the Constitution of America, and should exercise this freedom to be free indeed of that which brought us into bondage to the white race. We must think for self, do for self, protect self by unity of self and kind in the Universal Brotherhood of Islam. We must be a people seeking and accepting that which has the power to unite us and give protection for our unity. That power and protection can only be had and enjoyed with your belief in Allah and the Universal Brotherhood of Islam - this the white race knows. But, do not wait for them to tell you, for that they may never do.

YOU ARE FREE to think and do for self. You will be disappointed in waiting on your slave masters to think and do for you after being made free. They are not responsible for our failure in uniting on to self and kind. Naturally, they will try you with threats and the loss of jobs, food, houses and prestige. This, God permits them to do that you may be tried, but fear not such threats and trials when your salvation and future are at stake. They have no future in the hereafter. Their future and peace ended in 1914, and because of the lack of knowledge on your part, they, today, live on borrowed time. Universal peace and protection await you on your acceptance of Allah in the Brotherhood of Islam.

UNIVERSAL CORRUPTION

4-18-59

"Corruption has appeared in the land and sea on account of what the hands of men have wrought, that he (Allah) may then taste a part of that which they have done" (Holy Qur'an 30:41).

We cannot deny the fact that the Christian West is responsible for this universal corruption in the land and sea. From the same corruption that their own hands have wrought will come their doom. The Christians preach that which they do not do, and cannot do. Such as "Love thy neighbor." I have yet to meet one that loved his neighbor as he did himself. "Thou shall not kill." I have as yet to meet such a Christian. They even fight against each other, rob and kill each other, but yet represent themselves as world peacemakers - with what?

The great deceiver of the world will reap what he has sown. Have they not corrupted many people and nations under the false disguise as good, peace - loving Christians? The Christian West is full of the worst crimes, practicing her evils and indecencies to the fullest, and they seek to practice them on other nations as well. Universal tempters, even parading before the world their bold, half-nude girls and women - they are before your eyes in almost everything, regardless. Murder, gambling, robbery, drunkenness, drugs, adultery, lying - there is hardly any end to it!

THEIR LAND and seas are filled with deadly weapons of war, her islands of the sea she has filled with her corruption. Now she is hated and despised by all the nations of earth, for she is proud and boastful and desires to rule all people according to her wishes. Her religion (Christianity) is a curse to us (the black man) which is fill of slavery teaching. They have poisoned the Bible with their adding in and out of the truth. Now her doom is in sight. It is their own work.

They fill the sea with powerful, deadly ships, parking them off shore of the homes of other nations. They secure air bases on foreign soil to park deadly bomb - carrying planes within striking distance of those whom she thinks to be her enemies. Is not this the easy way to make enemies? Is this the act of a real Christian, the follower of Jesus who they preach came for the peace of mankind and to teach the sheathing of the sword and the turning of the other cheek? Where is a good Christian among this race?

They love meddling in other people's affairs, they are in every fight or war, regardless of whom or where; but yet crying, "Peace, peace," with every deadly modern weapon of war, brandishing them before the nations as a dare. Shall not the God of Peace and Justice deal with such trouble-making people as he did to those before you of old?

I warn every one of you, my people, fly to Allah and follow me!
Hurry and join onto your own kind. The time of this world is at hand.

WE MUST HAVE SOME OF THIS EARTH THAT WE CAN CALL OUR OWN

We have found the word of Allah to be true: "the non-Muslim world is disagreeable to live with in peace!" We tried, when we did not know our enemies, to live with them in peace, and could not. It is impossible, says Allah to me.

The Great Day of Separation has begun - the separation of white and black. We were created separately. The Bible and Holy Quire- an prophesied of a great separation of the people at the end of the world. "The End of the World," referred to in the Bible and Holy Qur'an, is the present world, ruled by the Caucasian for the past 6,000 years; is not the world that the righteous and the Black Nation can live together in peace.

The separation of the two nations must take place to save the grieved Nation (the Black Nation.) We the so-called Negroes, have 400 years of experience among this disagreeable people, and have never been able to please them, even though they own the country (America). We, their slaves, cannot get along in peace with them. We suffer the most savage brutality and ill-treatment than any people on earth. We are the most loyal and obedient people to these murderous people who actually do not have any good in them. If the poor so-called Negro is lucky enough, by the Divine Will and Help, to acquire a little property, he is envied by his slave master's children. Today, they (the so- called Negroes) are begging, as

445

always, for equal Justice, and will get the same old empty promises.

We need to be separated and given a place on this earth that we can call OUR OWN. If America wants her free slaves to remain with her, then why not separate the two people and give your slaves a chance to go for Self, and load us into ships, and ship us back to our people and native land? There, we will live in peace with our own kind, as God intended from the beginning of Creation, for here, we are a Nation without a home that we can call our Own, and are surrounded by our enemies who by nature cannot, and will not give the black man equal Justice until they see the fire of hell (and then only offer you equal Justice to get you into hell with them. BE AWARE OF THEIR PROMISES. The whole earth belongs to the righteous (the Nation of Islam) who will soon believe it or let it alone.

Sunday, July 29, 1959, in New York, we were greeted and welcomed by approximately 10,000 people and our subject was "Do the so- called Negroes Deserve some of this Earth that They can call Their Own?" Several hundred accepted, and it was a wonderful sight to see. I love the people of Harlem, they seem to want an end to the injustice, which the black man suffers, and so do I.

Let us have equal Justice and a home on this earth for ourselves and our future generations, or die trying. What is a home and life without Justice?

WE NEED SOME EARTH, AND MUST HAVE IT (PART II)

On our planet today, almost total disagreement exists between the people. All are involved in disputes over what they believe and what they think to be their own portion of this earth. Every kind of religious belief is involved. This cannot last much longer before there will be an explosion as long as the lighted fuse of disagreement keeps burning. But shall we be so foolish to sit by with our hands folded hoping and believing that our slave masters will ever be victorious and will care for their slaves in the usual way of providing work and soup in the bread line? This is foolish thinking! You must get on your feet and do something for self with the firm belief in Allah to guide you to success in finding a way for self and kind.

We need some of this earth that 20,000,000 so-called American Negroes can call their own, and go to work as never before to build a self-supporting Nation and not be a dependent Nation on another Nation as we are today. In America we are like the Bible's story of Lazarus charmed by the luxury of rich America and cannot turn our eyes from it to a direction for self. Such beggars will always be treated as a dog, kicked out of society, and unwanted by all industrious Nations. One does not want to take care of his own lazy children, if he happens to have any, so how much more does a Nation dislike caring for another who will not try going for itself?

447

For us to preach integration, inter-marriage, and social equality with our wise slave masters' children, who have already spotted us leprosy and robbed us of equal opportunity, is like putting the ox in a race with the well-trained horse. The square area of America, the educational system, plants, factories, government-owned, commercial and big business-owned farms, and controlled markets and prices, all belong to white America, not to mention white-controlled Christianity and its churches. You should unite with me and God and preach separation of our 20,000,000 beautiful men, women and children, for some of this good earth for us to live on that we can call our own, as our people here and all over the earth are doing.

The white Americans cannot have a sincere love for their over four hundred year old slaves over night, as some of them would have you believe. This is only falseness to deceive you to keep you from your own. Own which God Himself desires to give to you. We will not envy rich America, though our fathers and we, ourselves, helped to make her rich, but rather, envy the opportunity that we now have to become a great nation under the guidance of Allah (God) - as Israel had come under the guidance of Jehovah and Moses, His Servant.

Remember, you that so foolishly love mixing and having social relationships with the slave masters' children, they already have your families and homes raped by them. Everyone of you leaders and laymen of my people in America should unite with Allah and myself, His Messenger, to redeem our people from the hands of a people who only want to use you as a tool, and to forever keep the thought out of your head of ever becoming self-independent somewhere on this earth. But believe me, or believe the prophetic sayings of the prophets of old, the time is near and is at hand when you (the American so-called Negroes) will be forced to join up with your Own and seek a place of refuge in Allah, and a home that you can call your own. Waste your time drinking beer and whisky, dancing and playing games of chance, and committing all kinds of evil, and that day will come upon you as a surprise.

Your own Nation of Islam wants you and will treat you like brother and even better, in some instances.

WHAT WILL BE DONE WITH THE SO-CALLED NEGROES?

This question has been repeated again and again, by both the wise and the foolish. It was raised back in 1863. According to Prof. Carter Godwin Woodson, in his book "Negro Orators and their Orations," at that time, colonization seemed, to many people, to offer the only practical solution. An Englishman named Dodge preferred that the government get a large track of land in Central America, for this purpose. That Englishman, Mr. Dodge, should be living today to be this new President's adviser on "What to do with the Negroes." Such an adviser might help towards prolonging the life of both races.

A complete separation of the white and black, and a separate portion of this earth, for the so-called Negroes, is in accord with the plan of Allah (God). THIS IS THE ONLY SOLUTION. It is again the time that this problem, between the master and his slaves (the so-called Negroes), must be solved, or suffer the destruction of both the slave and his master.

Allah has said to me: "The Lost and Found members of the Black Nation, must be given the knowledge of Self regardless to the cost, and returned to their Own." The Hand of Allah (God) can easily be seen working in the solution of the problem of "What to do with the Negroes." Allah said to me, "If we, the so-called American Negroes (the Lost-Found members of the Tribe of Shabazz), will submit to Him, He would set us in heaven at once.

The great mistake, that the so-called Negroes are making, is not accepting this offer from Allah (God). IT IS PITIFUL: They are charmed by the riches of the slave masters and their unlikeness. This is holding the so-called Negroes to the white race, as the Jesus made it clear in a parable of the rich man and a lazy poor man, two thousand years ago. The rich man could not get rid of the poor man, not even by putting his dogs after the poor man. The poor man stayed until the death of the rich man. Maybe the death of the rich man would not have arrived, when it did, if he had been a little more merciful towards the poor at his gate.

TO MISTREAT THE POOR IS A SIN IN THE EYES OF ALLAH (GOD). The American white race has put their dogs, the police department, and F.B.I., on the so-called Negroes; not to mention their evil crooked politicians, the wicked unjust judges, the crooked unjust money-loving lawyers. All of these are making the Negroes their prey. Yet, the poor so-called American Negroes are too blind, deaf, and dumb to unite and seek a better solution to their problem. They seem satisfied to lay at the rich man's gate and beg. "WHAT MUST BE DONE WITH THE NEGROES?"

With thousand annually receiving diplomas and degrees, from high schools, colleges, and universities, should they stand by, charmed by the rich man's wealth and not go for themselves? Should we not say to Allah, I submit myself to Thee, or say to America, give us a territory to ourselves. If the West Indies, Ghana, and other African states want self-rule, should not 20,000,000 American

MEMPS.com

Negroes want something of their own? REMEMBER
THE QUESTION: WHAT MUST BE DONE WITH
THE SO-CALLED NEGROES?"

WHAT SHALL WE EXPECT TO SEE? A SPIRIT OR A MAN?

The Nations of the Earth expect the coming of a God Who will overcome and destroy all idol Gods and set Himself up as the Supreme God over all; for all Nations have made their own Gods, according to the Bible (Kings 17:29).

Many people have been saying for a long time that God is already with us. Most of the people believe God to be a "Spirit." If He is only a spirit, it is not necessary for us to ever look to see Him, only to feel Him, for a spirit cannot be seen; and, this has been the only God that we have had in the past.

Let us search the Bible and see if it teaches us to believe in the coming of god to be a spirit and not a man. The Bible teaches us of the spirit of God in many places; but only once do I find where it mentions God as being only a spirit (John 4:24). And, this came from a Prophet (Jesus), not from the mouth of God. If one read the previous verse (John 4:23), he or she will see that even Jesus could not have believed God to be only a spirit in these words: "But the hour cometh and now is, when the true worshippers shall worship the Father in spirit and in truth: for the Father seeketh such to worship Him:" (Here a Father is mentioned that we are to worship in Spirit, and not a God of Spirit, but worship God in Spirit).

Here it is made clear that the "hour cometh." This "hour" cannot be referring to anything other than the doom or end of the devil's wicked world of false worshippers, who

455

claim that they are true worshippers of the true God but are not. "For the Father (God) seeketh true worshippers." The devils and those who follow them deceive the people and are not true worshippers so Jesus could have only been referring to the time of the presence of God in person (THIS IS THE TIME). The World of Satan, the devil did not convert people to God, according to the parable of the wicked husband, whom the Lord let His vineyard out to (Matthew 21:33-41). In the 42nd Verse of the same chapter, Jesus makes another parable of the true worshippers under the "stone that the builders rejected;" that it became the "head stone."

It is the so-called Negroes who have been rejected by the builders of Governments (Civilizations), who are now destined to become the head in the new world (or government) under the Divine Supreme Being in Person. It is natural to say that God is the spirit of Truth.

WHAT MUST BE DONE?

The so-called American Negro must be taught the truth of this world's deceiver. (Gen. #:1, 13; Rev. 12:9, 15, 17, Holy Qur'an, 7:16-22; 17:62; 41:36; 16:63; 114:1-6). We must have equal knowledge of the devil, as well as that of Allah, the God of the righteous. This knowledge of the two Gods righteous and evil, was not to be given to you until the end of the time of the god of evil, the devil; Thessalonians-2:9, 19. Holy Qur'an 7:13,14,18.

The Black people must be taught to stop believing in the universal false teachings that these two Gods are Spirits, and not human beings. Then, and not until then, will the black people know the truth. The teaching that these two Gods are Spirits, was for the purpose of hiding their true selves until the time and end of the evil God, and his people. This knowledge has been a closely guarded secret among the wise of the nations for the past six thousand years. It has now been revealed by Allah in person. This is that TRUTH that the world must know, before the judgment of the wicked can take place. The devils know the time of their end. They have planned a mighty plan to deceive the Black Nation, (Black, Brown, Yellow, and Red) and especially the so-called American Negroes, who were reared by them. The Great Deceiver is mentioned in Rev. 20:8, and Holy Qur'an 17:62. they are the open enemies of the Black Nations, Holy Qur'an 7:22.

The Devils are the evil, filthy tempters of the nations of the world, and especially the so-called Negroes, whom the devils made blind, deaf, and dumb from birth. They did

457

that to deprive Allah, and His Messenger, of saving the so-called Negroes from their Doom. The devils are now deceiving the so-called Negroes under a pre-agreed plan.

Allah has said to me that this plan of the devils, is to tempt the Negroes into sexual relations, inter-marriage, and to make false promises of much wealth, and permanent prosperity. This wicked filthy plan is now in practice among the so-called Negroes and whites in a major portion of America.

The southern devils are the hardest to agree on this evil filthy plan to rob the so-called Negroes of the chance of seeing the hereafter. The hereafter is now being offered to the so-called American Negroes by Allah, through His Messenger, and the Nation of Islam.
Take a look at the open practice of fornication, and adultery, going on between the middle, and lower classes of Negroes and whites! Jesus, the last prophet to the Caucasian race (or devils), warns you in St. Matthew 26:41. The Holy Qur'an warns you against the devil's plans of deceiving you with their soft words, and love songs. This plan of deceit is going on among you at the present time. Look at the devils' acts and words openly on your TV and radio. Watch the soft language, and shoulder, and hip, patting, and the putting of arms around Negro women by the low filthy class of devils today. All this is done to deprive the so-called Negroes of the hereafter, as the devil deprived Eve and Adam of the paradise.

A little southern newspaper, "The August Courier" headlined a movement by the Methodist Church (so-called

Christians) to produce a mulatto race through Dixie. This means to experiment on the Negro women to get rid of the black race. Pharaoh and Herod's plan, in their time, to get rid of a nation, was child's play compared to this wicked, wise, devil of today.

I WARN YOU TO SAVE YOURSELVES BY ACCEPTING ALLAH, AND FOLLOW ME.

WHO IS THAT MYSTERY GOD?

FOR THOUSANDS of years, the people that did not have the knowledge of the person, or reality of God, worshipped their own ideas of God; and He has been made like many things other than what He really is. The Christians refer to God as a "Mystery" and a "Spirit," and divide Him into thirds. One part they call the Father, another part, the Son, and the third part, the Holy Ghost - which makes the three, one. This is contrary to both nature and mathematics.

The law of mathematics will not allow us to put 3 into 1. Our nature rebels against such a belief of God being a mystery, and yet is the Father of a son and a Holy ghost without a wife, or without being something in reality. We wonder how can the son be human, and the father a mystery (unknown), or a spirit? Who is this Holy Ghost that is classified as being the equal of the father and the son?

The Christians do not believe in God as being a human being yet, they believe in Him as being the Father of all Human Beings. They also refer to God as He, Him, Man, King and The Ruler. They teach that God sees, hears, talks, walks, stands, sits, rides, flies and that He grieves or sorrows, and that He is interested in the affairs of Human Beings. They also teach that once upon a time He made the first man like Himself, in the image and likeness of Himself, but yet they believe that He, Himself, is not a man or human. They preach and prophecy of His coming, and that He will be seen on the Judgment Day, but is not man. They cannot tell us what He looks like, yet man is made like Him, and in the image of God, and yet they still say that He is a mystery (unknown).

How can one teach the people to know God if he, himself, does not know God? If you try teaching the Christians that God is also a Human Being, they will say that you are crazy and that you do not believe in God, and you are an infidel. In the meantime, while they admit that He is a Mystery God (unknown), they teach not to make any likeness of Him, yet they adorn their walls and churches with pictures, images, and statues like Human Beings.

CAN GOD BE A MYSTERY GOD and yet send prophets to represent Himself? Have the prophets been representing a God that is not known (Mystery)? They tell us that they heard God's voice speaking to them in their own language. Can a spirit speak a language while being an immaterial something? If God is not material what pleasure would He get out of material beings, and of the material Universe? What is the base of spirit? Is the spirit independent of material?

ON THE 9th of this month the Chicago Tribune and a few other newspapers and magazines carried a false charge against me, that I was arrested in Detroit in 1934 for contributing to the delinquency of a minor. This is false, my record in Detroit can be found, and it proves that I was not arrested on any such charges. I shall do my best to make the guilty pay for such a false charge.

WILL AMERICA REPENT?

This is a great question. America knows her evil doings against us, but to repent of them, I doubt it greatly. She feels that if she tries to make up with us for her evil doings to us, she would be inviting her disgrace among the Nations of Earth. Her determination is to try and keep the so-called Negroes from believing in the True God, Allah, and the True Religion of Islam, which is our SALVATION. They are using many tricks to deceive the so-called Negroes, and they are falling for them.

False friendship is not able to stand up for very long; an enemy is just not able to put over false friendship for long. You should be able to know them and their tricks, as long as they have been putting them over on you.

According to the Holy Qur'an (60:1), friendly relations with enemies of Islam are forbidden. "Oh you who believe, do not take my enemy and your enemy for friends: would you offer them love while they deny what has come to you of the truth, driving out the Apostle and yourselves because you believe in Allah, your Lord?"

In this kind of doing, the foolish so-called Negroes will be trapped. There are even some weak Muslims who ignore this warning. Some go as far as to marry the enemies of Islam, and even hate me for teaching the truth of the enemies, but Allah is with me and I have no right to worry about the doings of the people after knowledge. The enemies do not love either you nor me. As the next verse teaches: "If they find you, they will be your enemies, and

463

will stretch forth towards you their hands and their tongues with evil, and they ardently desire that you may disbelieve." "They would slay you with their hands, and speak evil to and of you with their tongues."

You must remember that you do not like one who befriends your enemy. How much God dislikes you for making love with His enemies? The enemy does not have to be the real devil; he could be your father, mother, sister, brother, husband, wife or children. Many times they are of your own household (near of kin).
Today is the great time of the separation of the righteous (Muslims) and the wicked (White Race).

The wicked are not by any means asleep to the knowledge of the time. They are really on the job of trying to keep those who are blind, deaf and dumb to what is happening in that condition. They watch every step of the righteous (Muslims), seeking to harm them and their work of spreading forth the Truth. You must know the Truth whether you accept it or reject it!

Ask yourself these questions: (1) If Christianity is the religion of Jesus, why is it that the wicked (White Race) represents it instead of the righteous of Holy People of the East (Islam)? (2) Why has not the Holy City Mecca allowed it to be taught within her? (3) Why is not Jerusalem the Capitol of Christianity instead of Rome, Italy? (4) If Christianity was the religion of Jesus and the White Race is Jesus' beloved people, why did he preach the DOOM of the White Race and the coming of a new World?

This People will most certainly carry to their doom many of our people because of our people's fear and love of them. Look out of your doors or windows, and see the Black Woman sitting in the car in the arms of your and her enemy. He only wants to disgrace you and her, and keep her from seeing the Hereafter. You cannot have any such freedom with his women, and especially not in front of HIS DOOR. Love of them will get you HELL.

VOLUME I INDEX

467

180, 181, 189, 195, 196, 199, 200, 201, 203, 206, 207, 208, 210, 219, 225, 226, 228, 232, 235, 236, 239, 240, 242, 247, 255, 259, 260, 274, 282, 287, 288, 292, 301, 302, 303, 307, 308, 309, 311, 317, 323, 324, 325, 326, 331, 332, 336, 338, 342, 345, 348, 350, 353, 360, 366, 371, 372, 377, 379, 380, 390, 393, 396, 405, 407, 412, 414, 415, 425, 429, 434, 439, 440, 441, 446, 449, 458, 463, 464

Israel21, 34, 36, 37, 43, 83, 150, 167, 189, 215, 231, 250, 255, 329, 332, 360, 369, 370, 417, 418, 419, 448

Israelites.................................. 373
J. Saunders Redding................... 337
J.A. Rogers 95
J.B. Stoner......................... 313, 326
Jackson 112
Jacob... 418
James B. Kilpatrick............. 150, 250
Jehovah.......7, 21, 34, 35, 36, 43, 46, 150, 250, 329, 331, 332, 349, 359, 369, 370, 373, 383, 448

Jerusalem 464
Jesus8, 21, 25, 32, 36, 37, 40, 47, 57, 70, 112, 123, 139, 177, 180, 181, 196, 200, 204, 225, 228, 247, 259, 261, 264, 267, 268, 285, 287, 288, 293, 302, 307, 308, 343, 345, 360, 366, 369, 379, 383, 399, 404, 414, 415, 416, 419, 434, 444, 452, 455, 456, 458, 464

Jet Magazine.............................. 253
Jews 293, 308, 331, 345, 346, 359, 373, 415

Jim Crow 143
John 34, 171, 172, 173, 174, 175, 181, 199

John Hawkins 337
Joseph 329
Keyhoe................................. 17, 36
King..22, 23, 41, 150, 151, 152, 191, 203, 250, 251, 252, 257, 304, 461

Ku Klux Klan...... 313, 325, 326, 348
Laban 418
lamb 147

land 1, 2, 7, 27, 43, 65, 85, 89, 99, 109, 127, 134, 137, 143, 147, 148, 153, 154, 167, 208, 211, 214, 215, 218, 221

Latin.................................. 176, 192
Len O'Connor 413
Lomax... 3
Los Angeles ..19, 105, 108, 123, 124, 179, 181

lost 225, 226, 228, 239, 250, 261, 275, 303, 333, 334, 389, 395, 396, 411, 412, 418, 419, 439

Lost and Found 451
Louisiana 233, 234, 239, 323
lynching 313, 363, 396
Magog.. 47
Mahdi.1, 56, 174, 192, 206, 383, 387
Mary 366
masonry 405
Masons.............................. 203, 405
Mecca 7, 8, 106, 138, 348, 464
Messenger.i, iii, iv, v, 12, 39, 67, 74, 75, 106, 112, 117, 162, 171, 191, 195, 223, 227, 231, 233, 245, 246, 247, 278, 292, 293, 309, 326, 387, 425, 433, 434, 448, 458

Monroe 103, 112, 118, 121, 133, 134
Moses21, 25, 35, 43, 46, 57, 91, 112, 150, 157, 167, 195, 200, 204, 225, 246, 250, 255, 257, 258, 261, 264, 269, 270, 287, 298, 302, 329, 331, 332, 345, 349, 356, 359, 360, 366, 369, 370, 373, 415, 448

mud.1, 127, 136, 165, 169, 341, 361, 409, 414

Muhammad.i, iii, iv, v, 1, 19, 20, 22, 40, 46, 56, 66, 74, 82, 83, 90, 93, 100, 103, 106, 118, 121, 122, 128, 135, 139, 144, 154, 155, 157, 167, 172, 174, 176, 179, 180, 181, 192, 195, 196, 200, 204, 205, 206, 220, 223, 234, 240, 258, 277, 287, 293, 302, 320, 323, 324, 325, 326, 329, 331, 333, 335, 337, 341, 343, 348, 349, 352, 359, 371, 383, 413, 415, 418, 434

Muslims 231, 232, 233, 234, 235, 236, 239, 240, 241, 242, 260, 277,

VOLUME II INDEX

Thank you for purchasing this book. We trust the reading was rewarding and enlightening.

We offer various titles by Minister Nasir Hakim, as well a comprehensive collection of Messenger Elijah Muhammad's works. These works include:

- Standard Published Titles
- Unpublished & Diligently Transcribed Compilations
- Audio Cassettes
- Video Cassettes
- Audio CD's
- DVD's
- Rare Articles
-

You are welcomed to sample a catalog of these items by simply requesting a FREE archive Catalog.

Our contact information is as follows:

Secretarius MEMPS Publications

111 E Dunlap Ave, Ste 1-217 - Phoenix, Arizona 85012
Phone & Fax 602 466-7347
Email: secmemps@memps.com
Web: www.memps.com

Wholesale options are also available.

NOTES: